When journalist Ruth Montgomery first encountered the spirit world, she was a skeptic. But after a series of startling séances, she was convinced by the overwhelming evidence that life after death is a fact. Soon after, she discovered that she had been the medium chosen to disseminate their wisdom—and that through sessions of automatic writing, she could submit her hand to their will. Determined to fulfill her purpose, Montgomery obeyed her spirit guides and translated these passages. Today she is one of the most recognized authorities on psychic phenomena, and the most prolific representative of the spirit world.

A SEARCH FOR THE TRUTH

Ruth Montgomery

FAWCETT CREST   •   NEW YORK

To my father
IRA WHITMER SHICK
(1881-1953)
who continues to give me
loving counsel since he
passed to the next phase
of eternal life

A Fawcett Crest Book
Published by Ballantine Books

Excerpts from this book have appeared in *Ladies' Home
Journal* under the title "My Psychic Friends."

Library of Congress Catalog Card Number: 67-12986

ISBN 0-449-21085-5

This edition published by arrangement with
William Morrow & Co., Inc.

Printed in Canada

First Ballantine Books Edition: August 1982
Thirteenth Printing: December 1993

Contents

Foreword   1
1. A Born Skeptic   13
2. A Doubter's Dilemma   19
3. The Pencil Writes   37
4. A Spirit Goes House-Hunting   47
5. My Psychic Friends   55
6. The Golden Door   81
7. True Time Exists   91
8. The Selfishness of Grief   101
9. An Eagle on his Shoulder   107
10. A Do-It-Yourself Lesson   121
11. The Man in the Next Room   131
12. Love One Another   137
13. Walk With God   151
14. Mystery Stories of the Night   159
15. The Meaning of Christmas   171
16. A Spirit's Nose for News   179
17. The Ancient Wisdom   191
18. Voices and Visitations   209
19. "Intimations of Immortality"   237
20. This Wonderful Psychic World   245
Glossary   255

Foreword

This is a book about one person's search for the deeper meaning of life, a search that commenced a quarter of a century ago and still pursues that beckoning star. During those years I have authored numerous books in the psychic field, hopefully taking my faithful readers along with me on each progressive stage in my own quest for inner knowledge of man's relationship with himself and his Creator. *A Search for the Truth* marked my first adventuresome steps into the exciting world of the unknown, and because of the beautiful philosophy expressed by those mysterious discarnates who write through me, it is now being reissued by popular demand from readers who consider it a classic introduction to the entire field.

At the time that I wrote this book, I was a syndicated Washington columnist on politics and world affairs, busily traveling throughout America and the world in pursuit of hard facts that would make tomorrow's headlines. It was therefore a rather staggering risk to attach my well-known newspaper by-line to a subject that was only then beginning to tiptoe from darkened seance chambers into the searchlight of scientific laboratories. Yet the strong possibility of communication between the living and the so-called dead was also a story that needed to be told. And perhaps because of the breakthrough accomplished by *A Search for the Truth,* library shelves and bookstores are now crowded with hundreds of books on psychic phenomena.

In the 1950's, when I first attended gatherings of those interested in the occult, the audiences seemed largely comprised of little old ladies seeking messages from loved ones who had recently crossed through the door called death. Today, tens of thousands of well educated, smartly groomed citizens of both sexes and every race regularly attend psychic Seminars in every major city and on dozens of college campuses throughout our land. So many Oriental gurus, Yogis and philosophers have now established sects in America, and so many Americans have journeyed to the Orient to study in ashrams, that if Rudyard Kipling were still living he would need to revise his immortal lines, "Oh, East is East, and West is West, and never the twain shall meet." It is not communication satellites that have brought the two halves of the globe together, as much as the recently awakened Western interest in reincarnation and occult sciences that have long dominated Eastern thought.

The famous medium Arthur Ford did more than any other to excite my interest in the psychic, and with his encouragement I was able to develop a talent for automatic writing. From that mysterious source has since come much of the enlightening material for my books in this field; but because some people have undergone somewhat frightening experiences in their attempts at automatic writing, I should like to stress these safety guidelines:

1. Practice it only at the same hour each day, in order to establish a date with a superior discarnate who is willing to become your Guide.

2. Do not pick up the pencil until you have first meditated for ten or fifteen minutes, to place yourself in the proper spiritual attunement and to induce the alpha state through which the writing flows. Then murmur a prayer for protection or mentally enclose yourself in a protective circle of light.

It is well to remember that when we open ourselves to unseen forces, a mischievous or evil entity can contact us as easily as a benevolent one, unless we have attuned ourselves to a high-minded Guide who is alerted to our signal and will guard the opened doorway. However, Arthur Ford insisted that if we remain "God centered," or "Christ oriented," no harm can befall us through psychic delving.

In 1971 my great friend Arthur passed into spirit, and almost immediately thereafter joined "Lily and the Group" in helping to dictate material for my subsequent books: *A World Beyond, Companions Along the Way, The World Before,* and *Strangers Among Us.*

Mr. A, the remarkable healer described in the chapter of this book entitled, "The Ancient Wisdom," and can now be identified as William Gray of Berkeley, California, has also more recently passed on to the next phase of eternal life.

In the original Foreword to this book, I posed a series of questions: Why were we born? Did we live before, and is birth, like death, simply another step in a continuous progression of the soul? Do personality and memory survive our passage through the door that man calls death? Do we have a mission in life? Is there a Divine plan which to an extent prearranges the steps by which we earth-bound souls surmount our difficulties and eventually progress through other steps toward the eventual goal? What is that goal?

Jesus told us that the "kingdom of God is within" each of us. It is for us, then, to enlarge our own perception, and learn through daily meditation to listen to the "still, small voice" of conscience within. This process takes patience and effort, but the rewards are many. All of us are psychic, and through the utilization of our psychic talent we can develop self-reliance, greater awareness, and a sublime sense of Oneness with God.

If this book does no more than arouse us to the unlimited capacity within ourselves, it will have served some purpose. But, hopefully, it can perhaps further awaken us to the realization that the good we do here advances our soul's progression, while thoughtless acts retard it. Not one act or deed of ours goes unnoticed on the "other side." When we eventually cross that threshold ourselves, we will take up where we left off here. It is not up to God, but up to us to decide whether our next stage of life begins on an exalted or lowly level. Messages from those who have "gone on" make clear that the way to save ourselves is to lose thought of self in unselfish serice to others. If this precept could be accepted by all mankind, there would be no warfare or other acts of violence.

Charles P. Steinmetz, a celebrated electrical engineer, predicted in 1923: "Someday the scientists will turn their laboratories over to the study of God, and prayer, and the spiritual forces which as yet have hardly been scratched." In the four decades since World War II, we have seen a tremendous revival of interest in psychic phenomena. The crash program that Steinmetz foretold has not yet occurred, but a beginning has been made both here and in Russia. The church is exploring the psychical and parapsychological as never before, and pastors who a generation ago would not have dared admit to an interest are now busily organizing psychic study groups within their parishes.

The Reverend William V. Rauscher, rector of Christ Episcopal Church in Woodbury, New Jersey, says of the subject: "If we were to remove from the Bible all the accounts of mystical and psychical happenings, we would have very little left. Without the Resurrection experience, we would not even have a Church. The very things the New Testament speaks about involve psychical and parapsychological study: our community with Christ, the communion of saints, angels and archangels, the whole company of heaven, and the entire heritage of our mystical Jesus, and everything related to it in the world of the unseen demand scientific inquiry. I cannot think of Jesus walking on the water without thinking of levitation. I cannot think of the transfiguration of Christ, illuminating himself and glistening, without thinking of the whole meaning of the human aura, the halos around the saints in religious art; or the appearance of the prophets on the mount with Christ, without thinking of the reconstituting of matter, and in the resurrection to a physical form. I cannot think of prayer without thinking of some form of telepathy relating my mind to the mind of God."

Continuing, he declared: "Christian people must face up to the truth of their faith. These doctrines are either true or false. Either the communion of Saints is a reality or it is not. When we attend church services, do we not realize that there are more invisibles than visibles? If a person is convinced of life after death, his philosophy of life must change. In the Communist philosophy there is no room for this view. I believe psychical research could change this negativism. More and more the Church will have to become the laboratory of the spirit. In the church today we should continue to witness a new interest in psychical research, and all parapsychological studies. If any church is not interested, it is behind the times!"

In that spirit of open-minded inquiry, this book was conceived and written. I do not pretend to understand the mysterious laws that govern mental telepathy, clairvoyance, precognition, miraculous healings, apports, and apparent communication with those beyond the grave. I believe, however, that the search for this knowledge in no way conflicts with the tenets on which the church was founded. How many times through the ages have ministers quoted the twelfth verse from the fourteenth chapter of St. John: "Verily, verily, I say unto you, he that believeth in me, the works that I do shall he do also; and greater works than these shall he do; because I go unto my Father."

St. Paul, in the twelfth chapter of I Corinthians, admonished the early Christians: "The manifestation of the Spirit is given to every man to profit withal. For to one is given by the Spirit the word of wisdom; to another the word of knowledge by the same Spirit; to another faith by the same Spirit; to another the gifts of healing by the same Spirit; to another the working of miracles; to another prophecy; to another discerning of spirits; to another divers kinds of tongues; to another the interpretation of tongues."

These talents, like all others, were bestowed on man in order to be used and developed. Christ told us: "Ask, and it shall be given you; seek, and ye shall find; knock, and it shall be opened unto you." Unless we ask for further knowledge of God's universe, and seek for it, we cannot find it. Unless we knock, the door will remain closed.

CHAPTER 1

A Born Skeptic

I am a newspaper reporter, as skeptical as the average member of my profession. We have observed too many tricks, covered too many cleverly contrived courtroom defenses, and attended too many smoke-filled political conventions to accept at face value all that meets the eye. Because of my Methodist upbringing in small Midwestern communities, I am naturally dubious of anything that smacks of the darkened room and the occult. Yet no news writer can hope to be successful unless he is also blessed with an open and inquiring mind. This, I hope I also have.

Almost every family cherishes some folklore having to do with dreams, thought transmission, clairvoyance, or precognition. Eleanor Medill (Cissy) Patterson, the late publisher of the Washington *Times-Herald,* once confided that while taking an afternoon nap in her Dupont Circle mansion, she suddenly saw her former husband standing at the foot of the bed. "This was no drab, gray dream. It was brilliant technicolor," Cissy told me. "I was awake, and I actually saw him. He was wearing his gaudiest Polish uniform, with dozens of ribbons across his chest." As suddenly as he appeared he vanished, and Cissy rushed downstairs to tell her family about the chilling apparition. The next day a cable arrived from Poland, announcing that Count Josef Gizycki had died. The time given was the moment at which Cissy saw him standing beside her bed.

I had heard somewhat similar stories as a child. My

Aunt Lottie Cunningham once dreamed that a friend's house burned to the ground, and even as she recounted the details at breakfast, a neighbor brought word of the actual event. Grandmother sometimes spoke of her uncle, who dreamed so vividly of his mother's death that he leaped onto a horse and rode for two days to reach home. On arriving at Sumner, Illinois, he saw a funeral procession, and reined in his horse to inquire about it. It was for his mother, who had died the night of his dream.

If psychic qualities are inherited, I must have been skipped in my generation; or so I thought. Like everyone else I have had occasional hunches, particularly at race tracks, but mine never pay off. No dream of mine has come to pass. When Dr. J. B. Rhine introduced ESP (extrasensory perception) cards in the 1930's, I invariably tallied a miserable score. I knew so little of psychic phenomena that I had never heard of table-tapping until my sister, Mrs. Margaret Overbeck, saw it demonstrated at a bridge party during World War II.

Shortly afterward, in 1944, my brother Paul Shick arrived with his family to spend the night at Margaret's house, en route to a new assignment. Paul was concerned about his hotel reservations in St. Louis the following day. In answer to his telegram, the manager had replied that if the St. Louis Browns tied the Cardinals, and a world-series playoff was held the following day, the chances of available hotel rooms in that city would be nil.

Margaret told Paul of the new gambit she had seen at the party and lightly proposed that they ask the table how the next day's ball game would go. In the mood for relaxation they seated themselves around a card table, rested their palms lightly on its surface, and waited. Shortly, two of the table legs slowly rose from the floor. Margaret said this was the signal that the table was "ready to talk." Sounding braver than she felt, she instructed the table to tap once for *A,* twice for *B,* and so on through the alphabet, and to tell them the winner of the following day's game. Without hesitation the table tapped out "Cardinals." If true, that was good news, because the world series would end and

14

the hotel exodus immediately begin. Margaret next asked the final score, and then the numbers of the innings in which the runs would be made. Just for the fun of it, Paul jotted down the table's obedient responses.

The next afternoon, while driving along the highway, my brother tuned in the world series on the car radio. If the Browns tied the score, it would be pointless to drive into St. Louis that night. As he and his family listened, their amazement grew. The Cardinals were performing precisely as the table had foretold, inning by inning. When the Cardinals won and thereby ended the series, the final score was the same as the notation in Paul's billfold.

I was not present on this occasion, but after hearing about it through letters, I was eager to test the table at our next family reunion. Margaret and three others of us therefore seated ourselves on three sides of a card table, leaving the fourth side free to rise—which it soon did. The table then performed exactly as before, except that its alleged messages were not as readily authenticated as a next day's ball score.

Frankly, I thought that Margaret was manipulating the table, and waiting for us to catch onto the joke. This conviction increased when on returning to Washington I tried to demonstrate the phenomenon to friends. The table stayed firmly rooted to the floor while the participants shook with ill-suppressed laughter. Not until several years later, after I began delving into books on psychic phenomena for a newspaper series, did I discover that table-tapping is something more than a parlor trick. I then tried it again, and after the table gradually responded to my touch, I realized that whatever mysterious force was causing two of the four legs to rise and fall in answer to questioning was not consciously of my own doing. I have been as surprised as my friends when the table spells out names and incidents with which I am totally unfamiliar, but which often prove to be authentic.

By the time the table had begun to perform for me, I had attended a number of dark-room séances in pursuit of a newspaper series. I had also tried meditation and had received numerous purported messages via the ouija board. Shortly thereafter I was to discover that I could seemingly produce "automatic writing," when I held a pencil lightly above a sheet of paper, closed my eyes, and maintained a prayerful attitude of mind. Since then I have attended two seminars on meditation and dream analysis, have talked with outstanding leaders in the field of psychic phenomena, and have gradually become convinced that anyone who is willing to expend the time and effort can develop his own latent powers.

The source of automatic writing is as mysterious as life itself. To some the answer seems simple: that the thoughts are drawn from the subconscious of the person whose hand rests on the pencil. This may be true. If so, it fails to explain how events which are unknown to the writer find their way into his subconscious, or how future episodes can be accurately foretold.

There are certain dangers inherent in pursuing this lonely investigation. Unless a novice is well balanced, he runs the risk of subjugating his own will to that of another. The peril exists, whether the mysterious directing-force is indeed an entity now living on another plane, or whether it is a submerged personality within the mind of the one who holds the pencil. For this reason Hugh Lynn Cayce, son of the late great psychic, Edgar Cayce, warns against the use of automatic writing in his book, *Ventures Inward*. Others insist that if a person remains "Christ-oriented" while attempting to explore this fascinating realm, no harm can befall him.

During my own quest for truth I have run the gamut of emotions from amusement to semi-belief; from disillusionment to an awakening awareness that the human mind and the so-called hereafter are the greatest unexplored reaches for adventurous man. I do not pretend to know the answers today, any more than I did at the beginning of the search, but this much I have discovered: It is possible, with a little time and effort, to develop one's own psychic ability to such a degree that an exciting and stimulating new world begins to unfold. As it does so, one's spiritual awareness deepens and life takes on new dimensions. This has happened to me. It is why I am writing this book.

CHAPTER 2

A Doubter's Dilemma

A chance telephone call abruptly precipitated me into a fascinating new half-world of banging trumpets, supposed spirits in diaphanous draperies, drum-beating Indians, and long conversations with the purported voices of departed relatives. For sheer drama, the experience remains unexcelled. Much of it I cannot believe, but neither can I explain some of it by logical reasoning. I have since read more than a hundred books on the subject, both pro and con, but I do not pretend to be able to sort out the fraudulent from the genuine. Even Joseph Dunninger, the mentalist, who wrote an intended exposé of séances, added to the confusion by stressing that he is "absolutely convinced" that some of the mediums he "exposed" are sincere people who truly believe that they are transporting messages from the dead. Then how does he know for certain that they are not? Is there any way to be sure?

My own experience with mediums began on a dreary March day in 1956, when, despairing of seeing the sun again, my husband Bob and I decided to fly from Washington to St. Petersburg for a long week-end. I telephoned his sister, Rhoda Montgomery, of our impending arrival, and she asked if we would like to go to a séance with her. I had no idea what a séance was and would frankly have preferred to spend all the time at the beach, but I agreed to go, provided it did not take very long. Two days later, on meeting our plane, Rhoda said, "Ruth, your father is expecting you. He came through at a séance last night and said he was so happy that he would be able to reach you through us."

As my father had died three years before, I merely shrugged and remarked that she must have inadvertently tipped off the medium. This she emphatically denied. Rhoda reported that Dr. Malcolm Pantin, the medium, had given us a "trance" appointment, but would not demonstrate "direct voice" until we had become more experienced. Bob and I did not know the difference anyway. At the appointed hour we drove to Dr. Pantin's parsonage, entered the windowless séance room, and observed only a cheap card table with a group of folding chairs.

Dr. Pantin asked us to write several questions on a sheet of paper, but when he learned that I had scribbled a few notes in advance, he said I did not need to rewrite them. We laid the papers facing us on the card table, but before the medium seated himself opposite us, he told my husband to tie a thick black handkerchief, cut on the bias, over his eyes to seal out the light. We satisfied ourselves that Dr. Pantin could see nothing. My jottings were lightly written, and my scrawl is virtually undecipherable, so even my husband seated next to me could not make out my questions. It would have been almost impossible for Pantin, to whom they were upside down and several feet removed, to do so.

While we sang a hymn in the brightly lighted room, Pantin apparently went into trance. His head banged heavily on the card table; but after a moment he sat up, introduced himself as Pedro, a departed spirit, and spoke in a heavy Spanish accent. If fraud was perpetrated—and I do not believe that it was—Pantin is a superb actor who missed his calling in Hollywood. The blindfolded Pantin (or Pedro) groped for our question sheets, held them tightly between his two palms, and began to bring us messages from the "dead." He said that my father did not want me to worry about Bertie (my mother's nickname), because he was watching over her all the time. He recited facts about her that only I in the group could have known. Rhoda at that time had such slight acquaintanceship with my family that she did not even know Mother's first name, and could not have revealed it.

Pedro described a dark-green and midnight-blue plaid, and said my father wanted me to know that he "knew about it." (This meant nothing to me at the time, but on the way home Bob reminded me that the week before I had sent a plaid suit of that coloring to my sister Margaret.) Pedro told my husband that he was considering another job offer, which had recently been made to him. Since this had occurred the day before, and had been disclosed only to me, Rhoda could not have given away that information. The medium also gave Bob a message for a living brother, by name, and he warned Rhoda not to make the trip north she was planning, before May. There were too many dangers until the end of April, her Guide insisted, through Pedro. She ignored the advice, and the second day after her departure in mid-April, the car in which she rode was demolished. Only by a near miracle did she and the woman driver escape going over a mountain crest. Rhoda's collarbone was broken.

Four weeks after our séance with Pantin, my husband was unexpectedly called to St. Petersburg to make a speech before a business group. Now curious to know more about the psychic field, I agreed to accompany him if Rhoda could arrange a "direct voice" séance for us. On a bright April morning we again entered the séance room in St. Petersburg and inspected it even more closely than on our previous visit. There were no windows, and no additional furniture. The only draperies were black velvet ones, which in our presence were pulled across the locked door to block a glint of light. Four of us sat in a row, three aluminum trumpets stood on the floor in front of us, and Pantin faced us across the small room. At the end of the hour's séance, the trumpets had toppled over in various parts of the room, and one had banged to rest across Rhoda's ankle.

This time no questions were asked, or written. Pantin turned off the only light switch, and while we sang a hymn he presumably went into trance. In a moment, seemingly from the left corner of the room, a dignified male voice introduced itself through a trumpet as

Whitecloud, Pantin's Control in the spirit world. White-cloud greeted each of us by name, said that Maizie would take over the task of trying to bring in our relatives, and promised to return at the close for questioning. Then a high, piping child's voice from the opposite ceiling bantered with us for a few minutes until a male voice spoke to my husband, saying: "Robert, this is Father. This is Hiram." The name was correct. After a few minutes of surprisingly normal conversation, during which Hiram told Bob that the present arrangements for his mother were "the best possible, considering her advanced age and physical condition," Bob volunteered that he and Rhoda had been attempting to remember details of a house where they had lived briefly when my husband was a toddler.

"We were trying to recall how many steps led up to the front porch," Bob said. "It seems to me there were six or eight."

"There were exactly seven; I ought to know," Hiram chuckled. He added that Rhoda, who is older than Bob, should also be able to recall how badly the house needed paint, and how happy they were to move from it. Rhoda laughingly conceded that although she had forgotten it until then, the paint was peeling off in strips, and the family had been ashamed to live there until the Methodist parsonage was ready.

Next, Bob's two deceased sisters, Aseneth and Ruth, came in by correct name and conversed with us through trumpets. One, a former schoolteacher, confided that she was still teaching children, and "helping new souls who come over suddenly to adjust to their new surroundings." Both voices spoke of the beauty of their "plane" and said that Bob's mother "will soon be much happier here with us."

Suddenly Maizie's childlike voice said mischievously: "There's a gentleman here who wants to talk to his girl. He says he's her boy." The room was still. None of us could fathom the meaning, and in a moment Maizie rather testily repeated the remark. At that point Rhoda asked who she meant, since there were three women in the room.

"He wants *His* girl," Maizie insisted. "He says she'll know because he's her boy."

At this I cried: "Iry Boy!" This had been my pet name for my father, whose name was Ira.

"Of course," Maizie giggled, and a man's voice said: "Hello, Ruth. You don't know how wonderful it is to get to talk to you at last." He gave me a message for Mother and told me not to feel concerned about her, "because I'm working all the time to make things easy for her over there, and she's getting along fine."

I asked for any personal advice, and "Iry Boy" said that he certainly had some for me. "Now listen, listen," he began, using the repetitive phrase which he frequently had employed when he wished to stress a point, "stop going on all those trips all over everywhere, and stay at home more with Bob. It isn't good to leave Bob all the time. Your marriage is the important thing."

I confessed that even then I was planning a trip to the Congo the following month, and he chided: "I know, but what about Bob?" I said that he couldn't get away from work, but that mine was a business trip, and the voice grouched: "That's just what I'm getting at. Stop taking all those trips and thinking about your work so much." At least once or twice a year for a decade I had been making reportorial trips overseas, while Bob remained at his job in Washington. That fact could scarcely have been known to the medium.

After Dad relinquished the trumpet, a woman introduced herself as my Grandmother Judy and said that she was "very proud" of my writing, but worried about the trip that I was planning to Africa. "There's such danger," she sighed, "and I worry about you on those long flights over the water." This sounded typical of my grandmother when she had been in the flesh, but seemed an odd concern for a disembodied spirit.

Then began a soft beating of drums that swelled into a deafening cacophony, and the loudest voice that I have ever heard bellowed that he was Big Chief White Mountain, "Ruth's personal protector." I learned later that most spiritualists in this country believe we each have an American Indian as a "spirit" bodyguard.

"Me B-i-g Chief, me heap Big Chief, Ruth," White

23

Mountain boasted through the vibrating trumpet. "Me go wherever you go. Me protect you all time. Here, sit still and I show you how b-i-g and strong I am." With that, the trumpet banged me three times on the head, in the jet black room. Shaking with laughter, for a séance is remarkably relaxing, I asked whether he thought that I should go to the Congo. White Mountain indifferently replied that this was none of his business. If I went, he would go, too. It was as simple as that. He then withdrew, to the ebbing sound of the drum beat.

At the end of an hour we heard the medium sigh, cough, and finally speak. Then he flicked on the light and sleepily rubbed his eyes. The séance had ended, but my curiosity had not.

No one knew our identity when, on a Sunday evening shortly after our return to Washington, we dropped in unannounced at the Spiritualist Church of Two Worlds, accompanied by Mr. and Mrs. H. F. Seitz. Rev. Hugh Gordon Burroughs, after a brief sermon, announced that he had some "psychic" messages from departed spirits. He strode up and down the aisles mentioning names, each of which was gratefully claimed by some member of the audience, until he announced: "Amelia is trying to communicate with someone here." There were no takers. Next, from the rear, Burroughs suddenly walked to the front of the room to tell my husband that he had recently received an attractive new job offer. This, Bob admitted, was true.

Strolling across to "Hap" Seitz, the medium murmured: "William is trying to reach you." When our friend made no response, a woman directly behind him exclaimed that she knew "a William." This would have been an easy out for the medium, but he shook his head and insisted: "I see 'William' written across this man's chest. It has to be for him." Hap said nothing, and after a moment of quiet frustration, Burroughs continued with his message-bearing for others in the audience.

On our way home in the car, Tania Seitz rebuked Hap, saying: "Your father's name was William, and your mother's name was Amelia. Why didn't you admit it?" Bob and I, who had not known his parents' names, were astonished, but our friend said lamely: "I had momentarily forgotten that that was my father's name—he died when I was a small child—and my mother's name was pronounced Amalia, not Amelia." My husband and I were sufficiently intrigued by this to ask for a private séance with Rev. Burroughs; and in order to insure direct voice, I volunteered that we had already had such a séance with Dr. Pantin in Florida. The two men, it developed, were friends.

Judged by the multitude of voices and staggering detail, our first séance with Rev. Burroughs surpassed all others. Bob's two sisters and his father announced themselves by name, as did his maternal grandfather and an uncle, both of whom bore the identical name John Graves. This particular uncle had disappeared out West during the pioneering 1870's and was never heard from again by the family. Although this occurred long before Bob was born, the mystery had occasionally been discussed at clan gatherings for two generations. When my husband therefore asked "Uncle John" where his body was buried, the chuckling male voice replied: "I was the black sheep of the family, all right, but I had a pretty gay time out West. Sometime when you're driving through Wyoming, I'll lead you to my grave." This was fascinating, but difficult to check.

Father Murphy, the other-world Control for Burroughs when in trance, next introduced "a gentleman who wants to see his girl; he says he's her boy." Seeking "evidential," the investigator's word for proof, I warily requested his name; and as the purported voice of my father greeted me, Father Murphy supplied: "His name is Ira, isn't it?" We had quite a family visit, and when Dad's voice eventually faded away in the inky blackness, Father Murphy teased: "You used to call him Iry Boy, didn't you, Ruth?" True, but I kept wondering if Dr. Pantin might have alerted his friend.

My Uncle Charlie next took over the mysterious trumpet, sounding as wheezy as he had in real life. He said he had "just come along with your Dad to say hello," and this seemed logical, since his wife was Dad's sister. Uncle Charlie volunteered that "Will and Mary are here," and Father Murphy added that George, Elizabeth, and several other Shick relatives were also present in the darkened room. Since I could place none of them, the moment passed.

Afterward I wrote Mother to ask for possible identifications. She replied that Uncle Charlie's twin brother had been named Will, and his wife's name was Mary, but she thought the latter was still alive. George Shick was my father's favorite cousin from boyhood days, and Elizabeth was Dad's grandmother's name. It sounded like a real clan gathering, although many people have relatives by those names.

Bob's father, Hiram, sent his love to two other living offspring by name, told us that Bob's ailing mother "will be coming over to us soon in her sleep," and declared that he had recently been spending quite a bit of time in Russia. "I am trying to help persuade the Soviets to accept President Eisenhower's plan for pooling nuclear resources," he continued. "Perhaps you've noticed that you don't hear much recently about Red Chinese and Russian friendship. A rift is developing, and China will soon break away, just as Yugoslavia did." This prophetic utterance occurred in 1956. I commented that he seemed to have been doing a lot of traveling, but he assured me that it meant nothing "because there is no time or space on our plane."

One of Bob's sisters, after reiterating that she was still "helping souls who come over suddenly to adjust," confided that she was working on her vibrations so that she could appear to me in person. Teeth practically chattering at the eerie thought, I managed to assure her that she would be welcome anytime. To top the thrill-packed hour, Jack London announced himself to me, and said that he would be coming in from time to time to help me with creative writing.

During those first séances we could detect no noticeable slips of fact. Each feminine and masculine voice was distinctly different, and each had the age resonance and characteristics of expression that we remembered. If the stunt was a simple matter of ventriloquism, Edgar Bergen should look to his laurels. If the wealth of names and facts was merely the result of private sleuthing, the memory feat in a blackened room is impressive in itself.

A ouija board, that fascinating phenomenon of the toy stores, played a part in our next séance. Prompted by curiosity I purchased one, and persuaded Hap and Tania Seitz to place their fingertips on the pointer while I asked for answers they could not know. This, it seemed, would eliminate unconscious cheating. First I questioned the name of Burrough's Control in the spirit world, and the pointer correctly spelled out "Murphy." Then it delivered a message to "Ruth" from "Ira." At the next sitting with Burroughs, my father announced that he had come through to me "on the board the other evening," but this proved little, since I had foolishly mentioned the incident to the medium before he went into trance. I was accompanied to this séance by Rhoda, who was encased in a cast supporting her broken collarbone, and her alleged spirit Guide declared: "I'm not going to say 'I told you so,' but the signs were just not right for you to make the trip north at this time."

The account that Burroughs gives of his "adoption" by Father Murphy is intriguing. Now known as the "grand old man of spiritualism," Burroughs was orphaned in his childhood, and with almost no education went to Joplin, Missouri, to seek work in the coal mines. At the age of fifteen he was invited by his landlord to go to a séance. While they were there, Father Timothy Murphy made his trumpet debut and announced that thereafter he would guide Burroughs, and speak through him. Burroughs says the spirit priest told him that he had been born in Ireland, but was serving a Catholic parish in Chicago at the time that the great fire snuffed out his life. He now had unfinished business to complete through Burroughs, who later became a Spiritualist minister.

If Father Murphy's spirit does live on in this manner, he would make a good detective. Constantly seeking for evidential, I once asked my purported father-in-law what he did for a living while on earth. The spirit seemed not to understand the question. At our subsequent séance with Burroughs, however, Father Murphy took unsporting advantage of my husband by asking what his father did during the earth phase of life. Since it hardly seemed cricket to argue with a spirit Control, Bob reluctantly supplied the information that he had been a Methodist minister. Thereafter, Hiram was always identified to us as a preacher.

The alleged spirits of some deceased relatives materialized before us "in person" during a séance at Camp Silver Belle, a Spiritualist retreat in Ephrata, Pennsylvania. We know that we saw and touched them, but we are certainly unconvinced of their personal identification as disembodied spirits formed from ectoplasm. Too many errors of fact immediately preceded and followed the so-called phenomenon. Our relatives in real life were simply not such mixed-up people.

Eager to assemble sufficient material to write a newspaper series about mediums I asked Burroughs, who was president of the camp, to arrange appointments for us there. We had by now learned that we could rarely walk into a séance without proper introduction. Bob and I had been on the campground only an hour when we joined a public Message Bearer Service. As each person entered, he was asked to write a question to some departed relative on a supplied billet. Then, even before a handkerchief was tied across the eyes of the medium, he announced two "psychic messages" from "a preacher named Hiram" and "Iry Boy." This proved nothing however, since Burroughs could have alerted his fellow mediums to our arrival and supplied family information. I do not assert that he did so, but those two names were not on our unsigned billets.

We next enrolled for a séance with Rev. Elinor Bond Donnelly, and although three strangers shared the darkened room with us, our relatives beat theirs to the trumpet. Bob's father and two sisters came in by name and urged us to make no alteration in the arrangements for Bob's ailing mother. They assured us that they "watched over her all the time," and when I inquired whether she should be left in the nursing home where she had been for two years, they said that she should; but, unknown to Burroughs, she had been transferred five hundred miles away from it the preceding week.

Jimmy, the child who identifies himself as Mrs. Donnelly's Control, offered to show us his light, and a fuzzy sparkle which resembled the tail flash of a skyrocket fluttered through the inky blackness. Since the voice was emanating from a spot just in front of me, I slid downward and thrust out a groping foot. It struck something solid, which hastily withdrew. Almost immediately the voice asked: "Have we been able to touch one of you with our trumpet? We tried." I remained quiet. After all, nothing had tried to touch me. I had deliberately touched something as solid as a human being, which hastily moved away. It could not have been Mrs. Donnelly, provided that she was in trance in her chair across the room—but was she?

We next attended a public session conducted by Mollie Beck, a well-advertised clairvoyant who told my husband that she saw "a minister in a black coat and black bowler hat whose name was Hiram." Since my father-in-law had never owned a bowler hat in this life, it was nice to know that he was completing his wardrobe. The medium also said that "Iry Boy" was going to try to appear before me that evening, and with this encouraging news we kept our previously made appointment for the materialization séance with Rev. Bertha Eckroad.

While Miss Eckroad removed her bright red coat, exhibiting a form-fitting summer dress without pockets, I closely examined the room. It was empty except for fifteen camp chairs arranged in a horseshoe around three sides of the room. Across the other end, heavy maroon draperies formed the cabinet where Bertha would presumably go into trance. I inspected this with unusual care, and as far as I could determine it contained only the folding chair on which the medium would sit.

A second medium gave us important instructions. She said that after the overhead lights were turned out, a soft red bulb would burn in the lamp at our end of the room. If a spirit summoned us, we could approach and converse with it; but we must not cross between it and the cabinet, because this would sever its ectoplasmic connection and seriously harm Miss Eckroad.

By now we were tingling. The overhead light was extinguished, and while we sang a hymn our eyes became reasonably adjusted to the warm red glow from a cellophane-wrapped lamp bulb.

Before we could complete the second verse, a diaphanously clad figure emerged from the cabinet, gaily introduced herself as Bright Star, and said her mission would be to help our departed relatives materialize through the medium's ectoplasm. One by one, but never in pairs, the supposed spirits then strolled from the cabinet. As names were called, various ones in our group went to the center of the horseshoe to converse with their "spirit relatives"; and when I was told that my Grandmother Judy wished to speak with me, I eagerly approached a white-draped figure, peered into the aging face that I could not recognize, and viewed the type of long black hair which she actually retained until her death at eighty-three. Before departing, the spirit brushed my bare arm with the gossamer material which hung from the arms.

The parade of spirits resumed, and soon a voice announced that Aseneth wished to greet my husband and me. Together we approached a figure which was dressed much as the others had been, but had different facial features and hair coloring. She spoke softly of her pleasant life on the other plane, and when my husband observed that she must recognize the hymns we were singing, she agreed that she certainly did. As we resumed our seats and began the next hymn, we heard a high-pitched voice joining in from the cabinet. Bright Star said this was Aseneth demonstrating that she remembered our family songfests, but, if so, her voice had sadly deteriorated.

Assuming that we had had our share of spirit visitors, we had just relaxed when we were summoned to greet Bob's other sister, Ruth, "a former schoolteacher." The latter identification was true, and although my imagination was probably playing tricks on me, this figure seemingly bore a resemblance to my departed sister-in-law. After telling us of her "teaching duties" on the other plane, she started to say good-by, and I boldly asked if she could kiss me.

"Of course," she replied, cupping her left hand and kissing at me through that. The hand, which perhaps inadvertently touched my cheek, felt surprisingly human. She then kissed at Bob, but did not touch him, before disappearing through the parted draperies of the cabinet.

After the séance ended, I suggested to Bob that we jot down our impressions before discussing it. We both made these observations: the thirty or so spirits had somewhat different facial features and sharply contrasting hairdos, but appeared to be of approximately the same height, despite the fact that some were supposedly children whose high-pitched voices contrasted with those of the older spirits. No male adults made their appearance, although men comprised nearly half the audience. The figures wore similar gossamer garments, but were strictly three-dimensional, had distinctive voices, and walked like human beings. To a nonbeliever, the obvious impression was that either Miss Eckroad had spent a frantically busy seventy-five minutes changing her face and hairdo to impersonate a large cast of characters, or that accomplices had entered the cabinet, perhaps through a trap door. Lacking the weight scales and the cameras employed by more scientific investigators, which had helped to convince Sir Oliver Lodge and Sir Arthur Conan Doyle of the existence of spirit ectoplasm, we had no iota of proof for or against the scene we had just witnessed.

The next morning I discussed my grave doubts with Burroughs, and he urged that until I had further experience I should trust that I actually saw ectoplasmic figures of departed souls. Unfortunately, too many slips occurred during our next and final séance there. I had earlier requested a sitting with Virginia Leach Falls, an articulate young woman whose public lecture the day before was impressive enough to convince us that she would not need to resort to trickery to earn a living as a public speaker.

She turned off the lights, and after we had repeated the Lord's Prayer at her request, a merry voice identified itself through trumpet as Evening Star, the medium's Control. She first introduced my Grandmother

Shick, who said she hoped I had seen her in materialization the night before, but to her obvious surprise I said that I had not. It was my maternal, not my paternal, grandmother who claimed to have displayed her ethereal charms the evening before at the Eckroad séance. Next, my father declared his presence and said he too had tried to materialize, but since none of the supposed spirits were men, I had to protest that I had not seen him.

Two defeats apparently proved too much for the medium or for our spirit relatives, because although the next two voices were introduced as Bob's sisters, neither made the slightest reference to having greeted us "in person" the night before. In fact, although I asked Ruth when I would be able to "see" her, she replied that I must have patience because it was very difficult to build up sufficient power to materialize. She seemed unaware that she had touched and kissed me, and she made three other serious errors of fact about the family. When Bob's father came in by name, my husband asked him to sing a hymn and he replied with alacrity, "All right, son, what would you like to hear?" But after Bob warily suggested that he sing the one with which he used to open church services every Sunday, the voice hastily alibied that singing would require too much effort.

Throughout the séance a mysterious pinpoint of light darted around the blackened room, and a misty form once appeared in the spot where Bob's sister, Aseneth, presumably was speaking. Debunkers of spiritualism claim that it is relatively simple for a flashlight painted with lampblack to duplicate the mysterious darting light, and that a fluorescent petticoat can resemble a misty form when the outer skirt of a medium is lifted.

I am no expert, and although I am convinced that some of the antics we witnessed were faked, other aspects of the séance chamber continue to baffle me. How can the names of departed relatives emerge in widely separated locales, unless mediums maintain central card files with copies in the possession of all? If they do, how can they afford the expense, since the average fee for a séance is three to five dollars a person? How can a voice speaking through trumpet directly in front of us suddenly project from a far corner of the ceiling, unless the medium risks the sudden glare of a doubter's flashlight while treading noiselessly around the darkened room? If the stunt is accomplished by ventriloquism, such talent could surely command a better living on television or the stage. And what of the memory feat? Even if names are provided in advance, it is impressive that a medium can remember which relatives belong to whom when fifteen unrelated customers share a jet-black séance chamber.

It is my personal belief that nearly all such mediums have unusual psychic ability, but that some of those who have made it their vocation are tempted to resort to trickery when their powers are at low ebb. Certainly I remain impressed that Dr. Pantin's Control was able to introduce my purported father by saying, "Here's a gentleman who wants to talk to his girl; he says he's her boy." Only my sister and I had called Dad "Iry Boy." To whom else would such an introduction of a parent have made sense? But why, if our departed relatives actually are able to converse with us, do they make so many misstatements of fact? How could my husband's departed relatives fail to know that his mother had been moved to a distant nursing home if, as claimed, they were "watching over her all the time"?

Bob and I went to New Mexico on vacation after I had covered the Republican nominating convention of 1956, and while there we received word of his mother's death. We flew to Detroit for the services, and following our return to Washington, one final test remained. Realizing that Burroughs would have no way of knowing that Mrs. Montgomery was no longer on our plane, we reluctantly went to him for one last séance. No sooner was the room plunged into darkness than Father Murphy took over the "controls" and asked how Bob's mother was. Side-stepping the question, I replied that we had been traveling and were anxious to know. Apparently reassured, Bob's father and sisters made their trumpet appearances and said that Mother Montgomery's condition remained unchanged. "We are watching over her all the time," they reiterated, "and she will be coming over to us before long."

No Spiritualist can alibi that there may have been a delayed transition period, because during the same séance Father Murphy told me that "Elsie Robinson, the columnist, is here with us now." Her death announcement had appeared in Washington papers the day before, where the medium could have read it, but he had not seen the Detroit papers which reported Mrs. Montgomery's passing. It is only fair, however, to state that Burroughs was extremely tired that day, was preparing to leave on vacation, and had not wanted to give us a sitting because of that.

I completed a newspaper series about these experiences, which International News Service was planning to release with a fanfare of publicity. During the interval, I sat with a friend, Lydia Mithoff, at a ouija board. The pointer announced that it had a message for "Ruth" from "Ira," and rapidly spelled out these words: "Do not publish writing. You can do one proving life after death." Lydia had not even glanced at the ouija board, and I kept my eyes firmly averted except to read aloud each letter as the pointer stopped. It was not a message I wanted to hear, so I did not consciously influence its content. I cannot therefore explain it, or another message received shortly before.

My mother and her sister had been so distressed by my interest in psychic phenomena that they would have nothing to do with the ouija board which I had playfully given to Mother. They direly warned me against using the board, while at the same time insisting that there was "nothing to it anyway"; but I finally prevailed on them to try it together once, while I stood across the room to ask the questions. Almost resentfully, they placed their fingertips on the pointer, which began to move under their startled gaze. I asked for whom the message was intended, and as the pointer spelled out "Ruth," Aunt Mabel said accusingly, "Bertha, you're moving it."

"I certainly am not, but you're doing it," Mother retorted indignantly. Even as they argued back and forth, the pointer busily announced that the message came from "Ira," and then spelled out: "U C I love you."

I laughingly remarked that this was a rather neat abbreviation, but Mother and Aunt Mabel had had enough. Behaving as if their fingers were burned, they hastily left the board and refused to try again. I cannot honestly blame them, for I paid equally little heed to the ouija board request that I not publish my writings about the mediums. The debunking series appeared as written. It did not matter, because I was through with psychic phenomena anyway.

Or was I?

CHAPTER 3

The Pencil Writes

Despite my resolve to leave the psychic field to others, news of the Reverend Arthur Ford's arrival in Washington stirred my curiosity. Throughout my research on the subject at the Library of Congress, the name Ford had repeatedly appeared. He was America's best-known living medium. Sherwood Eddy, famous author, world traveler, and founder of the YMCA in the Orient, set forth in his widely read book *You Will Survive After Death* various messages received by him through Ford's Control, Fletcher, which he considered highly evidential. Numerous other authors and investigators on three continents lauded Ford's performances as a clairvoyant.

An ordained minister of the Christian (Disciples of Christ) church, Ford had undertaken a lecture assignment for Spiritual Frontiers Fellowship, a newly formed organization which he and some fifty prominent educators, professional men, and clergymen had established to probe psychic phenomena within the churches. (Its membership has since grown to two thousand.)

I attended one of his lectures at the Church of the Holy City in Washington, and afterward requested an interview with him about the fellowship. He set a time two days later, when the seminar would be finished, and at the appointed hour I knocked at the door of his hotel suite. The interview lasted half an hour. As I closed my notebook I asked his opinion of the ouija board, and Ford replied that some people had had good success in discovering psychic powers with it. I told him that after finishing a series on psychic phenomena, I had received a message purporting to come from my father, through the ouija board, which said: "Do not publish writing. You can do one proving life after death." I frankly added that the series was of the debunking variety, and Ford would therefore have been wise to show me to the door if he had anything to hide. Instead, he asked if I would like for him to see whether he could get anything for me through Fletcher.

At my affirmative nod he stretched out on the couch and knotted a black handkerchief tightly across his eyes. I asked if I should lower the lights, but he replied that they would not bother him. We were quiet for a time while I stared at the motionless figure across the room. He seemed to fall asleep, but suddenly his body jerked, his chin rolled, and a voice introducing itself as Fletcher began to speak. Thanks to the bright lights, so different from the dark-room séances, I could take copious notes on all that transpired. It is fortunate that I did so, for many of the names mentioned had as little meaning for me at the time as ancient Sanskrit, and I would consequently have forgotten them.

One of the gentlemen introduced by Fletcher persisted in talking about the troubles in Africa, and particularly in the Congo. "He is very disturbed about something that is happening where he lived in Africa many years ago," the Control relayed. "His name is Ed...no, no, it's Fred...Fred Bennett. He seems to have been an uncle. I think he was a preacher in Africa." I had never heard of him, and bluntly said so. Fletcher paused only momentarily before adding: "He says he didn't know you personally, but to ask your husband."

That evening when Bob came home from the office, I asked if he had ever heard of anyone named Fred Bennett. "I had an aunt who married a Fred Bennett," he replied, "but he's been dead since I was a child. How did you hear of him?" Ignoring his question for the moment, I asked what Bennett had done for a living. I shall never forget his response: "He was a foreign missionary in the Congo. Why?"

Unaware of this fact at the séance, I listened somewhat abstractly as other unknowns were introduced to me by the mysterious Fletcher. One was a man named Spence Irwin, who wanted to talk about the Near East, but I brushed him off rather brusquely. People I had known interested me more, and Fletcher seemed to sense it, because he said: "Another man is trying to come in. I have to get his name phonetically, because we don't use words over here. A man named Ina...no, but that's close. It's a three-letter word beginning with *I*. He's very fine, looks quite a bit like you. Must be your father."

I acknowledged that Dad's name was Ira, and Fletcher continued: "He sends you his love. Says he was quite ill before he came over, but then he came very suddenly. He didn't know it was that serious. He doesn't remember about dying, and says he hasn't found anyone over here who does. There is no dying. All of a sudden you're free, that's all. You're very sick and suddenly you're well. He says over here you have no ills. You're mature, but not old. His heart was bad, wasn't it? He had no thought that he would die, and no time to be frightened."

I was listening intently then, and taking down every word in my notebook, for Fletcher was remarkably accurate in describing my father's passing. An unusually healthy man, he had suffered a bout with pneumonia, but was recuperating satisfactorily when I telephoned long distance to talk with him before leaving for a newspaper assignment in Egypt. A week later Dad died suddenly of his first and only heart attack.

My mind strayed to that unhappy time, when word of his death reached me in Cairo and I flew steadily for two days and two nights to reach home in time for the funeral. Fletcher's voice, however, continued firmly: "He says you weren't with him when he came over here, but that you came soon, and he enjoyed his funeral very much. It was beautiful and simple, but he wasn't dead. He had merely gotten rid of his sick body. He says give his love to your mother. Is there someone named Bertie? He keeps saying Bertie."

I replied that this was his nickname for my mother,

Bertha, and Fletcher added: "He says you have nothing to worry about with your mother. She won't be coming over here for a good long time, buy your father says she's been having rather a difficult time this winter. One of her limbs is involved. A leg or an arm. It's been giving her trouble for quite a while, but it's not serious." Although I did not know it until I later checked by telephone, Mother admitted that this was true.

My father-in-law, Rev. Hiram Montgomery, sent messages for Bob; then Fletcher declared: "The next man is doing something. It's not exactly a typewriter I see. Jinx. Do you know Jinx?" I replied in the negative, but Fletcher was not to be squelched so easily this time. "Jinx says he knew you when you were just getting started in the newspaper business. Wait...now I get his full name. It's Jinx Tucker. He says he taught you something. He says he used to set his own stories up, not on a typewriter, but on a linotype machine. He keeps talking about football. Seems interested in sports."

Then I remembered him! Jinx Tucker had been the sports editor of the Waco *News-Tribune* in Texas during my cub reporter days there many years before, but I had not known him well. In fact, I did not know that he was dead, but when editor Harry Provence later verified this fact he further remarked: "I'll never forget Jinx. He's the only newspaperman I ever heard of who set his own stories directly into type on a linotype machine. He was also a printer." I hadn't remembered, if I had ever known.

The former president of Baylor University, my alma mater, brought greetings, and also a bit of medical advice from "a man with him whose name is Walter...last name sounds something like Morrson. He's here with Pat Neff, your college president." The doctor's name meant nothing to me, but Harry Provence later said that a Dr. Walter Moursund had served as dean of the Baylor Medical School in Dallas while I was a student on the Baylor fine arts campus in Waco.

Fletcher next said that "a Clyde Wildman, who used to be connected with schools," wanted to tell me that "someone who once lived near you, in a street or town

40

called Lafayette, has mysteriously disappeared, but he's over here now. He drowned. He was an offical of some kind...seems to have been a judge."

By then I was beginning to feel like an idiot child. I knew of no Wildman, nor of any disappearing judge since Crater, who was certainly not from Lafayette, Indiana, where I once lived briefly in my youth. The next day I telephoned the Lafayette *Courier-Journal* to seek possible clues. No sooner had I lamely begun to explain the purpose of the call than editor George Lamb declared: "That would be Judge Lynn Parkinson, of course. He used to live in Lafayette, but was judge of the United States Court of Appeals in Chicago when he disappeared last fall." He said that despite an intensive FBI search through seven states, the only trace found of the judge was his hat and umbrella, lying on the shore of Lake Michigan near the Lakeshore Hotel. For lack of proof of his death, the lifetime judgeship remained unfilled, and the Federal Government continued to pay his salary into his bank account.

The editor searched old city directories and found that Judge Parkinson had indeed lived only a few blocks from my family in West Lafayette twenty-five years before. What neither the editor nor I could then know was that a few weeks later the judge's decomposed body would be found floating on Lake Michigan. Wildman, it developed, had been a university president in Indiana before his death.

The séance with Arthur Ford was almost at an end. Fletcher introduced "a sweet old lady who seems to be of German descent, who says she was your grandmother. Her name sounds like Whitman, although that last syllable isn't quite right." My father's mother's maiden name was Jane Whitmer, and as this information does not appear in *Who's Who* or any other biographical listing for me, Arthur Ford could scarcely have researched it.

Fletcher then brought this message: "Your father says the most important story in the world for you to write is this: 'I live, and we are in a world of activity and growth. We are not living in a vacuum. I couldn't be happy if idle. I'd rather be out of my body than to

41

be an invalid, and I'd have been pretty much an invalid if I had stayed on there. I'm as vital and just as active now as when I was a boy.'" Fletcher added: "Your father liked to sing." (This was true.) "Now he's learning to sing and to develop the potentials he never had a chance to do there."

Dad (according to Fletcher) sent messages to my sister Margaret, and remarked: "She always hated to be called Maggie. She lives near your mother. You don't. She does a wonderful job of looking after Bertie. He sends her his love." All of these remarks about Margaret were true.

Ford then began to come out of trance. We said goodby, and in the days that followed I was able to check out the identity of all the strangers except Spence Irwin. Shortly afterward I wrote a Sunday feature about the experience, and as soon as the newspaper was published, people began calling long distance to tell me that Spencer Irwin had been the foreign editor of the Cleveland *Plain-Dealer*, and had made a trip to the Near East shortly before his death a year or two before. He had also known Arthur Ford.

A little pamphlet prepared by Ford for Spiritual Frontiers Fellowship stated that one of the principal methods recommended for developing one's psychic powers is meditation; and that a regular time should be set aside each day to clear the mind of worldly affairs while concentrating on a single symbol, object, or spiritual quality. I began experimenting with meditation, but had little success, for controlling a runaway horse is surely easier than commanding a restless mind to stand still. Sometimes an unusual peace seemed to envelop me, but this was invariably interrupted by the ringing of the telephone, the whir of the vacuum cleaner, or other household activities of the maid's. My mind was apparently too active for such stringent mental discipline.

I also tried my hand at automatic writing after reading the instructions in several psychic books. For minutes at a time I held a pencil lightly on a sheet of paper, but it remained stubbornly motionless. Having given the fascinating subject what I considered to be a reasonable test, I abandoned it, and busied myself with writing articles about the windup of Congress in the exciting election year of 1960.

This might have ended it, except that my good friend Hope Ridings Miller called one day to say that Gladys Moon Jones, the wife of an international lawyer, had broken her leg. Hope, a magazine editor who also is interested in the psychic field, continued rather breathlessly: "I called to commiserate with Gladys, and she said she was sure that the accident had a deliberate purpose—to force her to take time for psychic studies again. She's terribly interested in it, and I think she must be quite advanced. I asked if we could come over and talk to her about it."

A bit hesitantly, I agreed to go. My work schedule was heavy; but at least I could call on an ailing acquaintance who was also a member of the Women's National Press Club, of which Hope and I are past presidents. We spent an interesting hour listening to Gladys' vivid descriptions of her experiences in the psychic field, and agreed to meet again at the same hour the following week. Two more study sessions followed, and Gladys generously lent us books from her sizable collection on psychic phenomena. Reading these, I again became curious about automatic writing, and before setting forth for the Jones's residence, I idly picked up a pencil to try once more. Almost immediately the pencil began to race around the page, drawing circles and figure-eights with wild abandon. I could scarcely have stopped the nonsensical motions if I had tried. At last I dropped the pencil and drove to Georgetown.

No sooner had Gladys answered the doorbell than she said, "I have a surprise for you. I've just received some automatic writing which says, 'Ruth will be able to do this now.' Come, I will show you." She hobbled on her cast back to a chair, and I read what her pencil had written. Then I showed her my own ridiculous scrawls, which I had stuffed into my coat pocket. Gladys was elated. "This is authentic," she exclaimed. "It nearly always starts that way. The circles and figure-eights are their way of expressing joy that they are at last able to establish communication with you."

Encouraged, I sat down at her table to try again. Words gradually began to form, and soon a page was filling with messages from alleged relatives. I felt deeply perplexed. What was going on here? I held the pencil, yet it seemed to write without me. I had no thought of what was being expressed until I saw the words on the tablet. What was written was certainly not earth-shaking in its significance, but here was a phenomenon which clearly I did not control. Before I left, Gladys cautioned me to devote no more than fifteen or twenty minutes a day to automatic writing. This was extremely wise advice, because some people, on discovering the strange ability within themselves, let it become too time consuming. After all, we must live in one world at a time.

The automatic writing gradually developed strength in the days that followed; then an aunt who had died shortly before her wedding day, when I was three years old, took over the pencil by name, writing exultantly: "I love you. You are mine now. Now you are mine." This was disconcerting, to say the least, since she repeated the foolishly possessive phrases over and over again whenever I picked up the pencil and closed my eyes. Next, while I sat with eyes shut until the pencil stopped, she began to draw pictures through my hand, signing her own name to each with a flourish. They were whimsical and charming. Some were of animals, but most were of children in comical poses. None was a polished production, and most were rather childlike in their simplicity, but all exhibited a fluidity in drawing that I did not possess.

For a time I was amused, but I became increasingly vexed as the drawing continued to monopolize each day's sitting with the pencil. At last I firmly said aloud, "Aunt May, if you have messages to impart I will take them, but I will not waste any more time with your drawings." This made not the slightest impression on my father's kid sister who, I learned from another aunt, had been quite talented as an amateur artist in her youth. Aunt May continued to sketch until I would throw down the pencil in disgust and go on with my regular work. Our vacation fortunately put an end to it. During the weeks that we were away I made no attempt at automatic writing; on our return, a Guide introduced himself by drawing a lily, and announced that henceforth I would know him by that symbol.

He proved a stern fellow, this humorless Guide who now took over the pencil for ten or fifteen minutes each morning. He refused to tell me anything about himself, except that he had once been "a writer of great note" on my plane, but he began to give orders with the indisputable authority of a top sergeant. I was to stop smoking, he commanded, and also to forego cocktails. Time was too precious to be frittered in such fashion, and they were not good for me. I stalled, but "live and let live" was not one of Lily's favorite mottoes. His lectures via the pencil increasingly bespoke his irritation with me, and at last I stopped smoking.

A day or so later, the Guide wrote: "I want you to examine all the tobacco in your house, and see what it is that made you love it so much that you could not give it up before. Examine it as you would a lily, and see what made you want it. Look at it, feel it, smell it, and ask yourself why it had such a hold on you. Let nothing get a hold on you like that again." I had to concede that my husband's discarded cigarette butts were rather revolting in comparison with a lily.

I soon gave up cocktails, and then the next set of orders arrived. Years before I had stopped drinking coffee, after a doctor determined that I was allergic to it, but now Lily told me to discontinue tea, cokes and anything containing chocolate. The advice may have been excellent, but something in me rebelled. Who's life was this, anyway? I returned to my regular routine of a martini before dinner.

CHAPTER 4

A Spirit Goes House-Hunting

One day the pencil in my hand began to write, haltingly at first, and then with confidence. Racing across the pages of a notebook in barely legible script, it directed me to find a different house. "This is more important to our work than anything else at this time," it scrawled. "It should be very much older than the house you are in, with high ceilings and big rooms. This you know, too." As a matter of fact, I was becoming increasingly dissatisfied with the modern split-level house which we had bought five years before. I missed our hundred-year-old house in Georgetown, with its thirteen-foot ceilings and lived-in air. Since I had recently remarked several times to Bob that I would like to find a gracious older house, I thought that I must be writing my own subconscious thoughts with the pencil.

The pencil continued to speed back and forth across the page, writing: "The house should be located near the Georgetown area, and have much charm and beauty. You can find the house by looking in the want-ads today. It is very much to your liking, and has a little garden patio. Offer no more than seventy thousand dollars for the house, which is located near the library. You should find this house without delay on P Street." It wavered momentarily, and amended: "It is not on P Street but on R Street. It is advertised today, and should be inspected immediately. It is in the *Post* want-ads. Go at once and find it. Buy it. We will take care of the rest."

I had come to know that "we" referred to whatever mysterious force propelled the pencil. It does little good to argue with a Guide, or at least with the strong-minded ones who seemed to have appointed themselves my mentors. More meekly than I ever obeyed my parents, I now went to find the classified section of the Washington *Post*. No houses were listed for sale on R Street, nor for that matter on P Street.

Feeling strangely relieved, I returned to my desk and picked up the waiting pencil. Immediately it drew a lily, and wrote: "It should have been run today, but something went wrong. It will be in the *Post* want-ads this week. It is meant for you. Do not hesitate when you see it. Go ahead and buy it, and do not wait to dispose of your house. I promise that we will take care of that for you. Do not dilly-dally, but buy it. Godspeed!"

This was a rather chilling directive. Not only was I to tell my husband that we were buying a different house, but also inform that very practical man that we should not even wait to sell our own house first! I decided to say nothing about it. The next morning, I had no sooner picked up the pencil than the writing began: "Ruth, this is Dad. This is Ira. I want to tell you that the house you are to buy is not on R Street, but almost. It is near the Library of the Indianapolis Society. That is not the right word. I have it wrong, but it is not the public library. This is where you will buy, and it is the right one. I am allowed to tell you this by your Guide, so that you will know. It may be advertised now, but please look again in yesterday's paper. Now to your Guide. Love, Dad."

Without a moment's pause, but with a perceptible shift in the pressure on the pencil, the sign of the lily appeared, and my Guide wrote: "That is right, Ruth. I wanted your father to tell you, so you would understand about the error. It is not the public library that it is near, but another library belonging to an organization. It is near that, and the bridge. That is not quite in Georgetown, but near it. Try to find it in the ads."

I searched through the want-ads again, found nothing remotely resembling the location mentioned in the automatic writing, but marked a check beside three listings which gave no address. Then I held the pencil and asked: "Is it one of those that I have checked?"

The pencil sprang to life and nearly popped from my fingers as it wrote exuberantly: "Yes, yes, it is the one with the ormolu. Get it today. It is for you."

Feeling rather foolish, I dialed the listed telephone number of the real estate agency. A woman answered, and when I inquired about the house-for-sale advertisement that mentioned "French ormolu hardware," she surprised me by exclaiming: "My dear, I'll bet you would have come to see it yesterday if you had known the address, wouldn't you? That stupid *Post* left the address out of the ad. It was supposed to be there." A slight shiver tingling my spine, I asked where it was located. "It's on Massachusetts Avenue," she caroled. "Right on Sheridan Circle. You know where that is dear? R Street stops there for the Circle."

The location was exactly, then, as the pencil had described. I knew the area well. The Q Street bridge into Georgetown was a scant block to the west. Little more than a block in the other direction stood the imposing National Headquarters of the Society of the Cincinnati, a patriotic organization with its own museum and library. The mistake in name would have been an understandable one for my father to make, even if still in this plane. He had had two brothers. One lived in Indianapolis, the other in Cincinnati. It could almost have been a slip of the tongue. By now thoroughly intrigued, I made an appointment to see the house, and as an after-thought asked the price.

"My dear, they have been asking a hundred and twenty-five thousand for it," the agent cooed, "but the owners simply have to sell, so I do think you could get it for eighty-five. Come and see it, anyway. I'll meet you there in an hour."

Feeling somewhat deflated, I returned to my desk and the pencil. Lily, announcing himself with exuberance, wrote: "That is the place! They will come down on the price. You must buy it. It is the one for you, and it has what we need for our project—height and space

49

and big rooms. Tell her you will pay seventy thousand dollars, but no more. Then we can negotiate."

After a slight pause, the pencil began anew: "It has a little patio, and you can alter one of the rooms to make it our work place. This will be the front one on the lower level. It will be just right for our project. It is ready for our use, except that we need one big room instead of two. Knock out the partition and take out the fireplace, so we can have a wide area of space. Then we can have sessions there with people who need us and want our help. This is a very private place to meet, away from the rest of the house. That is why this house will be so good for our work. We must act promptly, so that our work is not delayed. Please rush this, I beg you. Now, go—go—go—go."

I went, and it was eerie to find everything exactly as the Guides had described. The ceilings were lofty, the rooms spacious, and the details of moldings, cornices, marble mantles, and ormolu hardware were masterpieces of French artistry, created in another day when craftsmen took pride in their handiwork. The front room on the lower level did indeed have a fireplace, a false one that was readily removable, whereas the five others in the house were real. The room had a private entrance from the street, and was certainly "away from the rest of the house." In the rear was a charming little garden patio, precisely as foretold.

Unfortunately the house also contained four flights of stairs, and the dining room and kitchen were on the third floor. It was this which decided us against it, despite the very real temptation of its beauty and charm. Bob and I, after giving it careful thought and admiring the exquisite detail, decided that it simply would not do for us.

My Guides forcibly argued otherwise. An impasse developed, for under the prodding of my husband I became as adamant as they. Repeatedly I explained that whereas it was no trouble for a discarnate spirit to flit up and down a stairwell, Bob and I still lived in bodies that had to make the climb. So would the delivery boys, and the maid. The logic was all on my side, but the Guides were not to be swayed. During one of our ensuing arguments via the fast-moving pencil, Lily wrote: "I must insist that you buy it. It was meant to be your home. It may be inconvenient, but it is the way you were meant to live. There is no way to avoid it. Why struggle against the inevitable? It is yours. Take it and be happy in it, as you will be. This is your destiny. It is yours, and you must not shirk it." When I winced, the pencil commanded sternly: "Now, go to see it again. Make your offer of seventy thousand dollars, and let's get on with our work."

I went to see the house again, and loved it, but still could not bring myself to sign a contract for such a fantastically unaccommodating abode, particularly when our own house had not even been put on the market. At last Lily seemed to relent a little. "Let it go for a few days," he wrote one morning. "It may just possibly be that we could find another equally suited to your cause. This is not to be taken as a denial of what I have told you, but I hope we can find something that will please Bob as well as us." The next day, the powers that controlled the pencil remembered their promise. "Let's concentrate on finding one that is to Bob's liking as well as ours," the pencil wrote beguilingly. "This is important, because Bob is to play a big part in our project."

The Guides seemed unusually understanding. Thus encouraged, I sallied forth to inspect some houses which other real estate brokers had to offer, but everything was anti-climatic after the unsurpassed beauty of the Sheridan Circle residence. Tired and disappointed; I picked up the pencil; which wrote: "It is going to be difficult to find anything you want except that house, Ruth. It is made for our work. The house is truly ours, and Bob will soon love it too. Please buy it now."

Lily had begun to sound like the most persistent real estate agent in the business. He told me to pay seventy-five thousand dollars if necessary, but when I asked whether we would be able to realize that much from our own house sale, he tantalizingly replied: "You are not to worry about that. I will take care of that myself. It will be sold in good time, and for a good price. This is true. Now, go ahead and get the other one."

The plaintive arguments with my Guide continued

for several days. Once, without the familiar opening sign of the lily, the pencil wrote: "Ruth, this is Dad. I want you to do what the Guide says. He knows what is best for you. He always has your interest at heart and is here to help you. He is very wise and wonderful, and wants to do what is right. He is for you on this plane what I wanted to be there. He will look after you from here and will be for your good. Let him tell you what to do, and always do it. This is as it should be. Believe me, I know. I wish I had known it when I was there."

Another time a message from "Dad" had this to say: "You are one of the fortunate ones who has been chosen for this work, and it is very necessary that you obey. I know it is not always easy, but it must be done if you are to fulfill your life mission. Do it, Ruth, do it. Believe me, I know, and I want you to succeed. It is a wonderful thing that lies before you if you will do as bidden. This is all now. Ira."

At the urging of the pencil, I persuaded Bob to go with me to see the house once more. Afterward Lily rhapsodized: "The house is perfect for our project, and is what you need to advance spiritually and mentally. It is not for you alone that I ask you to move. It is for the sake of our work together. It will make of you a new person, dedicated to good and to helping others." I asked if he could tell me anything about this mysterious work that lay ahead. He replied that he could not until I had "made the next step" and the "conditions were right."

I wanted to know his identity, and whether he had been a newspaperman in this life. Slowly the pencil wrote: "No, I was not a newspaperman. I was a writer of great note. I cannot tell you more at this time."

Piqued, I prodded: "If I take the next step, will I be able soon to know who you were?"

"We shall see," he replied noncommittally.

A few mornings later the writing began with great verve: "This is the day you will get the house. I am so happy about it. It is for you and Bob, and our work. This beautiful house was made long ago for this purpose, but the previous owners have been incapable of this kind of communication. Now relax. We will take care of the rest, including the sale of your own house."

The real estate agent, totally unaware of the aid she was receiving from my unseen pen pals, unexpectedly dropped by the house that day with the head of her agency. They brought a contract which they urged me to sign. "Just offer something," she wheedled, "and we will see what the counter-offer will be."

I telephoned Bob at his office, listened again to the logic against it, but with trepidation signed a written offer for seventy thousand dollars. In a little while the agents returned with a counteragreement. The owner would accept seventy-five thousand. Almost before I realized it we had compromised on seventy-two thousand five hundred dollars, and the deal was sealed.

Lily was jubilant. The agents had no sooner departed than the pencil in my hand began to twitch, and the Guide wrote: "Oh, how wonderful! Now we can truly begin our work. Now we can begin to serve others, as we were meant to serve them by our Creator." I started to drop the pencil, but with a flurry it added: "I will handle the sale of this house, so you will not lose on it. It is not going to bring what you are asking, but it will be a fair price. God bless you!"

Two days later, on a Sunday, the pencil surprisingly wrote: "Your house will sell this week. You are not to worry about it. It will go for seventy-five thousand dollars, and that is fair. Do not hesitate to accept it. It will not bring more, so why wait? Now rest, relax, smile, and prepare for the week ahead."

We had no prospects for the house, having not yet listed it for sale, but we had decided to ask eighty-five thousand dollars. The next day an out-of-town friend called and said that she and her husband were in Washington to find a furnished house for leasing. His business interests would be bringing them to the capital rather frequently for the next two or three years, she explained, and they both disliked hotel living.

I gave her what leads I could about rental houses. I also mentioned that we had just bought another house and would be putting ours on the market. She knew our house rather well, having been there to parties when in Washington, and she asked if she could bring her husband to look at it. I told the maid to admit them in my absence, and two days later they purchased the house. Their offer was twenty-five hundred dollars less than Lily had predicted, but since we would not have to pay a realtor's commission, and it had indeed sold within the week, the Guide's batting average stood at one hundred per cent. A month later we moved to the house on Sheridan Circle.

CHAPTER 5

My Psychic Friends

Nearly everyone can recall a hunch that came true, a
dream that seemed to foretell an event, or an occasion
on which he apparently picked up another's thought
wave. How many times has a friend telephoned just as
you were preparing to dial his or her number? How
often have you found yourself thinking of someone who
long ago passed from your life, only to encounter him
on the street that day? But occasionally, a person who
has had no previous brush with extrasensory perception experiences an isolated incident of such dramatic
impact that he cannot thereafter question the existence
of some powerful force which man does not yet understand.

On a rainy January night in 1943, the wife of General Nathan F. Twining was asleep at her home in
Charlotte, North Carolina, when a sound "like a clap
of thunder" awakened her. Opening her eyes, she "saw"
her husband standing at the foot of the bed, although
she knew that he was halfway around the world, commanding the Thirteenth Air Force in the Pacific Theater of war.

"I saw Nate's face and hands clearly, even to his
West Point ring," Maude Twining recalls. "Then, as I
watched, his fingers lost their grip on the footboard,
and he gradually disappeared. The experience was so
eerie that the hair literally stood up on the nape of my
neck."

Too disturbed for further sleep, she went to the

kitchen to brew a pot of coffee. Her next-door neighbor, noticing the lights burning, telephoned to ask if one of the children were ill. Mrs. Twining told her of the disturbing vision, and the neighbor came over to sit with her until daybreak. The next day Mrs. Twining received a long-distance call from a friend, whose husband was also an officer in the South Pacific, asking if she could come down to visit for a few days.

"I had difficulty suppressing my alarm, because I felt that she was being sent to me for some reason connected with Nate," Maude confesses, "but her three-day stay was uneventful. Then, two hours after she left, I received official notification that Nate had been missing for over three days at sea. Although she and I had not known it at the time, her husband was in charge of the widespread search for Nate's plane, which had gone down the night of my vision."

An oil slick, and pieces of the airplane in which General Twining and fourteen others had been traveling from Guadalcanal to Espiritu Santo airbase, had finally been sighted the day that Mrs. Twining was notified. The following day, searchers spotted two life rafts lashed together, and a navy hydroplane managed to rescue the severely sun-burned, ravenous men after four days on the storm-tossed seas.

General Twining knew nothing of his wife's strange vision on the night that his plane went down, but in his first letter to her after the ordeal, he wrote that just before the plane crash-landed in the angry Pacific during a raging typhoon, he clearly "saw" her looking in at him through the rain. The plane then hit the waves with a rending crash, broke in half, and sank within thirty seconds. Twining, as commanding general, was the last to leave the wreckage, and as his hands grasped the side of the already crowded life raft, he noticed the gold wrist watch which his wife had given him slip from his wrist.

"Maude will be mad as hell," he thought wryly while the watch disappeared into the briny deep. His West Point ring remained on his finger.

Psychic experiences seem to become more prevalent

during wartime, perhaps because of the strong emotional link between those who are facing constant danger in the battle zone and their families at home. Mrs. U. Alexis Johnson, the wife of our former Ambassador to Czechoslovakia and Thailand who is now Ambassador to Japan, had a series of psychic promptings early in World War II.

Because of gathering war clouds, she and their children were evacuated from Mukden, Manchuria, late in 1940, but Johnson stayed on as U.S. Consul until the Japanese placed him under arrest the same day that they bombed Pearl Harbor, on December 7, 1941. Mrs. Johnson had meanwhile taken a house at Laguna Beach, California, and one March day in 1942 a neighboring couple told her that their radio could pick up broadcasts from the Orient. Knowing that she had learned Japanese while her husband was a language officer in Tokyo during the 1930's, they suggested that she drop in some evening to translate the Japanese-language broadcasts for them.

Mrs. Johnson thanked them, but thought no more of it for three months. Then, at 9:50 P.M. on June 8, an inner voice told her: "Go at once and listen to the Meinards' radio." She rushed down the beach to the neighbors', discovered with some embarrassment that they were having a party, but nevertheless said that she wished to hear their radio. Her host hospitably began turning the dial of his high-frequency set, and she suddenly cried: "There, get that station! They said Mukden, and that's where my husband is."

The station came in clearly just as a Japanese announced in heavily accented English: "In a few minutes you will be hearing from an American official, Mr. U. Johnson." A hush descended over the room, and at exactly ten o'clock a familiar voice spoke across the airwaves, saying: "This is U. Alexis Johnson in Mukden. If anyone hears this, will he please contact my wife, Patricia, in Laguna Beach, or my parents, Mr. and Mrs. Carl T. Johnson in Glendale, California, with this message: I'm well, getting enough to eat, and hope to be exchanged by way of Lourenço Marques, Portuguese East Africa. I send my love to my dear wife and three darling children, and hope they have not forgotten their daddy."

Mrs. Johnson says that although a number of kind strangers later relayed word to her, not one of them had the message quite right. Two interminable months passed before Mrs. Johnson received official notification that her husband was sailing on the *Gripsholm* with the first exchange of prisoners. She went to New York to be on hand for his arrival, but a letter from the FBI requested that she not meet the boat because her husband would have to remain on board for two days to help clear the repatriated Americans.

She had every intention of obeying those instructions, but as she walked along Broadway the day that the *Gripsholm* docked, an inner voice again prompted: "Go to the ship." Rushing down a stairway to the subway, she reached the ship just as an old friend descended the gangplank and called out to her: "Hi, Patricia! He's right behind me!" In another moment she was in her husband's arms.

After a brief reunion, Johnson returned to the ship to help with identifications, but arranged to meet her at the hotel the following morning. To help her endure the tedious wait, friends thoughtfully invited her to dinner and the theater that evening; but as the entrée was served, something told her to call the hotel. Obeying, she asked to be connected with her room, and her husband's voice sang out: "I'm here! I don't have to go back to the boat anymore." Except for the psychic nudge, she would have missed their first evening together in two years.

Mrs. Johnson recalls that at the age of eight she followed the instructions of another inner warning. Because her mother was ill, she had been visiting her aunt and uncle for a week at their home in Bethesda, Maryland; but one evening as they started upstairs to bed, she suddenly announced that she had to go home. No amount of urging could pacify the child, so her uncle wearily hitched up the horse and buggy, and drove her to Washington. By then it was midnight, and she was hastily put to bed, but the next morning she went to her mother's room for a happy reunion. Ten minutes later, her mother peacefully died.

A series of extrasensory experiences also befell another well-known woman during World War II, although not through her own psychic ability. India (Mrs. Herbert) Edwards of Washington, a close friend of the Lyndon B. Johnson and Harry S. Truman families, is affectionately called the Queen Bee of the Democratic party, because of her long-time roles as Presidential advisor and as Women's Director of the Democratic National Committee.

On the night of December 29, 1943, India was awakened by a long-distance call from Wendover Field, Utah, informing her that her nineteen-year-old son was on a missing bomber that was overdue at the base. She spent a sleepless night, and early the next morning telephoned her son's godmother, Mrs. Inez Boulton, to tell her of the missing plane. "I just know John is dead," she wept.

"No, I'm sure that he's alive and well," Mrs. Boulton replied with confidence, "because last night I 'saw' him on my stairway, and he said, 'Aunt Inez, tell Mother not to worry. I'm O.K.'" But Mrs. Boulton had misconstrued the meaning of his words.

Search parties combed the wild Utah countryside for several days before spotting the wreckage of two planes which had collided in midair. There were no survivors. In a few days an officer personally delivered to Mrs. Edwards all of John's effects, except a signet ring that had been given to the young second lieutenant by his fiancée. Queried about it, the Air Force officer said he was sure John had been wearing it when he died; but, since the bodies of the airmen were badly mangled and burned, their coffins were not opened by the families.

The key to John's jewelry box was also missing, and one day when Inez Boulton and India's mother, Mrs. India Gillespie, sat at a ouija board, the pointer suddenly spelled out this message: "The key to John's jewelry box is in his glasses case." The women went immediately to the carton containing his effects, removed a pair of dark glasses, and shook the glasses case. Out fell the missing key; and inside the jewelry box, which it unlocked, was the signet ring.

Several weeks later, Mrs. Edwards returned home late and found a note from the maid instructing her to call a Mrs. Blank in Connecticut regardless of the hour. (Mrs. Blank was a nationally known woman whom she had not seen in many years.) India returned the call about midnight, and the woman began apologetically: "India, I don't know whether you are aware of it, but my daughter is quite psychic. She tries not to receive messages, but sometimes they are forced on her. I'm visiting her here in Connecticut, and when I walked into the library this evening, she jumped up and asked, 'Mother, do you know somebody named India?' I told her that I'd never heard of but one person by that name, and my daughter said, 'Her son John wants to get a message to her. He says it's urgent. Tell her to stop grieving that he died in this country rather than in battle, because he was doing just as valuable work here as he could have done overseas. He says the more she sorrows, the harder it is for him to keep from being earthbound.' India, did you have a son named John?"

Mrs. Edwards sorrowfully told her of his plane crash in Utah, and confessed that she had been grieving because her son had died before he could use his military training in battle to help America win the war.

"John, despite his youth, was such an expert bomber that the Air Force was using him to train others, instead of sending him overseas," Mrs. Edwards recalls. "My natural grief over his death was heightened because I felt that if he had to go, he would have preferred to give his life for his country in combat. This message helped greatly to straighten out my thinking."

Others have also been aided by voices which seem to come from beyond the grave. Peggy Farnsworth, the wife of a foreign service officer, was driving her mother and an aunt to Los Angeles after attending her father's funeral in Fresno. Exhausted from lost sleep and emotional strain, she dozed off at the wheel. As she did so, her foot apparently pressed down on the accelerator, and suddenly she heard her father's voice shouting,

"Peg, Peg," in his familiar, cautionary tone. Instantly awake, she discovered that she was rounding a curve on the Ridge Route at eighty miles an hour. A sheer precipice dropped from the road at either side. Except for her deceased father's "voice," they would probably have been killed.

Roderick Burnham of Los Angeles once had a dream that was clearly clairvoyant. At the age of sixteen he was staying alone at the family home in California while his parents and a younger brother were at Maidenhead in England. His father, a famous Indian scout who had also served as Chief of Scouts in the Boer War, was on a government mission there, but the school term prevented Roderick from accompanying the family. One afternoon, on returning home from classes, such a strange uneasiness gripped him that he went to his grandmother's house to spend the night. Toward midnight he dreamed that he saw his young brother come out of the house at Maidenhead, walk onto the pier, and drop a little homemade canoe into the Thames River. The canoe promptly sank, and as the little boy hunched forward for a better look, he toppled into the river without a sound.

Roderick awakened screaming and ran into his grandmother's room to tell her of the nightmare. The next morning, a cable from his father informed them that his brother had drowned in the Thames. Later messages disclosed that no one had seen the child fall, or heard him cry out, but his body was found in the water beside the pier in front of their house. Allowing for the difference in time zones, he was last seen alive shortly before Roderick's dream.

Mental telepathy is sometimes particularly acute in times of emergency. Two sisters, members of a prominent Washington family, were at home alone one day when a hospital attendant telephoned that a traffic victim had been brought in unconscious. "We don't find any identification on him," the caller said, "but he roused once and spoke your father's name. Can you come over right away?"

Jane and Virginia (as we shall call them) quickly hailed a cab, and during the drive to the hospital the former silently prayed, "Dear Lord, don't let it be Freddie," while the latter kept silently repeating, "Don't let it be Jack."

On arriving at the hospital, they saw to their relief that neither of their two brothers was involved. The injured man was an employee on their father's estate. They gratefully arranged to take care of the man's medical bill, notified his wife to come to the hospital, and then returned home. As they entered the house the telephone was ringing, and when Jane answered she heard Freddie's voice asking, "Sis, are you all right?" She cautiously asked why he wanted to know, and he replied: "I was running the tractor a while ago, when I heard your voice calling me. I looked all around, and thought you must be playfully hiding behind a tree, because I couldn't see you; but when I kept hearing your voice, I came to the house to call. Are you in trouble?"

Severely shaken, she told him why she had been silently repeating his name. A few minutes later the telephone rang again. This time it was the other brother, Jack, asing if anything had happened to Virginia. "I was flying down to Richmond, when I repeatedly heard her calling me," he explained. "It was so vivid that I finally turned the plane around and came back to Washington. Is something the matter?"

Significantly, each brother had heard the voice of the particular sister who, without the other's knowledge, had been silently repeating the name of her favorite brother.

Many children have a strongly intuitive faculty, or sixth sense, which unfortunately diminishes as adult pressures force them into accepted molds in the world of so-called reality. That this suppression of a natural gift can be harmful seems to be borne out by an occurrence in a Los Angeles public school. Mrs. Natalie Keller Cleveland was teaching a seventh-grade art class composed of thirty-five boys who were all low achievers in academic subjects, and was discussing a

problem in design, when a student complained.
do we always have to use our imaginations? Why can ʋ
we draw something that's real?" Others chimed in with
similar protests, and Mrs. Cleveland asked, "So what's
real?"

The first student said real things were "things you
see." With a little prompting, others decided reality
was also "things you feel, smell, taste, or touch."

"How about being sad or happy or angry, is that
real?" the teacher asked. After some hesitation the boys
agreed that moods were real, but when she asked if
dreams were real, their faces reflected a complexity of
doubt. She next asked if a desk was real, and the students all shouted "yes," but their thoughtfulness grew
as she posed the question of whether the desk was still
"real" if it was taken apart and perhaps made into a
door frame.

After they had mulled over this problem for a time,
Mrs. Cleveland wrote "extrasensory perception" on the
blackboard, and inquired whether anyone knew its
meaning. Silence reigned until one boy ventured that
it meant mind-reading. Nodding, the teacher added:
"Not only that, but sometimes it is a feeling that you've
been in a place before, or it's like knowing that something is going to happen before it does. Sometimes it's
knowing that something is happening far away."

At this the boys began talking at once, all trying to
recount experiences of their own, or ones they had
heard about from family and friends. Then one boy
politely raised his hand. An epileptic, he was one of the
lowest achievers in the below-average class. "Is there
really a name for knowing what is going to happen
before it does?" he asked hesitantly.

"Yes, it is called precognition," Mrs. Cleveland replied, and wrote the word on the blackboard.

The boy, painstakingly copying the word on a piece
of paper, said, "I didn't know. I thought something was
wrong with me, because it happens to me all the time."

The bell rang then, and the students filed out of the
room, still chattering. As the school term continued,
Mrs. Cleveland noted marked improvement in several
members of the class, particularly the epileptic boy.

emed to have released him, and from the ⸻ class he rose rapidly until he graduated as ⸻ student two years later.

⸻ ave no proof that this wouldn't have happened a⸻ way," Mrs. Cleveland says, "but never have I seen greater relief than when this child found that there was a normal, accepted word for his secret experiences, which he thought had set him apart from others."

Hope Ridings Miller, editor of *The Diplomat* magazine, recalls that at the age of five she was awakened one night by the sound of excited voices. Her mother was telling her father of having dreamed that her diamond ring was missing, and after checking her jewelry box, she discovered that the dream was true. Hope and Dr. Alfred L. Ridings joined in the frantic search, but since they had returned to Sherman, Texas, the day before from California, it seemed probable that the ring had been lost en route.

A few nights later, Mrs. Ridings dreamed again of the ring. This time, she said, "someone with a familiar face" told her to look in the fourth finger of her glove. Because she particularly liked gloves, and had a large assortment for every occasion, she had to examine a number of pairs before finding the missing ring in the fourth finger of one of them.

Ten years later, Mrs. Ridings was attending a Circle meeting at the Baptist church in Sherman, when she sensed that something was amiss at home. Leaving the meeting, she almost ran the three blocks to their house, and after glancing into several rooms, found her daughter unconscious in the bathtub. Like most of their neighbors in those days, the Ridings family had an instant gas heater for warming water, and the flame had gone out while Hope was taking a bath. Except for her mother's premonition of danger, she would have been asphyxiated or drowned.

One of our neighbors was Ambassador Bulend Usakligil, who occupied the beautiful Turkish Embassy residence near our own home on Sheridan Circle. One night at a dinner party he told us of a precognitive experience which befell him during his diplomatic tour of duty in Rumania, in 1938. He had received word of the illness of his brother, Vedat Usakligil, and while taking an overnight train to his bedside, dreamed that his brother entered the compartment, pulled out his watch, displayed the dial, and said, "I have to leave you now. I have come to say good-by."

The Turkish diplomat awakened with a feeling of unease, snapped on the light, and looked at his wrist watch. It was a few minutes before five o'clock, the precise time which his brother's watch had indicated in the dream. On reaching his destination, he learned that Vedat Usakligil had died a few minutes before five o'clock that morning.

Mrs. A. Burke Summers, the wife of our former Ambassador to Luxembourg, has understandable reason to believe that some people have precognitive ability. As a high school student in Walla Walla, Washington, during World War I, she made a trip with her mother to the family ranch near Yakima, and they stopped en route to visit friends in Spokane. Their hostess, finding it impossible to keep an appointment with a local psychic, suggested that Helen go instead. Helen Salisbury Summers says that the neatly dressed, attractive psychic did not know her identity, but that she told her these three things:

* If you call this telephone number in Seattle at ten o'clock tomorrow morning, you can prevent your young brother from enlisting. He will be fibbing about his age.

* Your return trip home will be delayed, because you will come down with a contagious disease that will cause quite a furor.

* You will marry a high school sweetheart, but not until each of you has crossed both oceans. Before graduating from college you will be tempted to give up school and move to the Orient, but you will not do so.

Helen was sufficiently impressed to insist that her mother call the Seattle telephone number at ten o'clock the following morning. Although Mrs. Salisbury pooh-poohed the idea, she reluctantly consented, and learned that her fifteen-year-old son was in the Marine recruitment office at that moment, swearing that he was eighteen. The youngster was ordered home to Walla Walla, where his mother had assumed that he was, instead of to boot camp.

Mrs. Salisbury and Helen continued on to the ranch, but after riding horseback together one afternoon, Helen suddenly felt impelled to go into town for the night. Her mother argued that they would be leaving the next day anyway, but Helen's sense of urgency was so great that Mrs. Salisbury told the ranch manager to drive her daughter to the home of friends in Sprague.

"I had never felt better in my whole life," Helen Summers says, "except for that strange feeling that I had to be in town. During the night I awakened with a raging fever, and the friends rushed me to a nearby hospital. Doctors at first thought that I had typhoid fever, but pandemonium broke loose when they discovered that they had a case of highly contagious smallpox on their hands."

The third prophecy by the palmist-numerologist also came to pass. During Helen's junior year at the University of Washington she became engaged to Burks Summers, the son of Congressman John W. Summers, whom she had first dated in high school. That summer Burks accompanied a Congressional junket to the Orient, and was offered such an attractive career in the export-import business that he and his fiancée seriously considered getting married immediately and moving to China. Dissuaded by their parents, they postponed the wedding until after college graduation. By that time Helen had made trips with her family to Europe and the Orient, and Burks had made another overseas trip, to Austria. Each had crossed both oceans!

Despite the remarkable accuracy of the woman's predictions, Helen made no further attempt to contact her. After her marriage to Burks they moved East, and in September of 1930 were living in a Philadelphia apartment when friends telephoned that they were coming down from New York to see a psychic who had been recommended to them. Helen agreed to accompany them, as did her sister-in-law, Mrs. Paul Summers, who lived in the Philadelphia suburbs; but at the last minute the latter, who was pregnant, decided not to go.

Helen went anyway, and after the psychic looked into a crystal ball she told her: "I see you, the first week of January, standing at an open grave in the cemetery. A woman in your family will die, and it will completely change your life." Helen was unimpressed. As she told friends on the way home, even if her mother or mother-in-law did die, it would not alter her life in any dramatic way.

Mrs. Paul Summers gave birth to a baby boy in late December, and was due to go home from the hospital Christmas Eve. The day before, she began to run a high temperature, and during the first week of January died of pleural pneumonia. Helen Summers, who was childless, had never held a new baby in her arms until she went to the hospital to take Paul, Jr., home to his widowed father and three-year-old sister, Virginia. There was only one thing for Helen to do. She and Burks moved into his brother's house in the suburbs, and she devoted the next twenty years to mothering two children. Her life had changed indeed!

Shortly before the outbreak of World War II, the Summers' moved to Washington and plunged zestfully into Republican politics at the national level. In 1948, a local psychic whom Helen had heard about at a party told her: "You're going to have a very unusual experience. You will propose a plan that will meet with considerable opposition from other women, but three important men will help you put it over, and I see you standing in a large arena filled with thousands of people, while other thousands clamor to get in. You are surrounded by red-white-and-blue bunting, and American flags are flying. Bands are playing, but it's not the Fourth of July."

Helen believes that she gave the prophecy no further thought; but the following year, while serving as co chairman of the annual Lincoln Day Congressional Dinner, she vowed never again to work on "anything as silly as a few hundred Republicans just talking to each other at an expensive dinner." When the League of Republican Women asked her to serve again as co-chairman the following year, a sudden thought popped into her head, and she said: "I will, provided we can have a big rally, with only box suppers for food."

The other officers of the women's league flatly rejected the idea, but when Helen later mentioned it to Congressmen Joseph W. Martin, Jr., and John Dondero, they were enthusiastic and asked her to prepare a format. She subsequently engaged Uline Arena for the evening, persuaded John Willard Marriott, a well-known Republican restaurateur, to furnish box suppers at cost, and asked actor George Murphy to serve as master of ceremonies for a gala variety show. Murphy, later to become a United States Senator from California, was eager to cooperate if he could be released from other commitments, and Helen managed that, too.

On February 6, 1950, eight thousand jubilant partisans jammed the arena, while another five thousand people milled around outside, unable to get seats. Bands played, flags fluttered, and red-white-and-blue bunting bedecked the arena. The woman psychic had apparently experienced a precognitive vision of the first Lincoln Day box-supper rally, which was to set the pattern for many more to follow.

Paul Summers, Sr., Helen's brother-in-law, remained a widower for more than a quarter of a century, until after Paul, Jr., had graduated from college and married Jill Faulkner, daughter of famed novelist and Mrs. William Faulkner. The elder Summers subsequently married Minnie Lee Wire, an attractive widow, who has a strong psychic sense. Minnie Lee was entertaining a guest one afternoon in 1944, when, she says, "I suddenly felt all life draining out of my body, and I could scarcely breathe. This frightening condition remained with me until midnight, when I received word that my sister, Mrs. Robert Young, had died in San Angelo, Texas, at the exact time that I suffered the attack."

In the late 1950's she experienced a similar sensation, which lasted for several hours. She then learned that her favorite uncle, E. W. Williams of Lubbock, Texas, who had served as trustee for her father's estate, had "passed on at the moment of my seizure." In June of 1962, after attending the college graduation exercises of her twin daughters, Ramona and Rosemary Wire, in Massachusetts, she was driving back to Washington, when she suddenly became so weak that she felt as if she were dying. "I could scarcely breathe during the remainder of the trip," she recalls. "On reaching home we discovered that my brother Guinn "Big Boy" Williams (a character actor who played the role of a cowboy in such movies as *Dodge City* and *Virginia City*) had died."

The only other time that the normally healthy, energetic Mrs. Summers suffered such an experience was on March 14, 1966. She was looking forward to a party that evening at the Arthur Bergmans', but suddenly felt that "all the vitality was being drained from my body." In a few minutes her husband telephoned to check the time of their social engagement, but on hearing her voice, asked with some concern if she were ill. She told him of her unaccustomed weakness, and while he rushed home, the administrator of a hospital in San Angelo, Texas, telephoned to say that Mrs. Summers' mother had passed away only shortly before.

Minnie Lee says of the curious episodes: "In every instance, when a member of my family has passed away, my vitality was at such low ebb that it was difficult for me to breathe. As life left their bodies, it seemed almost to leave mine, for each time my disturbance occurred at the actual time of their death in another city."

Newspaperwoman Virginia Kelly, the wife of Rear Admiral Thomas J. Kelly, says that the first "navy wife" she ever met, when she went to Annapolis as an eighteen-year-old bride, was the wife of Admiral David C. White. The two women became devoted friends, but after their husbands were transferred from the Naval Academy they met less frequently, and only through occasional Christmas cards did the Washington-based Kellys know that the Whites eventually settled in Hauula, Hawaii.

Virginia had not seen Ruth White for eighteen years,

when, on the night of June 22, 1966, she dreamed that her friend came to her apartment and said, "I've just come from the hospital." She awakened with such a feeling of depression that she almost called the Whites in Hawaii, but put the expensive impulse from her mind. That afternoon she took a nap, and dreamed an almost identical dream. Again she thought of placing a call, but did not do so until the following morning, after discovering that the same dream had recurred for the third time in two days.

Mrs. White answered the telephone in person, and when Virginia asked how she was, her first words were, "I've just come from the hospital." Virginia then made known her identity, and learned that her long-time friend had suffered three heart attacks since Christmas.

The strangest precognitive dream that I have encountered among my friends came to Mrs. Donald Mixsell of New York on the morning of August 24, 1939. The former Virginia deHaven, a graduate of the exclusive Finch School, had gone to Paris on her honeymoon in the mid-1920's, and she and her weathly bridegroom liked France so well that they decided to settle there permanently. They took a Paris flat on the second floor of a building with an elevator, and after the birth of their son, David, a couple of years later, they returned to the States only once a year.

Shortly after David's fourteenth birthday, Mrs. Mixsell booked passage on the liner *Normandy,* in order to put her son in school at Lawrenceville, New Jersey. The morning that they were to sail, she awakened from a deep sleep and discovered that she was sobbing into her pillow. The maid, entering with her breakfast tray, observed the unaccustomed tears and asked what had happened. Mrs. Mixsell then told her husband and the maid of this dream:

"For some unaccountable reason I was raging with anger as I rushed up the steps to our second-floor flat. In my fury I pressed hard on the doorbell, rather than using a key. The door was opened by a strange man, who looked extremely guilty and kept rubbing his hands together. He was short of stature, had dark curly hair, and was wearing American-type sports clothes, rather than French. He ushered me into my own flat as if I were a prospective tenant, and I thought to myself, 'How dare he behave like that, when this is my flat and my furniture!' We walked into the main salon, and instead of seeing my green-and-white flowered slipcovers on the sofa and chairs. I noticed that they were covered with sheets, as if the owner had been away. In the center of the room was a trunk. Then I awakened, with the most horrible sense of foreboding that I have ever known."

It was apparently this feeling of despondency that had caused the tears, and when they continued to flow all the way to the boat-train, her husband stopped and bought her a pair of dark glasses to conceal her swollen eyes. Mrs. Mixsell had intended to return to France in two weeks, but almost immediately after the *Normandy* docked in New York, war broke out in Europe, and she could not return. Her husband left Paris soon afterward and joined her in New York as soon as he could secure passage on a blacked-out ship.

Five years later, when David reached his nineteenth birthday, he was inducted into the United States Army; and two nights before his division shipped overseas, he had a farewell dinner with his mother at the Stork Club. Plastic swizzle sticks were served with their champagne, and David playfully held a match to his until it softened. Then he bent it into the shape of a man, and smilingly handed it to his mother, saying: "Here's a fetish for you. Keep it with you, and it will bring you good luck."

A few months later, the Mixsells received notification that their only son had been killed in action. Utterly devastated, Mrs. Mixsell locked herself in her room and refused to see friends, but when her brother mentioned that a certain woman had called, she unexpectedly announced that she would see her.

"I don't know what possessed me to do that, because she was only a casual acquaintance," Mrs. Mixsell says, "but I have always been grateful that I yielded to the sudden urge."

The woman arrived, and taking her by the shoulders, said: "Listen, Virginia, you've got to snap out of this grief, because I have something important to tell you. I was at Pennsylvania Station this morning to see my son off to war, when, glancing across the tracks, I saw your David looking at me. At the same moment, I inwardly heard him ask me to tell you that you must be brave, because you are needed. He said you can't let yourself go now, because you have the opportunity to be a perfectly wonderful woman...or a terrible one. You know which way he wants you to choose."

Somewhat apologetically, the woman drew an inexpensive turquoise bracelet from her purse, handed it to Mrs. Mixsell, and said: "I don't know why I was told to give you this, but I was. It's just a little trinket made by the Indians, which I picked up in New Mexico several years ago, but for some reason you're supposed to have it."

Comforted by these words, Mrs. Mixsell pulled herself together and tried to resume a normal life. The following week, she and her son's godmother were discussing David's religious beliefs when she remembered the fetish that he had fashioned from the swizzle stick, and went to the bedroom to get it. As she lifted the lid of the old jewelry box in which she kept odds and ends, an unusual shaft of light suddenly shone through the window, illuminating a cheap ring that had lain forgotten for many years in the box.

Recalling that David had bought it for her on his first boyhood trip to the Southwest, she picked it up, and uttered a startled cry. Rushing to get the bracelet from the bureau drawer where she had tossed it after accepting it from the acquaintance a week before, she compared it with the ring. Not only did the square-cut turquoise stones exactly match, but even the Indian carvings on the coin-silver bracelet and ring were identical. It was as if David had clearly said to her, "Look, Mom, I'm still here and able to communicate with you."

The war finally drew to a close, and as soon as civilians were allowed to book passage, Mrs. Mixsell sailed for Paris. Finding that her own flat was occupied, she checked into the George V Hotel, and immediately sought to regain possession of her property. Through official sources she learned that a major in the German Gestapo had occupied it during the war, and since the liberation it had been appropriated by an American colonel. She repeatedly tried to establish contact with the latter, but since he was unwilling to be dispossessed, the colonel artfully eluded her calls. It was weeks before he reluctantly set a date when she could see her flat. Consequently, by the time she reached the apartment building she was so angry that, disregarding the elevator, she ran up the steps and pressed hard on the doorbell.

"The door was opened by the colonel, who looked decidedly guilty, as well he might!" Mrs. Mixsell declares. "He had no right to be there, but what stunned me was that this was the man I had seen in my almost-forgotten dream six years before. He was short, had curly dark hair, and was dressed in sport clothes instead of uniform. When he even began rubbing his hands together, I was so startled that I brushed quickly past him into the salon—and nearly fainted! My green-and-white slipcovers had been laundered so many times during the occupation that they were loose-fitting and faded white. They actually resembled sheets. But more incredibly, in the center of the salon stood a trunk!"

Now, at last, she understood the reason for the despondency and tears which had accompanied the dream. Before it could become a reality, the world would be plunged into its most devastating war, and her only son would die in battle.

The wife of Senate Majority Leader Mike Mansfield seems always to have been gifted with a sixth sense that alerts her and her family to peril. A typical example is this: One day her husband, on arriving home from the Capitol, parked the car in front of their house rather than pulling into the garage. Mrs. Mansfield, sensing danger, rushed out to meet him, calling: "Darling, please don't leave the car there, or it will be struck." At that instant another automobile zoomed over the hill and crashed into their parked car.

Major General Leigh Wade's wife, Helen, also has a psychic attunement which has often evinced itself on city streets. Born and reared in Washington, D.C., Mrs. Wade frequently thinks that she sees a friend, discovers her error, and then actually encounters that friend within two or three blocks. She recalls that in her teens she and a school chum, returning from the movies one Saturday afternoon, saw the friend's mother walk out onto her porch; but before she could greet them, Helen exclaimed: "You don't need to tell me. My father has just died, hasn't he?" Although her father had been hospitalized in Baltimore, his sudden death that afternoon had been totally unexpected.

General Wade is not surprised by his wife's intuitive flashes, because he had heard many accounts of an aunt's clairvoyance during his boyhood. He recalls that the day before Christmas in 1908, his aunt, Mrs. David Lee of Edgely, North Dakota, wrote a letter to his mother, Mrs. William Wade, in which she told of her intuitive feeling that someone in the Wade household had just died. She said her impression was that the death was by drowning.

"Mail delivery between North Dakota and our home in Cassopolis, Michigan, took four or five days in that era," the general recalls. "By the time we received the postmarked letter, we had already held funeral services for my brother Herman. On the afternoon that my aunt wrote the letter, he and a cousin broke through thin ice while skating on a nearby lake. Both boys were drowned."

Jackie Martin, a celebrated photographer-reporter and former war correspondent, comes from a family with such a strong psychic bond that each member seems to sense when another is in danger. "This sixth sense is like an extra pair of arms or eyes for us," Jackie explains.

In 1941, Alice Rogers Hager, a well-known writer on aviation, was invited by President Getulio Vargas to visit Brazil and make the first definitive study of the nation's aviation system. Jackie Martin was asked to accompany her as a photographer, and these two members of the Women's National Press Club spent three months collecting material for thirty magazine articles, in addition to two books—*Frontier By Air* and *Brazil, Giant to the South*—for which they later received the Order of the Southern Cross. During that memorable tour of Brazil, the women and their Brazilian pilot were flying up the rugged coast from Florianopolis to São Paulo in a one-engine, twelve-year-old Ballanca which had an altimeter and compass, but no radio. Beneath them was a solid bank of clouds, which fortunately began to thin as their watches told them they should be approaching São Paulo.

Their pilot opened his window and began to bank sharply from side to side, while scanning the ground, until he sighted a railroad track which he hoped would lead them to their destination. Nightfall was close at hand, and just as thick fog was again enveloping them on all sides, he spotted a small town. Searching desperately for an open space to land, he skimmed so low over the main street that the women could see anxiety written on the faces of the townspeople. While the pilot continued his low dives, they noticed that the only open field lay under water. Their only hope was a small football field with high-voltage wires at one end, and at the other end a solid bank of houses.

Jackie, her eyes on the pilot during these frantic maneuvers, suddenly saw her mother's face, serene and smiling, between them. "I took off my dark glasses, believing that the lenses might be causing a strange refraction," she recalls, "and I also looked away, thinking that the cold fear which possessed me might be affecting my vision. When I looked back toward the pilot, my mother's face was still there, smiling reassuringly. Then I heard her voice saying: 'And underneath are the everlasting arms. Underneath are the everlasting arms.' Her face faded away, and I was filled with a sense of quietude. I knew that we would emerge safely, because my mother's words had reawakened my faith in the Divine Presence."

The plane rushed toward the football field at sickening speed, cleared the wires by inches, but struck the limb of a dead tree—which sheared off one wheel. They came down hard on the other wheel, swung crazily around, and smashed a wing. But the brakes caught, and as soon as the switches were cut the door of the wrecked plane was opened from the outside by frightened Brazilian villagers. The moment she reached São Paulo by car, Jackie announced that she must cable her mother that they were safe. Alice, by now sufficiently recovered from her fright to think logically, observed that this was unnecessary, since their families would not even know of their misfortune.

"Mom knew," Jackie replied quietly, and dispatched the cable. After their return to Washington, she told her family of the experience, and turning to Mrs. Philip Martin said, "You did know, didn't you, Mom?"

"Yes," Mrs. Martin replied, and confessed that when she sensed the impending crash, she had opened her Bible to Deuteronomy 33:27 and read: "The eternal God is thy refuge, and underneath are the everlasting arms."

Buell Mullen, a distinguished muralist whose paintings on stainless steel adorn the Library of Congress, the United States Naval Academy, the national headquarters of the American Chemical Society, and numerous art galleries, was born with a twin sister. Modrea died when a year old, but Buell insists that during her own preschool days, the twin returned nearly every day to play with her.

"She told me not to tell our parents, or she wouldn't be allowed to come again," Buell says, "and I kept my promise. We played together, and I saw and heard her as clearly as I could my German nurse; but when I was nearly six, she announced that she wouldn't be coming regularly anymore, because she had to go on to another place. I was desolate! Mother called me in to lunch, but I couldn't eat; and for several weeks thereafter I had a severe illness which doctors couldn't diagnose. Finally one of them asked Mother if I had lost a close friend, or pet, because I seemed to be in a deep shock of grief. Mother, a Scotch Presbyterian who knew nothing of my loss, replied in the negative. I gradually recovered, but in times of peril I have since received advance warning which I feel comes from Modrea and mediums have often described a twin standing beside me."

Attracted to psychic study because of this experience, Buell later took a development course from Arthur Ford. During one of the dark-room sessions she "saw a fine-looking young man standing in a blazing light, as if in a theatrical spotlight." No one else in the class saw the phenomenon, but Buell had such total recall of his features and expression that she went home and made a sketch of him. She took it to class the next week, but neither Ford nor the other pupils recognized the face that she had drawn. She left the sketch on a shelf in the classroom, and a few days later it fell to the floor while Ford was hunting a book for the Roman Catholic Bishop of New Jersey.

The Bishop, stooping to retrieve the paper, exclaimed: "Where did you get this portrait of Tom Kelly? I've been making inquiries for one everywhere, but the only picture his wife has was taken when he was ill, and is not a good likeness. This one is splendid!" Tom Kelly, it developed, had begun life as a Catholic, but during his world-wide search for knowledge of the spiritual world had converted to Buddhism; then he rounded out his life as a Quaker at Pendle Hill. He had been dead twelve years. With Buell's permission, the Bishop had the picture framed and delivered to Tom Kelly's widow.

The artist had another odd experience one summer while visiting a friend at a Lake Michigan resort. She was writing a letter when her pen, without her conscious volition, suddenly wrote: "Beware Jack. Beware Jack." Buell's hostess had recently fled in terror from her husband, Jack, when he threatened to kill her and their child. She assumed that he was still in Canada, since Canadian authorities had promised to notify her if he left home. However, when Buell told her of the warning, they decided to take no chances; the two women, the child, and her nurse barricaded the doors, alerted the chauffeur to block the driveway, and loaded a rifle. The dogs were then turned loose to guard the approach. The next day the friend's cousin called from a nearby beach and asked: "Why didn't you tell me Jack was coming? I saw him last night at the inn, and he was in a towering rage." They learned that although he had driven by the cottage that night, perhaps because of the dogs and the blocked driveway he had not attempted to break in on his family. He later died in an insane asylum.

Gladys Moon Jones has had several experiences involving strange forces that we do not yet comprehend. Four days after her mother suffered a stroke which totally paralyzed her speech, Gladys and her brother were at the bedside when Mrs. Moon calmly and clearly spoke one word three times: "Now. Now. Now." Then she died.

While she and her brother remained at the bedside silently grieving, Gladys suddenly "saw" her mother beside her, and heard her lilting laughter as she said, "Well, you are looking at me." Until then Gladys had forgotten that many years before she told her mother: "I will never look at you after you're dead, because I'll want to remember you as vividly alive."

Her mother's I-won-the-bet attitude was so amusing that Gladys laughed aloud. Her brother, thinking that she was becoming hysterical, looked at her sharply, but when she told him that their mother had just spoken to her, he replied: "Yes, a moment ago she also reminded me of a private joke between the two of us."

Some years afterward, Gladys was typing a magazine article late one evening, when, she says, "My hands went limp and then were taken over by some presence that began typing even more rapidly than I had done." In a few moments she read these words, "Thank you for reading my poetry to your friends the other day."

Unable to recall what poetry she had been reading, she asked, "Who are you?" and the presence typed, "I am not a dead one, not a spirit gone on. I am living now."

Gladys asked if she knew him, and the typewriter wrote, "No, but we are going to meet soon. You shall know me by the yellow flowers on the floor." This sounded so nonsensical that Gladys, wondering if her mind were befogged, gathered up her papers and went to bed.

At a theater party in New York the following week, Gladys was introduced to a young woman whose name she promptly forgot, but who came unannounced to her hotel room the next morning. She asked if she was "interrupting anything," and when Gladys smilingly remarked that she was writing a poem, the stranger blurted: "I know a poet you must meet. I'll telephone him right now, and introduce you."

Before Gladys could catch her breath, she was being presented via telephone to Joseph Auslander, who politely invited her to attend a reading of his verse at the Poetry Society that evening. She went, and found herself deeply moved by his reading of "A Letter to Emily Dickinson," from his then-new book, *Letters to Women.* Afterward, as she introduced herself to him, she had the eerie feeling that a shy, timid voice utterly unlike her own was telling him, through her lips, that she liked his reading.

On an impulse, Auslander asked her to drop by his house the next morning and said that if he were not back yet from an appointment, the door would be unlocked. Gladys went the next day, and when there was no answer to her knock, she walked in, There, in a streak of April sunlight, stood a large bowl of yellow tulips on the floor! Only then did she recall that she had been reading Auslander's poetry to friends shortly before the evening that the automatic writing on her typewriter said she would see "yellow flowers on the floor."

What power arranged the odd, interlocking circumstances? Why had a strange young woman brought her into the company of Joseph Auslander, who, when he returned home, was as puzzled as Gladys by her strange account of the message about the flowers? Could it have been the spirit of poetess Emily Dickinson who planned the sequence of events, and who seemed to speak through Gladys in a "shy, timid voice," telling Auslander that she liked his reading of her letter? Who knows?

offered to publish it, if Chloris would pay for
it. That was language calculated to her poet's mind.
But, she—

A.J. Shenstone lived in New York the first week when
Chloris was reported to a young writer whose name
she brought jingling, but who came introduced to her
notice upon the next morning. She asked if art was
interesting anything, and when Chloris smilingly
remarked that she was writing a poem, he frankly
replied, "I know a poet, you must meet. I'd enjoy the
talk, right away, and introduce you."

Being Chloris could catch her breath, she was being
pressed via telephone to Joseph Anstather, who politely invited her to hear a reading of his verse at the
Poetry Society that evening. She went, and found her
self deeply moved by his reading of J. Barlett's Emily
Dickinson, from his chat new book, came and to work in.
Afterward as she introduced herself to him, she had
the safe feeling that a girl, used confusedly, unlike
her own, was taking him, through her, upset that she
liked his reading.

On an impulse, Anstather asked her to drop by his
house the next morning and said that if he were not
back at from an appointment she does want to the
room. Chloris went the next day, and when there was
no answer to her knock, she walked in. There in a
chair of April sunshine, sat a Paris Dove, sound
asleep on the floor. Why then did she laugh at a shiver
as she had been reading, Anstather? How to friends and de-
dire, the avenue. After the appointment with no ever
typewriter and she would see yellow flowers on the
floor.

Willpower arranged the odd, mud-looking objects
changed. She had as a sense young woman by that her
like the company of Joseph Anstather, who when he
changed come, was as moved as cheery by her image.
Women of the message about the flowers. Could it have
been the spirit of poetess Emily Dickinson who planned
the sequence of events, and who wanted to speak
frankly. Chloris in a shy, strange voice, telling Anstat-
hader that she liked his reading of her letters, who
knows.

CHAPTER 6

The Golden Door

Shortly after Bob and I settled into the Massachusetts Avenue house that Lily had selected for us in the fall of 1960, a new Guide appeared. He was not to replace Lily, he explained, but to supplement his teachings. He identified himself by drawing a donkey in one continuous line, and since Lily always announced himself with a picture of a flower, there was no problem in telling them apart. Further, their manner of expression was quite different. The Donkey Guide seemed more concerned with spiritual matters and was less dogmatic than his colleague.

One of his first instructions was that in my daily meditations I should try to visualize "a Man of God on a donkey." I was not succeeding too well, and in a few days he gave me more explicit information. I was to picture the scene in the desert near Jerusalem, on a dark but starlit night. The Man of God was "on a mission of mercy to help others, because that is the true purpose of life."

From time to time during this period Gladys Moon Jones, Hope Ridings Miller, and I held study groups for interested friends in "the room away from the house," which the Guides had designated for that purpose. The false fireplace had been removed, but we had not otherwise enlarged the room. One day, the pastor of a church, knowing of my interest in psychic matters, called to ask me to help a young woman who said she had been contemplating suicide, but who paradoxically had an overwhelming fear of death. I knew nothing about her, but she began telephoning frequently, and I finally invited her to one of our meetings. Gladys led the general discussion, after which I tried my hand at automatic writing, and the pencil declared that the girl was disguising her true fears. Actually, it said, her troubles were centered around an older, married man whom she must relinquish because he was an evil influence on her. I have no idea whether this was true, but when I read it to her she looked startled and made no attempt to deny it. She never called again.

By this time the automatic writing, to which I devoted only fifteen minutes each morning, was flowing so rapidly that I had difficulty in deciphering it afterward. I have a rather illegible handwriting, and the Guides' scrawls were even worse. One day Lily, while controlling the pencil, wrote: "This writing can hardly be read. We think now that we have developed sufficient strength to type through you, so go to your typewriter."

I opened my eyes and stared blankly at the notebook. The pencil began again, as Lily wrote commandingly: "I said, go to your typewriter—NOW." He was certainly a bossy fellow! I walked across the hall to my desk in the library, turned the switch on the electric typewriter, placed my fingers on the keys in touch-typing position, and closed my eyes. I have before me the first words that were typed that day. With reasonably few mistakes, but with little capitalization or punctuation, Lily wrote precisely as follows:

This is the way we will work hereafter take our message down this way because you can read it better. x you are losing so you are losing so much of what we wrote because you cannot read the handwriting this will stay with you hereafter put a sheet of paper in the machine before you begin to write we will give you any thoughts that we have lower the back on your typing chair it is too high to give you support now relax we can type no yes we can type.

Each morning thereafter I seated myself at the type-writer and closed my eyes. Then, after silently praying for protection from evil forces, I sought to lift my mind to a higher plateau and free it of worldly intrusions. Since I have always used the touch system, the typing presented no problem, but I never knew what word was coming next until it began forming itself on the paper. Whatever force propelled my fingers typed rapidly, seldom hesitating over the choice of a word. It soon became apparent why the Guides had resorted to the type-writer. Without the restrictions imposed by a slower moving pencil, they could produce two or three single-spaced pages of philosophical dissertation in the daily fifteen-minute sitting; and they made clear that my role was not to be limited merely to acting as their unpaid typist. I was also to disseminate their message to the world, by means of books.

The unseen writers blithely continued to ignore the man-made rules of punctuation, but their grammar was flawless, and I could not help but admire their remarkable fluency of expression. During this period I was utilizing my spare time to write a book about Mary McCarran, daughter of the late Senator Pat McCarran, who had been a nun for thirty-two years, until she renounced her vows to care for her widowed mother and invalid sister; and sometimes I would labor for days over the same number of words as the Guides could produce in a few minutes.

The Guides scrupulously refrained from giving me any assistance on the book, or on my daily newspaper columns; but after the book was completed, and the publisher and I were vainly trying to find a suitable title, they suddenly came to the rescue. Without the slightest hint on my part, Lily broke into the "lesson" one morning to write: "The book should be called ONCE THERE WAS A NUN, by Ruth Montgomery. The subtitle should read, 'The Story of Mary McCarran.'"

That afternoon the publisher telephoned from New York, and I asked whether he had yet had an inspiration for a title. When he replied in the negative, I ventured: "What do you think of ONCE THERE WAS A NUN?"

After a slight hush, he exclaimed: "You've got it!

That's the perfect title!" The subtitle was eventually altered to read, "Mary McCarran's Years as Sister Mary Mercy," but the title remained unchanged.

The summer before, Bob and I had purchased two ocean-front lots at Middlesex Beach, Delaware, and were having a six-bedroom cottage erected. We considered it a good investment, since by renting it to vacationers during the height of the season we could use it the rest of the time virtually free of cost. Two weeks before the cottage would have been completed we drove over for last-minute decisions. Three days later a freak storm swept it away and severely damaged most of the coastline from Georgia to New York. Insurance companies refused to reimburse any of the property owners, and the loss of forty-three thousand dollars was a financial blow to us; but Lily seemed remarkably unsympathetic.

His only comment was: "We want you to write books which will take your time from such things as that, and also repay the value many times over. Get to work, Ruth, and do not go off again on a tangent which is as time-consuming as that would have been. That would have distracted you and Bob from things that are much more important to your future and your soul's development. You are to help others. Keep this in mind hereafter, and don't get involved in time-wasting projects like that cottage."

How sad, I mused, that my Guides were always so eager to help everyone except me! As a mere human I could not seem to shake off the feeling that money and physical relaxation were important, too. What was the use of having a body if we could not give it some creature comforts now and then?

A few days later, Lily for the first time took note of the séance I once attended in Florida. "The Indian, White Mountain, is here now," he wrote. "He says to tell you he is still watching over your personal safety, but could not save the cottage, since you were not in it. That is out of his department, he says. He is laughing at that last crack. Your father is also here, and he says his heart aches for you, because he knows what it is to

84

lose a dollar; and he remembers his concern when he lost forty of them, but later found them in another suit. He says to keep your chin up. He admires your courage, and does not want you to get discouraged by temporary setbacks. You will recover some of your loss, and will go on to bigger and better things." As a matter of fact, we later found that we could deduct some of the loss from income taxes, and when the shoreline gradually returned to near-normal, we were able to sell the lots for the price that we had paid.

Lily added these sterner thoughts of his own: "You let too many worldly things interfere with your concentration on spiritual development. It is a shame that you do, because these worldly blows are as nothing over the long stretch. The only part which matters is how well you prepare yourself for the next stage of life by making the most of your time while there. We want you to help others through our teaching."

On April first a surprise awaited. As I sat at my typewriter, expecting a Guide to begin writing, a new hand seemed to be directing the keys. The typing was less fluent, but the message read: "Good morning on April Fool's Day, Ruth and Bob. This is Hiram. This is Papa"—the name by which my father-in-law's children had usually called him. "This is a new experience for me, typing, but we'll see what we can do. This is a Sunday morning, and I want you to go to church every Sunday from now on. Put God first in your lives, children. Believe me, I know. ˈFrank"—his earthly nickname for Bob's mother, Frances—"is here and sends her best. She is still a little confused about where she is and why, but coming out of it at last. She had a hard pull to adjust, because she was so worn out when she came over, poor girl. She'll be all right soon, never fear about that. We all make it sooner or later, but it's so much easier if you prepare for it in that life, than to wait and have to do it all over here. Ruth has made a good beginning, but has far yet to go. Bob must join in trying to make the connection between the two phases of existence. It is really easy if you put your minds and souls to it. Now run along, both of you, and get ready for church." How like a Methodist minister he still sounded!

The next week-end we drove to the shore to see what was left of our property and of other cottages in Middlesex and South Bethany. On our return Lily commented: "It was good that you went, and saw the impermanence of human building. You must build toward the next phase of life, and develop your spiritual graces without worrying about the very brief period of one's life that he spends on earth. It is merely preparation for this phase of life; and we, of course, are preparing for the next phase of ours. That is why we are so anxious to help others through you on that plane. It is part of our spiritual development here, and you are retarding us when you refuse to make yourself available. Do you understand a little better now why it is so important for you to cooperate?" I felt rather ashamed that I sometimes overslept, or was too rushed in the morning to give the Guides the typewriter for fifteen or twenty minutes.

A few days later, they asked me to begin meditating on "the soul of man and his place in the hereafter." They stressed that this was important, because it would make the crossover period that we call death less tedious, and would permit a more accelerated advancement in the next plane. "The faster that we can convert earth-souls into transfigured spirits," they wrote, "the more rapid the progress will be toward a fusion of the whole. This may not be clear to you just now, but as you progress in your meditation we can lead you through a transfiguring series of experiences which will divulge the cause for which we are working.

"Time is wasted in *this* phase of existence, as well as in YOUR phase. That is what I am trying to tell you as a first lesson. In other words, the over-all plan for this universe is so immense that it is tragic to waste even the minutes that it takes to adjust to a new form of existence here. Time is the most precious commodity in life, and the one thing that can never be restored to the squanderer. Time, dear Ruth, is more valuable than all the gold and diamonds in your world. Time is not only healer, mentor, teacher, and progressor, but the very stuff of the universe.

"To waste golden moments is to cheat yourself of something greater by far than your life there, for whether or not you live long on that plane is immaterial. You live on and on and on, but the time that is wasted in your soul's development can never be regained. Always you are held back by the squandered moments which could have been used to help your soul's progression to the infinite plane beyond which there lies the promised land: the Golden Door through which none must return to serve further penance.

"This is the ultimate goal toward which we all must strive, and the more rapid your progress there, the less time you will have to spend here in the tedious tasks which are essential to a soul's salvation. We tell you this, that you may spread this message to others, and that you may be spared the tasks that we have had to perform here; the frustrations of trying to work through earth-people like you, who will not follow our bidding, but on whom we must depend gradually to work our own way through that portal for which all hearts yearn.

"This is the final peace that all men seek: the reunion with our Maker, and the ultimate tranquillity. That is the way and the life, the place for which all mortals struggle, and for which we were first born to reach. It may sound far-fetched to you now, dear child, but let me tell you this: the vague stirrings of hearts and yearnings of man are tied to that place from which man never returns. It is the Golden Door, the portal of God, and this stage in which we now find ourselves is nothing more than a single step in the gradual advancement toward that goal.

"It is so silly for some people to believe that life stops with the transfer from your world to ours. The step is so slight as to be barely noticeable in the evolution of the soul. The next step, where we are, is no more than the passing through an open door. The long struggle lies ahead for us, as well as for you. We are novices along this road, and have far to go before we reach that sublime place where time at last will mean nothing, and our souls will be in blessed union with that of our

Creator. How far we must travel, and how weary the road depends on how much people like you can assist us in our mission of helping others; for make no mistake about it, that is the only way: the helping of other lost souls to advance along the path toward perfection."

Those thoughts are too deep for me. I did not originate them, nor did I compose their phraseology, but I set them down here as a mere reporter who has been assigned a specific task.

On Easter morning Lily launched into a fascinating dissertation on life in the hereafter. He began by pointing out that that day above all others has significance for Christians, because "the risen Christ is living proof that life goes on after what we call death." He said that while pastors were preaching that life continues into infinity, the word "infinity" needed some explaining.

"We here in this plane are not much closer to the infinity than you are there," he began. "We are merely one step farther along in the great progression of the soul. We here on this side of the thin veil are less earth-bound than you, but still so near to earth that we must try to compensate for our faults in that life, and help others there before they come over. This binds us nearly as closely to your earth-world as you, who are further handicapped by its limitations of time and space. When we here advance to the next stage, we will become less concerned with the earth problems, because we will by then have compensated sufficiently for our own short-comings to take on a much higher task. The next phase will be far more ethereal and far more concerned with goodness as such.

"The next step in our progression toward infinity is one which we eagerly await, for it leads a step nearer the ultimate goal, where we at last are pure and whole. To achieve it we must pay many penalties for the things we left undone in your plane, and try to keep others from like sins of commission and omission. This is a long and arduous pull, and although we are much happier and freer here than there, the contrast between our stage and the next one is so great that we strive always to make this crossover period as short as possible.

"The important thing for you there to know is the utter unimportance of material things, inasmuch as your body plays such a brief part in your soul's upward climb. It is regrettable that those on earth do not fully understand the ridiculous quality of striving simply to clothe the body in fine furs and jewels, when it is the soul that is naked and needs nurturing. Do not be troubled by whether you are a society queen or a rich man's darling. Rather, turn your thoughts to the short time remaining in which you may compensate for your sins and help others find the way to God. You can have no higher mission there than to pass on to others the truths which you have been learning here. You have already wasted so much of your precious life-span that it goes without saying you have not another moment to lose. Now, off to church..."

The next morning Lily had some advice for my husband, who could scarcely have been less interested. Bob objected strenuously to my interest in automatic writing and did not even want to hear about it. My Guides nevertheless gave me occasional messages for him, and after a personal one at this time, Lily wrote rather gaily: "When a person looks younger to himself in the mirror, he is also apt to act younger, so why let yourselves become old fogies before your time? The day of long white beards went out with hoop skirts and bustles. Be dramatic! Act with the vigor of youth, conquer the world in which you live, so that you will be ready to push forward with equal zest to conquer the worlds that lie ahead. It is for the young in heart that the world was made, so be young, act young, feel young, and push forward with great ambition and *joie de vivre*. Rise each day with a song on your lips and a melody in your heart. Meet the world with a greeting of good cheer. Time enough for long faces in the grave, but not before. No one cares what expression your body in the grave will bear, because it is no longer a needed part of you."

Shortly thereafter Lily announced that he was ready to impart a new lesson. He began it this way: "The time that you spend there is recorded here as firmly as a leaf imbeds itself in a rock and is discovered a million years later, still reflecting the flora of an age. Not one whit of what you do there is missed here, or unrecorded in the progression of your life through all the stages of your development. When you fail to aid a soul in torment, or when a person reaches out to you and is spurned, you are imbedding that picture of yourself in the rock of ages. Is it the picture of yourself that you want the world to see forevermore?"

Perhaps I had recently been guilty of some heedless act, for Lily addressed me by name, writing: "Ruth, how much better it would be to take that extra moment of time, of energy, of strength, or money to aid the person in trouble, than to brush busily by, saying, 'I do not have the time today,' or 'Do not bother me so often, please.' The greatest thing in life is the aid that you extend to others, in order to help them upward and onward. This is more a spiritual than a physical need, so the most important help you give is by inspiration and example, but there are times when nothing takes the place of a helping hand as well.

"The only thing that you can bring with you to this life in which I am now is the good that you have done there. We do not hold against you the unaccountable and incredible mistakes of your past life; but they do not help you forward, and that is the loss. To progress, you must do good. To retrogress, you fail to use your talents and God-given qualities of love and solicitude. Help your fellow man. Guide and uplift him. Teach him God's blessings, and show him that this is the way and the light. Those who help others are the ones who form the aristocracy on this side over here—not the ones who sit in the seat of the mighty on your side of the veil."

CHAPTER 7

True Time Exists

The guides made no attempt to conceal their disgust when I failed to keep our appointed date each morning at nine o'clock. My family, on the other hand, did everything possible to discourage me from continuing with the automatic writing. Mother, with her small-town Midwestern background, felt that if it were not actually the work of the Devil, at least people who heard about it would think that I was mentally off-balance. My engineer-trained husband feared that it might harm me in some way.

I could not personally see how the inspiration derived from such a high-minded philosophy could have other than beneficial effects, no matter from what source it came; but it troubled me that whenever I became beset with doubts, and asked the Guides for evidential material which could be checked, they either disregarded my request or gave me seemingly wrong information. Their interest, they insisted, was in helping worldly people find the road to salvation, not in trying gimmicks and stunts.

Sometimes I would retaliate by skipping the sessions for weeks at a time, but, inevitably, something would pull me back to it. One of the most exalted messages I have ever received came after one such disruption. The Guides began it in rather offhand fashion, writing: "We want you to visualize the perfection of the lily. Sample its fragrance, and gaze upon the exquisite detail of its lemon throat and regal stem. The study of this one symbolic flower will teach you more of God's ways than any number of books. This flower reaches always toward God. Its head is high, its throat erect, and its face is turned toward the heavens in rejoicing. From its radiant being emerges an aroma more breathtaking than fine incense. It has sturdiness, together with obvious grace and charm. It has purity of line, and is uncluttered by false ornamentation. The lily is goodness personified. All who would strive to be as the lily will have no difficulty with their present life, or the next stage which you call the hereafter."

They next launched into an intriguing discussion of immortality, which seemed to hint at reincarnation, writing: "Actually we are no more the 'hereafter' than you are, who sprang from a previous stage which you cannot recall. The very thought that thinking human beings sprang fully developed in that one state of existence would seem laughable to any except you earth-people, who are accustomed to accepting everything at face value. You who are more advanced and sensitive have lived through many previous phases, while some of the more doltish varieties had only primer training in a previous step. To that life which went before, you are as much the 'hereafter' as we here are to you. The hereafter goes on and on, my dear child, until at last you and we and all of us eventually pass through that Golden Door where longing shall be no more, where perfection has been attained, and where we are at last one with God, our Creator. This voyage through the various stages of life can be as rapidly performed, or as slowly drawn, as you make it, depending on your own contribution there, here, and in all of the various steps. The progress depends on you, not on God, who has given all equal opportunity, although not all have the same opportunity at each level of their advancement."

Then came a philosophy, new, at least to me, concerning poverty and hardship. "Remember," they wrote, "that some people are in different stages of living than others. The ones you call the unfortunates may not be unfortunate at all. It may be simply their way of achieving goodness and oneness with God more rapidly than you, because if they sacrifice more, and live more abundantly for others, they are far more fortunate than those of you with mink coats, chauffeured cars, and the countless temptations that beset your trail through the maze of parties and working hours.

"Some who seem unfortunate may also be in an earlier stage of advancement than you. A part of your own mentality may once have been struggling along as they are, in a previous life. Theirs may be simply a later start, for not all of us were created at once, and created equal in the usual sense of the word. As each was created out of God's love, he was given certain tools or talents with which to make his path through life, and return at last to God. How those talents are utilized determines when the long journey shall end, for time is a precious commodity which can no more be recovered than the rain which falls on parched soil.

"Time is of the essence indeed, my dear Ruth, and it is that for which there is never any substitute. You delay your life's voyage by each moment that you fritter away in useless pursuit of sheer pleasure, or in every lost opportunity for helping others to save their souls; for each time that you lend a hand to another groping soul like yourself, or one of a still lower level of ordination, you have helped by an accountable degree the advancement of your own soul toward God."

The Guide paused momentarily, and then resumed: "Our striving here in that respect exactly parallels yours, although we can see more fully than you, and are in a better position to evaluate our acts before it is too late to change our course. We have what you have there, without the hampering temptations of the body, and with a broader outlook of the path that lies ahead. Given that glimpse of the path ahead, as we have had and as we want you to give to others there, it is far easier to shoulder one's burdens, to climb the rugged rocks, and to stand ready at all times to shift your own burden in order to lighten another's."

It was here that Lily launched into his remarkable dissertation on creation, which, as far as I have since been able to determine, is unique. "Each new little entity that is created out of God's Goodness joins in that endless pursuit of perfection," he declared, "yet hungers all along the way for the lost particle which once knew perfection. No sinful thing was ever created by our God and Maker. The entities that became all of us were once segments of His Glorious Self, and as each radiated off from Him it became a little breath, with a chance to grow and develop into a real and significant unit that could shine in God's true grace. These little entities set boldly along the path that would lead back to their Maker, but along the way the temptations proved too strong for all of them. In varying degrees, judging by the way each had strengthened his own God-given character through trials, denials, sacrifices, and faith in the goodness of man and God, each little particle progressed through different stages.

"Some of these included life on your plane. Others have not yet been born into your plane, and some may progress so well here that they do not have to include that step in their soul's progression. Earth is a hard test, because temptations lie in wait for every mortal. Because the Son of God was able to reject those temptations, He is able to return to the earth again and again, without any of its hampering limitations of time and space and body. This Man of God can be found in many areas of your world at any time that someone with sufficient faith calls forth to Him. He can stay when needed, and go when the task is done, without again having to wear the mantle of the earthly body.

"He is perfection incarnate, and there are others who have stood so well in the sight of God, because of their understanding of God's will, that they too can be called by those who need them there. Some, as I have said, were able to forego that trail, because in other levels they proved so pleasing in God's sight. Others have been saints on your plane, or only simple people who helped their neighbors more than themselves, never for a moment knowing publicity in your life. They, like we, are intent only on doing good, but they are far more advanced than we who are still striving to compensate for our earth-life mistakes. This is all for now."

As the message ended, my arms dropped into my lap, and I sat in amazed contemplation of the paper before me. Where had such a stirring idea originated? Certainly it was not mine, nor had I ever learned such teachings in church, school, or library. How freely the words had flowed! How effortlessly the unseen author had phrased the chronology of his lesson. If true, it opened the window on an entire new concept of creation and the ultimate goal of man.

The lessons continued each morning. Constantly the Guides harped on the theme of service to others, "which must be done not only in a spirit of charity, but as a burning need to fulfill one's own mission." We must, they said, be more interested in helping others than ourselves. In so doing, we would automatically be advancing our own cause. "That was the message that was brought to your world eons ago by Christ and other religious leaders," they wrote. "The message has not changed one iota. It remains as it was then, when Christ said 'love one another.' This is not *one* way to advance spiritually, but the *only* way."

One morning, as the mysterious typing continued its preachments, I dared again to ask the Guides who they were. Rather reproachfully they replied: "This question which interests you so much is truly not important. The most that we want of you is cooperation in helping others. We were writers, and that is why we want to work through you, who are of our calling. The interest between us is such that we can work well through you, if you will give this regular time each day to the joint enterprise. We want you to be the success in life that we were not, by helping others and bringing this message to them through your own writings. As writers we were fantastic successes in the worldly sense, yet what we failed to do was help other people. We were too busy pouring out our torrents of words and enjoying public acclaim. We should not have been so concerned for fleeting earthly fame, but for the survival of the souls of all of us.

"Let us impress upon you that we are all of one progression. We are as you will be, and you are as we once were—and not so long ago, at that. There is nothing which separates us now except the thin barrier of the mind. We see you as you are, but you do not yet

95

possess the ability to see us as we are now. Without the impediments of bodies, we are so much freer than you that we are able to help in ways that you can never help yourselves, as long as you are there in that component. We are eager for you to learn by our mistakes in that life; for by aiding you we can progress, just as you will progress by helping others in your own life. The most important thing that you will ever learn is this: *To live for self alone is to destroy one's self.*"

The Guides capitalized that passage—as they capitalized all other words which are here printed in italics—and then continued: "The miracle of birth is wasted on any soul who misses that all-important message. Better to have remained as a spirit entity and foresworn the chance for advancement through the earth-test, if you are unwilling to dedicate yourself to helping others. When you turn your face against another who is yearning for aid, then you are turning your back on the one road which leads to your own salvation."

The Guides struck the paragraph key, and I sat waiting with closed eyes. They seemed in some way to want to underscore what they had just written. After a few seconds they began again: "This does not mean that you must so utterly give of yourself to some other person that you are drained of strength and balance, and the power of decision. Let no one so consume you that you are no longer an entity in yourself. That person will be damning his own chances for salvation if he tries to consume you, so don't let him do that to himself. Gently but firmly force that person to stand on his own two feet, with his sights set on the heavens. There are a great many people who will need you throughout your busy, useful lives, so do not let some one person monopolize your attentions and ministrations. Be ready to help those in need of your words and deeds, but this does not mean supporting those who are shirking their own tasks or refusing to exert themselves for others."

This time the typing stopped cold, and only the faint hum of the electric typewriter broke the stillness of the room. Oddly enough, when the typing resumed it was to declare: "This is not exactly what we meant to say here. Ruth is trying to interject some thoughts of her own. Ruth, stop a moment and drop your hands. Meditate for a moment, and then give us a freer hand, please."

I tried to do as directed. After a few minutes I replaced my fingers on the keys, and the Guides wrote: "We will now begin that last part again. It is important for us to make clear that those who need you most are the ones who are groping for *spiritual* knowledge; the lost souls who actually yearn for the true road, but seem to lose their way. It is to those that you must minister. Let not your time be consumed by those who merely seek earthly advancement and the better physical comforts that money will buy. The hungry ones are not nearly as pathetic as those who starve for spiritual goals and fail to grasp the light. There are many who can give food to the poor, and medicine to the sick. Few there are who have grasped the far more important truths which will save their very souls. The ones who are most to be helped are those who truly yearn for goodness. If you turn your back on another soul in need of you, while simultaneously using that time for your own advancement in some earthly way, this will wipe out your gains for many days and times. You must remember that the time to help another soul is the time for your own advancement. Do not squander it, because it may not come again. Each opportunity to help another should be regarded as a prize jewel in a crown. Welcome and cherish it."

The writing again stopped. Although discarnates lack physical bodies, the Guides ordered me to air out the room. "You should always be in ventilated places, so that you can breathe freely," they cautioned. "This cigarette smoke is foul for you, even when it is not your own." My husband had apparently left a telltale trail of it behind him when he had left my study a short while before.

I opened a window, and the mollified Guides then advised that the easiest way to get that particular day's message across would be to "think of a bird on the wing, which floats and swoops and sails, just as the human soul will do when it is no longer entangled with a body.

The bird is of the world you are in; yet it is totally unentangled by the ground. The nearness of your plane to ours is the significant thing we want to impress on all of you today. We occupy the earth, as well as the sky and the heavens. We are striving to break our ties with the earth, to free ourselves for the next phase; yet we cannot sever the tie until we have completed the good tasks that we should and could have done on your plane. How much better it will be for you, and for your soul's progression, if you can live there as you would if you could but view it from here."

One Sunday the Guides delivered an edifying treatise on life hereafter, beginning in this novel fashion: "The sermon for today, if we were occupying a pulpit, would have to do with immortality. We should begin by saying that it is the one reality in an otherwise somewhat unreal world, for that is what your phase actually seems to us here. The fact that you are hampered by physical barriers, and stopped by man-made laws as well as walls of earth's formation, lends to it a slightly unreal note.

"We are here too, you know, yet totally unbound by any of your limitations. The rules of God are all that control us, and they are so simple, sane, and obvious that none needs to memorize them. They exist! That is enough to know. They exist! We obey them because they are there. None can disobey them without so obviously harming himself and his soul's progression that none in this phase of life would even try. Immortality is the one reality, because it is a part of time.

"Time is the indestructible quality that exists throughout eternity. True time exists and has being, like God Himself. It measures your progress through life by how well you make use of the quality of time. To waste time is to waste your very life away, for this unrecapturable quality has no resale use. It cannot be reused, because it never backs up or retreats. It marches forward, bringing you ever nearer to the next phase, when the opportunities of that phase of your life have been squandered or utilized, depending on your own self. We are not trying now just to save *you* that shocking loss, my dear girl, but rather we are thinking of the entire race of man, which has a right to know that the quality it is squandering is forever lost to all.

"'Take Time To Be Holy,' says the old hymn, and that is so true! Take time for the important things that truly matter, but take not time to fritter and squander and burn. Do that which is necessary to provide for self and family, but let not yourself become so immersed in the pursuit of money that that pursuit of God is lost. The only thing that can be taken with you to the next phase of existence is time, that common yardstick which measures what you have accomplished there in terms of goodness and kindness to others. The worldly successes do not even register on that stick of time, for they are of no possible use in the next phase. We who made names for ourselves in your world—and we did— find them of no value here. That is why we are reluctant even to speak of our earthly identity, because it might seem to be a boastful utterance that could be misunderstood by you.

"We want you to feel no particular thrill that we were once renowned personalities there, because actually we failed. Had we been truly successes, we would not have to be doing that which we are now attempting—to save thoughtful people through you. Had we lived useful and fruitful lives there, we would have accomplished so many good things that we could have by now moved on to an earth-free existence in a still higher phase of our progression. As it is, we must try to atone for the good works that we left undone while on earth.

"The time for every man to think about his future is while he is living in what will become his past. Regard each day as an unblemished page in the book of life. Let no ink or mud spot or smudge of dirt blemish those pages. Take them with you, spotless, into the next stage and you will have advanced far beyond your wild est dreams. The best thing to remember is this: *Greet each day as the untarnished future, and handle it as carefully as if it were already a published record of your past.* That thought, held closely, and lived, will keep your attention pointed straight ahead, and not deterred by the temptations of the world."

CHAPTER 8

The Selfishness of Grief

A close friend had recently lost her husband and was inconsolable. I tried to reassure her of the continuity of life, and gave her books to read on the subject, but neither her pastor nor I seemed adequate for the task. At one of the daily sittings, the Guides abruptly waved aside the regular lesson to talk about Nora's problem.

Referring to her deceased husband, Richard, they wrote: "He is here now, and anxious for her grieving to stop. He would be supremely happy if he could find some way to help Nora over this difficult adjustment period. His own philosophy was always such that he could accept the will of God. The parting is brief in any event, but Nora has a long time by earthly standards before she joins us. It is therefore most urgent that she stop her weeping and anguish of heart, turn her face to the task ahead, and fill her heart with the joy of living and of helping others. To be on the same level with Richard in this life, she must prepare in that one. He was an unusually able student of life and living. He had a great spirituality and therefore stepped so easily from that phase into this, that to reach him at this level requires her equal dedication to spiritual truths."

Urging me to "help Nora comprehend that every moment she now wastes in looking backward is another golden opportunity squandered," they continued: "To gain eternal life she must understand that life must be surrendered there. Why would anyone want to detain Richard, when he had fulfilled his mission on earth and was supremely qualified for the next great step in his life's progression toward ultimate perfection? This man had fulfilled his destiny. He had done it well.

"He wants Nora to understand that although he was loath to leave the woman he adored, the time had come for him to take the next step upward. He wishes her to know that he is with her at all times that she thinks of him, and that he will watch over her as tenderly here as there. She will never walk alone as long as she continues to need or want him. She is his sweetheart through eternity. This is the particular message that he wanted us to bring to her through you."

I paid a visit to my family, and after my return the Guides brought a second message for Nora: "As she realizes more and more that each of you is there merely for testing and advancement, not just to stay and stay, she will eagerly wish to put forth every effort to make her own testing period count. Her grief will seem empty and meaningless when she realizes that we are as much with you people there as we could ever have been in the flesh. There is nothing which passes through her thoughts that Richard is not sharing today, more intimately than while he was in the flesh. One person cannot fully know another until each has passed on to the next stage, where true union is possible—if each desires it to an equal extent. In this way, love continues through eternity."

On my birthday, the Guides said that Dad had something to say to me. My father announced himself as jauntily as ever and, using his pet name for me, wrote teasingly: "Hi, Sis. Well, I remember you when you were a puny little thing, but what a difference now! Guess a few of those pounds could be spared, eh, Sis? Well, it's a great day to remember, and you have made me very happy. Once in a while you've been a little feisty and scrappy, but over-all you've been my gal, and I expect you know that I love you. Be a good girl. Look after your mother, and remember that what you do there is what counts over here. The bad things total up, and have to be paid for later. Remember that the upward climb is easy if you think of the other chap first. I wish that I had had the opportunity the rest of you have, through these writings, to know that the time there is a testing ground not to be squandered. The worst thing to do is to spend it thinking about earthly gains and money-grubbing, because those are the least important goals. Look up instead of down, and find the stars. What's the difference if the other fellow looks a little better than you do, or has more money in his pocket? Does he have a better chance to help others, and to save himself by so doing? That is the question to ask yourself. Don't spend so much time trying to advance yourself in prestige and honors that you forget the other fellow, who needs an uplift from you."

Dad then brought a personal message for Nora, which proved to be such excellent advice that it has aided other bereaved friends in the years since. Declaring that she needed to be "straightened out" on the purpose of life, Dad wrote:

"Richard had passed the test of the earth-life, and was ready for the next step. It is wrong of Nora to try to hold him back with her tears and grief, because that keeps him too earth-bound, and we all have missions here to perform. Try to make her understand that she is slowing his progress by demanding so much of his time. She must develop the poise and womanliness that can let him go gracefully. The letting-go is not a permanent thing, as you know, but a mere releasing of his talents for his next progression.

"Whenever she wants him he is there, but how much better it would be if Nora did not want him quite so often. That is the mistake: for a person there to grieve so deeply that she cannot release the person who crosses over, so that the soul's progression can continue in orderly fashion. She will never lose Richard, because the love they share binds them eternally together; but like a woman who must let a man go to the office eight or ten hours a day to make a living, she must now be willing to release him for regular periods, so that he can do the work we all must do here. He will be there in any emergency when she calls, but she must release him as freely as a mother releases a child who starts school. That is the mark of maturity."

This latter part was a new idea to me, and I was

frankly amazed at my father's new depth and seeming perception. I had always adored him. W had been pals, and occasionally fellow conspirators when my seldom-aroused mother laid down the law in the family. Dad and I were much alike in our perennial optimism that everything would turn out all right if we just didn't worry about it. Mother was a worrier, who wanted every move carefully planned in advance. Dad and I were quick-tempered in our youth, but our fits of anger were as brief as April showers. Mother, slow to anger, was equally slow to forgive, and it annoyed her that after we had blown off steam we immediately forgot what the tempest had been all about.

For this reason I had never considered Dad a very introspective person. Obviously we both lacked some quality that would have prevented our causing occasional outbursts from my normally sweet-tempered mother. That is why Dad's dissertation on Nora surprised me so much. The "Iry Boy" I knew in the flesh could never have authored such a subtle analysis, nor could I have done so. The idea was far-reaching in its implications. It brought home to me, as nothing else had done, the utter selfishness of grief.

I pondered this equation for a few minutes before again placing my fingers on the typing keys. The writing began at once, but with slightly different pressure. This time it was the Guides who wrote: "Ruth, what your father has just told you is well put. If you are able to make Nora understand this, it will help tremendously. She has depths that she has not yet tapped. She has maturity that she has not yet reached. She has beauty of soul that will flower as a rose once she realizes that grief is a lack of faith, that it is pure selfishness, and that the woman admired in this realm above all others is the exquisite creature who loses herself in thought of others. Grief exists only when it is nurtured too well. If we would think of others before ourselves, we would be too busy to wallow in tears. Those tears are for ourselves; not for others.

"Tell her that to prove her love for Richard she must surrender him as regularly as she would if he had earthly chores to do at an office. His work here is far more important than that which occupied him there, and he has no wish for her to tie herself to that. He knows a great deal more about the true meaning of life now than at the time he was busying himself with tax reforms. That was a pastime that has little permanent appeal, for the soul is unclothed, and owns no dime.

"To clothe the soul is to hamper it, unless it is with pure love of fellow man. Richard needed an interest to keep him alert and active until his days on life were through, but he never once lost sight of the ultimate goal, which was soul's salvation. Decent living, thoughtfulness of others, and a helping hand were needed. This is the work he would have Nora carry forward; not to become bogged down in his office work, organizations, and chores. She is a magnificently endowed woman who can earn her own high pinnacle in that phase, as Richard did, by adopting his sweetness and spirituality, and thinking of others first."

The typing hesitated and then continued: "This, my dear Ruth, is something that you too must learn to the nth degree, and there is no better place to start than here at this typewriter. The time is now. The hour is late, because you have not yet properly started on the course that leads to ultimate salvation. Your days are numbered on the earth, but only in the sense that all days are numbered from the moment that a new baby cries. By your earthly calculations you have a long row yet to plow there, both Nora and you, but no wasted moment can be retrieved in that life or the next, so waste not. Begin this day to live your life with such perfection that the inspiration you provide others will set them on the same marvelously dedicated course that you should follow."

Recalling that this was my birthday, the Guides added: "What a time to begin this new course; to say to yourself, 'As of this day and forever forward, my thought will be of others. My heart will be attuned to others' needs. My life shall be dedicated to aiding others find salvation.' What a turning point this day can be for you, if you will only make it so."

CHAPTER 9

An Eagle on His Shoulder

Arthur Ford occasionally returned to Washington to conduct seminars on behalf of Spiritual Frontiers Fellowship. Although I could not spare the time to attend them, on two different occasions I invited the famous clairvoyant to meet with small groups of interested friends at my house. Each time, the Reverend Mr. Ford tied a handkerchief over his eyes and went into trance through a method of self-hypnosis which he had learned from a yogi. The room was brightly lighted, and I made tape recordings of the conversations.

The guests were always strangers to the medium, who did not know whom to expect until they arrived. One of the gatherings included an outstanding member of Congress, the wife of a top-ranking Senator, an editor, a television moderator, and a state legislator. Fletcher, Ford's mysterious Control, had messages for each. He told editor Hope Ridings Miller that she had been born in a little town with an odd name, which to the former French-Canadian that Fletcher claimed to have been sounded like *bon homme,* meaning "good man." Hope's birthplace was Bonham, Texas!

He described a high hedge around her childhood home, saying that a doctor had tenderly cultivated it, and that it had seemed remarkable for a hedge of that variety to flourish in such arid climate. "But he watered it regularly, even when there sometimes wasn't sufficient water for other things," he added, and Hope readily verified both the hedge and the tender-loving-care.

107

"Your father was that doctor," the voice emanating from the larynx of the slumbering medium continued. "You seem to be surrounded by doctors. You married one, and your father says to tell him to try"—here Fletcher gave the technical name for a little-known drug—"in the project he is working on that has to do with aging. I've been working on it over here and find that it will help considerably." Hope was indeed the daughter of a deceased physician, and her husband, Dr. Lee Miller was the resident physician at the United States Soldier's Home, a retreat for aging veterans, in addition to his regular medical practice.

Fletcher next addressed Deena Clark, moderator of an NBC television show called "A Moment With," saying: "A man wants to talk to you, whose name sounds like Christ, but that can't be quite right. He keeps talking about Lottie, and wants to express regret for some unhappiness he may have caused while he was in your plane." Deena acknowledged that Lottie had been her father's nickname for her mother, Charlotte, from whom he was later divorced. Her mother was still living, and her deceased father's first name was actually Christos, a fact that none of us had known.

The late Senator Pat McCarran identified himself by name to the wife of Senator Mike Mansfield, and gave her some interesting advice for her husband, whom he had known well during their years together in the Upper Chamber. The other women similarly received messages from departed relatives or friends, by name, and since the medium had not known my guest list in advance, he could not have consulted reference books.

During one of Ford's visits, I arranged for him to have a private sitting with my friend Nora. To avoid any suspicion of foreknowledge, I refrained from telling the medium her name until she arrived at his hotel suite, volunteering only that she had recently lost her husband. Since she was not a public figure, he had no way of recognizing her or of knowing her circumstances. At my suggestion Nora took copious shorthand notes after Ford went into trance. With its miracle of recorded detail, that séance turned out to be one of the most evidential that I have encountered. Not until Nora later read me the verbatim transcript did I learn for the first time of marital difficulties within her late husband's family and of many activities in which they were engaged. Through Fletcher, Richard gave Nora expert advice on the settling of the estate and the disposal of certain personal properties, including the yacht, which he identified. His children by a previous marriage were discussed by name, as were his brothers and sisters. Every reference checked out with complete accuracy.

The amazing story of Arthur Ford has been related in numerous other books, including his engrossing autobiography, *Nothing So Strange*. A native of Florida, he had been a divinity student at Transylvania College in Kentucky at the time of our entry into World War I, when he enlisted and quickly became a second lieutenant. He was based at Camp Grant when, on awakening one morning, he "saw" the roster of those who had died there of influenza during the night. Thinking to shake off the curious dream, he walked over to the adjutant's office to see the actual list, which was just being posted. To his dismay he discovered that not only were the names those which he had foreseen, but they were even in the same order as in his dream roster.

The flu epidemic was then raging throughout the country, and each day the list of victims at Camp Grant grew longer. For three nights in a row, Lieutenant Ford continued to "see" each day's roster before it was posted. Having never heard of clairvoyance, he hesitated to mention his strange experience to his buddies, for fear that they would consider him insane. On the fourth morning, however, he ruefully told them the names that he had just "seen" on awakening. They went with him to check the new roster, and every name appeared in the order he had given them.

After the war Ford went back to Transylvania, and in addition to his divinity courses he also enrolled for psychology classes. There he learned that many saints, and such religious leaders as John Wesley, Martin Luther, and Dwight Moody had been endowed with psychic powers. He became acquainted with the work of the Society for Psychical Research in England, and with the experiments of such scholars as Frederick W. H. Myers, William James, Sir Oliver Lodge and Sir Arthur Conan Doyle, who had become convinced of communication between man and the world of the spirit.

After Ford was ordained a Christian minister, he filled several church pulpits, but his growing interest in psychic phenomena gradually led him into the lecturing field. He developed rapidly as a "sensitive," and by the time I made his acquaintance he was perhaps the best-known living medium. He had traveled throughout the world giving demonstrations of clairvoyance, but in recent years was concentrating on helping ministers and divinity students to recognize the validity of psychical manifestations within the churches.

One evening my husband and I attended a Ford séance at a Washington rectory, where the only others present were eight men of the cloth. Among the discarnates whom Fletcher introduced was a mother of three, who said that before her recent death she had been married to the pastor of a Washington church—which she identified by name. She described the physical condition—a brain tumor—that caused her death, and gave other intimate details of her life on this plane. None of the pastors had heard of her, but when we telephoned the church and spoke to its rector, he readily confirmed that his wife had died a few days before of brain tumor, leaving three children. He said he had never heard of Arthur Ford, and rather curtly added that he had no interest in the psychic field.

During the séance, Fletcher reminded me that at a sitting the previous year he had said President Kennedy would be killed in a moving conveyance while away from the White House. I had forgotten it until I rechecked the tape recording. Now, only a month after the assassination, Fletcher flatly informed me that only one southern state would go uncommitted to the Democratic convention the following summer—Alabama—and that President Johnson would easily win election to a full term. He was right, of course. Alabama did not even list Johnson on its ballot, and its unpledged slate of delegates cast all votes for Goldwater, while LBJ won the election by a landslide.

A week before the election, on October 28, 1964, I received a telegram from Walter Voelker, an engineer-inventor who had attended a Ford séance in Philadelphia the evening before. The wire, which I have before me, reads: "Harold Ickes via Ford predicts Goldwater electoral vote 43 minimum 52 maximum." The Old Curmudgeon of New Deal days had apparently become a shrewd political prognosticator since his demise. The Goldwater electoral vote turned out to be 52.

At a garden party in the summer of 1964, a friend inquired of me about Arthur Ford's health, and an attractive woman in the group asked if I knew him. When I replied that he had recently visited us, she said that she had read his book and would like very much to meet him the next time he came to Washington. Nearly a year elapsed before his return, and by then I was unable to recall her name. Fortunately my husband's memory is better than mine, and I therefore telephoned to invite Ruth Newburn Smith to my house.

I carefully refrained from telling Ford the identity of my expected visitor, and I knew so little about her that I could have supplied no details if I had wished. On her arrival I introduced her as "Mrs. Smith," and the medium went almost immediately into trance. Fletcher was seldom in better form! For the next hour he leafed through the pages of her life, and as I later learned, gave surprisingly evidential details.

Mentioning her father first, Fletcher said: "He's rubbing his heart—he came over quite suddenly—but he lived to be quite old. A man with him was sick longer. He was confined to bed for some time." (Fletcher later made clear that this was her first husband.) "You have a son over here, too. He's been here seven or eight years, hasn't he? You and he had been talking about the possibility of communication after death. Your son traveled a great deal. He was not very old—just a young man in his late twenties—but he knew he was coming over here. Your boy says he is glad you don't make the mistake of thinking of him as gone. He is very much

111

alive. He says he has tried to come into your consciousness many times, but has never been successful except on one occasion several years ago, when he hadn't been here very long, and then you weren't sure you saw him. He tells you to re-create the same conditions as those existing when he reached you before—a detached state between waking and sleeping—so he can give you a sign of his presence.

"I keep seeing an eagle, a symbol of a flyer. It is something he did. He places the eagle on his shoulder. It is wings. Your son was in the service. He puts his hand to his head—speaks of a crash. He did not suffer. It was quick. He had a feeling that he was not destined to stay too long there. He had been studying survival and parapsychology. He says, 'Tell Mother I have all the answers now that I ever needed. There was no pain, and no lapse in consciousness. It is the same world, with different dimensions, but not in another plane or planet. We have no time or space problems, but we have to immerse ourselves in psychical energy to communicate with you.'

"You had tragedy and long nursing. Your first husband was immobilized a long time. You were sitting beside a river alone. All you had was your boy."

The son gave Mrs. Smith other, more personal, messages before yielding his place to her close girlhood friend, who identified herself by name, mentioned people they had known, and called one of them by a peculiar nickname. Her remarks clearly demonstrated that she had a continuing, intimate knowledge of Mrs. Smith's activities. Until that day I had known nothing of Ruth Newburn Smith's personal life, or that she had suffered bereavements and been married previously. She was obviously cultured, poised, and intelligent, and because this was her first experience with a medium, I suspected that she had had an inner struggle before deciding to attend the sitting that day. Because of her admirable composure, I could not discern to what extent Fletcher's messages had been accurate; but later, while writing this book, I found the courage to ask her. This is what she wrote for me:

"In 1957 my son, Lieutenant Robert Gordon Sedam,

112

a red-headed Marine jet pilot, was transferred from his fighter squadron in Atsuki, Japan, to Floyd Bennett Field on Long Island to be near his father, who was dying of acute leukemia. In 1958, a year after his father's death, Red showed me a review of Arthur Ford's then-new book, *Nothing So Strange,* and asked me to buy a copy immediately. Red was enthusiastic about everything in life, but often discussed with equal enthusiasm his belief in life after death.

"Before I could buy Arthur Ford's book, Red's jet went down in dense fog in the Atlantic off Long Island, two weeks before his scheduled discharge from the Marine Corps. In spite of a five-day sea and air search, no trace of the plane or pilot was ever found. I bought Arthur Ford's *Nothing So Strange* and read it to tatters.

"The following year I remarried and moved to Washington. Because of a painful back ailment, diagnosed as a bone infection, I was ordered to bed for three months, after which time I was to have bone surgery. I had agreed to follow this procedure. Much to my amazement, late one night as I was about to fall asleep, I saw Red's face in my darkened room. I heard no sound, but mentally 'heard' the urgently repeated suggestion: 'Get another X ray! Get another X ray! Get another X ray!' I could scarcely believe my impressions. Feeling rather foolish, since I had already been X-rayed several times, I consulted a different surgeon. On the basis of new X rays, the diagnosis was completely reversed and bone surgery was ruled out.

"For the first and only time in my life, I sat with a medium in June of 1965. Ruth Montgomery introduced me to Arthur Ford only as Mrs. Smith; and shortly after he went into trance, a voice introducing himself as Fletcher said, 'You have a son over here. He's been here seven or eight years, hasn't he?' He then mentioned several facts known only to Red and me, as well as accurate descriptions of people and events in my life, past and present. He also asked that I try to re-create the same conditions as those when my son 'reached me before,' so that he could again give me 'a sign of his presence.'

"Accordingly, on the night of July 28, 1965—the

seventh anniversary of the night Red's jet had gone down—I got into bed, turned out the light, laughed, and said in the tone Red and I used to use with each other, 'O.K. Speak up. Say something!' In a matter of minutes I felt impelled to go into an adjoining room containing several shelves of books, among them several dozen paperbacks which had belonged to my son. Having no desire to read a book, I asked myself what I was doing in there, and went back to bed. Unaccountably, I got up again, went in and looked at the books, and returned to bed. A third time I involuntarily arose, went in, and looked at those books.

"This time I pulled out one of Red's paperbacks at random. The title was, *The Universe and Dr. Einstein,* a book I had never read and never intended to! As I opened the book, a small piece of paper fell out. I had never seen it before, but in my son's unmistakable hen-scratched writing was this statement: 'I am thoroughly convinced that the immortality of the human soul and its relation to God is a reality, but in a way not yet conceived by man. I also feel that electricity and/or electromagnetic forces are the basic powers of the universe and human life.'

"Was this Red's way of convincing me, as he had insisted so many times while here, that life does go on after death? I don't know, and until now I have never mentioned these occurrences to anyone but my husband and Ruth Montgomery."

Mrs. Smith showed me the paperback book, the slip of paper on which her son had written his conviction of immortality, and the eagle on the Marine officer's insignia he had once worn on his lapel and which she now wears on a charm bracelet, together with his pilot's wings and other family momentos. She said Red had been dead for seven years (Fletcher had said "seven or eight"), and that he had been twenty-six years old when his plane crashed (Fletcher had correctly said "late twenties"). She added that after her first husband's death, she and her son had often discussed the possibility of communication and that Red had certainly "traveled a great deal."

I asked her about the others whom Fletcher had

mentioned. She replied that her father had died suddenly of a heart attack while traveling on a train, but had been only fifty-two. Her first husband had been hospitalized for a number of weeks before his death of acute leukemia. The curious nickname employed by the schoolgirl friend during the sitting was one which she immediately recognized. And what about Fletcher's odd remark, "You were sitting beside a river alone. All you had was your boy?" Nodding, Mrs. Smith responded: "Until I remarried and moved to Washington, my house was on a river, and my only other son was away at college."

General and Mrs. Albert C. Wedemeyer gave a dinner party one evening for Arthur Ford at Friend's Advice, their historic estate near Boyd, Maryland, which has been in Dade Wedemeyer's family since one of her ancestors built it in 1800. During the evening Ford went into trance, and Fletcher introduced an assortment of discarnates, including two Chinese who said they had known the general when he was commander of the China theater, and chief-of-staff to General Chiang Kai-shek from 1944 to 1946. Fletcher also brought a message to Wedemeyer from "Buffalo Bill" Cody, his grandfather's cousin, for whom Cody, Wyoming, is named, although the rest of us had been unaware of Al's family relationship with the famed army scout; and another to a woman in our group, from her father. "He regrets now that he took his own life," Fletcher said, and the woman blanched. Afterward, she said it was a family secret that he had committed suicide.

Dade Wedemeyer recalls that at a previous sitting with Arthur Ford in New York, when General Jimmy Doolittle and newspaper columnist Danton Walker were also present, Fletcher spoke of her deceased sister and others by name. Then, turning to Walker, he said a woman who had died of a ruptured appendix was telling him that "Danton would know about an unplucked chicken," and that a man with her was "standing in a ship and talking about Marsha—no, Martha."

"Incredible!" Danton Walker exclaimed. After the séance, he told them that when his mother was dying of a ruptured appendix at their country place in the South, their Negro cook rushed out and killed a chicken, then placed it, unplucked, on his mother's stomach. He said the primitive superstition of the area was that an unplucked chicken would draw out the poison and cure a stomach ache. He added that his mother's uncle had been a seafaring man who during the Civil War had captured two Yankee ships off Martha's Vineyard and thereafter never stopped talking about it.

On another occasion Ford sat for Gwendolyn Risedorf of Massapequa Park, New York. She had never before met the medium, but as soon as he went in to trance, Fletcher introduced her seventeen-year-old son by name, described the nature of his death (which was not a natural one), correctly identified him as a ham radio operator, and told of his stature and personality traits. To Mrs. Risedorf, however, the most remarkable part of the séance was Fletcher's repeated reference to her "Jewish" background. She questioned him closely about this, and then told him, "I don't know of any Jewish strain anywhere in our family."

Fletcher imperturbably replied: "Well, your mother—Lulu, isn't it?—tells me her husband was Jewish. The man she married was Jewish."

"Then it suddenly struck me like a bolt from the blue!" Mrs. Risedorf declares. "It was not my father that Fletcher had been talking about, but the man my mother (Lula) was married to when she died. My stepfather was Jewish, although I never think of him as a Jew, or even as a relative since my mother died. Naturally Mother would be speaking of him, though. How could Arthur Ford, who did not even know my identity, possibly have picked up that link, unless Fletcher was actually in communciation with her?"

Arthur Ford is one of the most modest, dedicated men I have ever known. A devout Christian, he abhors the trickery to which some mediums resort when their psychic powers are not at peak performance. Although gentle and unassuming, he is so well informed and knowledgeable that people sit spellbound while he discusses everything from the Bible to Christian yoga and

Carl Jung. His financial means are extremely limited, but he believes so keenly that psychic manifestations should be recognized in the pulpit today, as they were in the early Christian church, that he gives freely of his time and energy to religious groups. A number of outstanding Episcopal ministers are among his most ardent fans, as are clergymen of nearly every other sect.

Ford is primarily a trance medium rather than a psychometrist, but once I handed him a pocket watch and asked if he could tell me anything about its ownership. He held it between the palms of his hands for a few minutes and then began to massage his arms as if they ached. "The watch belonged to your father," he said. "He obviously suffered a great deal with pains which shot down his arms from the shoulders to his hands. I know, because I am picking up his agony."

My father had seldom been ill until he died of his first heart attack. In his later years, however, Dad would often get out of bed in the night and run hot water over his arms and hands to ease the frightful ache for which his medical advisers had no cure. Since only our immediate family knew this, Ford could not have learned it by normal means.

Any doubt that Arthur Ford was actually in trance during his séances vanished, as far as I was concerned, one day at our house on Sheridan Circle. He had stopped by for lunch, en route from Philadelphia to Florida, and after we had chatted a while, he said that he would like me to ask Fletcher a few questions on his behalf. "There are some decisions I must make," he explained, "and since I'm always asleep when Fletcher is talking, I don't have a chance to ask him myself."

I gladly acquiesced, and Ford gave me his list of questions. Then he stretched out on the couch in the library, tied a silk handkerchief across his eyes, and went into trance. Fletcher soon announced his presence and started to bring me a message from a former newspaper woman who had recently arrived on the next plane, but I broke in to say that I had some specific questions to ask Fletcher on behalf of Ford. What, for instance, should he do with his sizable collection of books, since he had just sold his house in Florida and would be living out of suitcases for a time?

Fletcher seemed rather uninterested, I thought, in helping the man who had been his faithful mouthpiece for nearly a half-century. His answer was rather indifferent, and when I next asked whether the medium should visit a clinic in New Mexico for a thorough physical checkup, Fletcher snapped: "He'd better do something. If he doesn't, I can't work through him much longer. He should not lie down flat like he's doing now, and he knows it. It's bad for him. He's in great pain this minute and doesn't know it; but he will when he comes out of trance."

Alarmed, I asked what I should do for him, and Fletcher replied: "Just get him up on his feet as soon as you can. He'll know what to do then."

Fletcher started to introduce a departed relative of mine, but I was too worried about Arthur to pursue the conversation. If he was in danger, I felt that we should not be draining his strength. He looked as peaceful as a slumbering child, but I asked Fletcher to bring him out of his trance. As the spirit Control withdrew, and the familiar look of consciousness began to return to Ford's face, he suddenly clutched at his heart and groaned in agony. The pain could not have been feigned, for beads of perspiration popped out on his forehead, and his suppressed moans tore at my heart.

Badly frightened, I rushed to him and said that I would help him stand erect. It was not easy to bring him to his feet while he was doubled over with pain, but as soon as he stood, he asked me for a drink of carbonated water. I quickly provided it, and he put in his mouth a pill carried for use in the event of such an anginal attack.

Arthur Ford, whose own psychic powers are widely acknowledged, has sometimes triggered extrasensory reactions in others. For instance: On May 10, 1966, after completing a series of lectures at a Spirtual Frontiers Fellowship convention in Chicago, he was chatting in his Palmer House suite with Arthur Shefte, an old friend, when he suddenly lost consciousness. Shefte knew him well enough to recognize that this was not a yoga trance-state. He therefore called the hotel doctor, who summoned an ambulance and began administering oxygen. As Ford was being carried from the room on a stretcher, his telephone rang. Shefte, answering it, heard a voice say: "This is Margueritte Bro. I was awakened from a nap just now, by a voice which said, 'Arthur Ford is in very serious trouble. Get in touch with him immediately.' Is he all right?"

Mrs. Bro, who collaborated with Ford in the writing of his autobiography, *Nothing So Strange,* was forty miles away, at her home in Park Forest, Illinois, at the time of his attack.

Ford required hospitalization for several weeks because of an embolism, after which he returned to his home in Philadelphia to convalesce. Then, feeling considerably stronger, he spent the week-end of June 24 with John Lawrence, an award-winning CBS-TV commentator, and his wife at their home in nearby Chestnut Hill. After everyone had retired for the night, Lawrence heard his dog barking and clawing at the door to Ford's room, and went to investigate. When his houseguest failed to respond to his knock, he opened the door and found Ford lying unconscious on the floor beside his bed. The famous medium regained consciousness thirty hours later in the Chestnut Hill hospital, having suffered another embolism.

Some guardian angel was apparently watching over Ford, who ordinarily lives alone, for he was fortunate enough to be in the company of friends each time that he had an attack.

CHAPTER 10

A Do-It-Yourself Lesson

In the summer of 1963, I attended a seminar on meditation and psychic development at the headquarters of the Edgar Cayce Foundation in Virginia Beach. My newspaper editors had agreed that it would make an informative series, since my mail indicated a growing public interest in extrasensory perception, so I went both as student and reporter. In my previous research on the subject, I had read a great deal about the late Edgar Cayce, the most documented seer who ever lived, and of his seeming ability to tap the cosmic consciousness when in trance. Millions are familiar with the work of this remarkable man through such best-selling books as *There Is A River,* by Thomas Sugrue, and *Many Mansions,* by Gina Cerminara.

Born on a Kentucky farm in 1876, of old American stock, the devoutly religious little boy was making such slow progress with his schoolwork that one evening his father grilled him for hours with a spelling book. At 10:30 P.M., when he still was misspelling the words in his lesson, Mr. Cayce disgustedly knocked him from his chair. As the boy fell he seemed to hear a voice saying, "If you can sleep a little, we can help you."

Edgar Cayce begged for a brief respite, and after his father grudgingly left the room he fell asleep with the book under his head. Awakened in a half-hour to resume the grilling, the lad not only knew the next day's lesson perfectly, but could correctly spell any other word in the book. Thereafter he slept on his other textbooks at night, and through some strange process of osmosis knew their entire contents by heart, including the number of the pages on which any answer could be found.

In his young manhood he lost his voice. Doctors could find no cause or cure, but he eventually healed himself while under self-hypnosis. His latent psychic talent then developed rapidly, and through better-educated friends he heard for the first time such words as clairvoyance and precognition. He discovered that in a self-imposed trance state he could correctly diagnose illnesses and prescribe successful treatments, despite his total ignorance of medicine when awake. As his fame spread, sick people called from all parts of the nation, and even doctors began beating a path to his door. He did not need to meet the unknown patient in person. If the writer specified where he would be at the time of the reading, Cayce could locate him psychically while in trance, and make the diagnosis.

Suddenly, one day, the readings took a new turn. The voice which emanated from Cayce during the trance state began to tell patients about their lives in previous incarnations. The deeply religious man was dumbfounded when told what he had said. Having never heard of reincarnation, he did not see how he could reconcile such a strange philosophy with the Holy Writ, until he turned to his well-thumbed Bible and found that in the book of Matthew, Jesus had indicated to his disciples that John the Baptist was the reincarnation of Elias. From them until his death in 1944, Edgar Cayce gave many thousands of physical and life readings, verbatim copies of which are on file at the headquarters of the Association for Research and Enlightenment (A.R.E.) in Virginia Beach. These are being carefully indexed under the direction of his elder son, Hugh Lynn Cayce, by dedicated men and women who are devoting their lives to making the great seer's spiritual teachings available to a hungry world.

A.R.E. Study Groups have spread throughout the nation, and at the Virginia Beach headquarters several seminars are held each summer. The first one that I attended was jointly sponsored by A.R.E., Spiritual

Frontiers Fellowship, and the Institute for Research in Psychology and Religion. The last is directed by Dr. Harmon Bro, a Harvard-educated psychologist and university professor, who with Hugh Lynn Cayce and Arthur Ford conducted the week's study in which I participated. My classmates included ordained ministers, professors, lay leaders, doctors, a construction tycoon, an engineer, a folk singer, an insurance executive, and housewives, who, having developed mysterious psychic abilities, were asking themselves "What is happening to me?"

Meditation, we were taught, can awaken us for the first time. It can change our lives. It can revolutionize the world. "Psychic" stems from the Greek word meaning soul, or breath of life. All of us, then, are psychic, but as with music or art, some have a greater flair for it than others. Just as any normal person can be taught to paint or play the piano so all of us can learn through basic techniques how to develop our latent psychic ability.

"Meditation is absolutely essential to mankind," Hugh Lynn Cayce told us. "I could go out and sell it for the by-products alone." Through disciplined meditation, during which we deliberately seek a higher level of consciousness, Cayce says that we can acquire the ability to:

*Hear a speech or sermon all the way through, without woolgathering or losing a word of it.

*Focus the mind on relaxation, and fall instantly asleep as our head hits the pillow.

*Awaken at the exact time that we previously instructed our subconscious.

*Sit down anywhere—in a crowded bus station, on an airplane, in an automobile—and go to sleep at will, waking refreshed at whatever time we desire.

*Derive amazing new energies for all sorts of strenuous tasks.

*Lean against a tree, hear its sap flowing, and the churning noises of its life energy.

*Completely relax the body and mind, thereby easing inner stresses.

*Sharpen the senses so that we can hear music never

123

before heard, see auras of color surrounding others, involuntarily change our taste for certain types of food, and understand our dreams.

If an amateur decided to scale Mt. Everest, he would naturally seek advice from a professional and secure proper climbing equipment. If he were wise, he would also take along trusted companions in the event that he slipped or needed another's rope to save himself. It is the same with meditation. Cayce advises all who would develop psychic awareness to join a study group and follow tried rules of discipline, such as those which he learned through the trance instructions of his father. These sound deceptively simple, but to put them into practice may require the hardest work of your life.

To prepare for meditation in the Cayce manner, you should first study and memorize an affirmation, such as those imparted in an A.R.E. book called *A Search for God*. A typical one is this: "Create in me a pure heart, O God. Open Thou my heart to the faith Thou hast implanted in all that seek Thy face. Help Thou mine unbelief in my God, in my neighbor, in myself." Such other affirmations as the Lord's Prayer or the Twenty-Third Psalm may be used instead.

Seek a quiet place, and sit with spine straight to perform each of these exercises three times: Bow the head forward until the chin touches the chest, and drop it backward to rest on the top of the spine, returning it after each exercise to an erect position. Next twist the head three times to the lower right, straining to see the right heel over the shoulder, and repeat to the lower left. Afterward, loosely roll the head three times clockwise in a wide circle, and then counter-clockwise. Breathe deeply three times through the right nostril, exhaling each time through the mouth, and repeat with the left nostril. Lastly, chant in a low monotone the letters "A I E R Om." You will find that a vibration sets up with utterance of the "Om."

Now you are ready to begin the meditation, either in a chair, with spine erect, or prone on your back. Picture in the mind's eye the memorized affirmation, seeing it as carved in stone or written on a blackboard, but do not mentally repeat its words. Your mind will repeatedly stray; chase it, and bring it back. Continue the same concentration daily for ten minutes, at the same time and place. At first the body will develop itches and twinges. Ignore them. A series of faces may flash before the inner eye. Keep going deeper into meditation. Don't pause to look at the faces, because you are seeking a higher level of consciousness than this. Allow the spiritual energy to move upward until it makes contact with the cosmic energy flowing from God.

"Let the real soul take over," Cayce counsels. "One day you will suddenly reach the state of silence and light. You will know when you have experienced it, because there's nothing like it; but this is the mere beginning of true meditation. This is when you begin to encounter God. Your hate and self-pity are removed. You are cleansed from within. Beyond the silence and light is the sudden knowing of the nature of all things. It is not a loss of consciousness, but a heightening of awareness. There is an awe, as you come into the presence of something far beyond Self. There is a sudden realization of something you must do, of something left undone in a relationship with another, which must be completed before you can come into the Presence of God. Meditation becomes a way of life."

Having experienced true illumination, no one is ever quite the same again. Dr. Richard Maurice Bucke, whose book, *Cosmic Consciousness,* published in 1901, has become a classic in the literature of psychic phenomena, wrote that an individual who has known illumination is "almost a member of a new species." He describes the sensations as "a state of moral exaltation, an indescribable feeling of elevation, elation, and joyousness, and a quickening of the moral sense which is fully as striking and more important both to the individual and to the race than is the enhanced intellectual power. With these come what may be called a sense of immortality, a consciousness of eternal life; not a conviction that he shall have this, but the consciousness that he has it already." Dr. Bucke cites impressive "evidence" that not only such immortals as Buddha, Jesus Christ, St. Paul, and Mohammed experienced illumination, but also Dante, William Blake, Walt Whitman, and Francis Bacon; and perhaps Ralph Waldo Emerson, Alfred Tennyson, Henry David Thoreau and others. *Cosmic Consciousness* is a book worthy of study.

The early Christian church was founded on psychic experiences, and both the Old and New Testaments describe angelic visitations. Arthur Ford says that "the psychic stream is the common denominator of all religions; every world religion has been born out of it." Although Ford himself is a medium, he warns against "using a medium as a crutch." He believes that people should "develop their own psychic talents, and learn to make the contact themselves." Disagreeing with those who assert that it is dangerous to "open up one's psychic," Ford says: "If you are God-centered, and your motives are right, you are perfectly safe in exploring any part of the universe. This is what Paul taught in the twelfth to fourteenth chapters of First Corinthians." St. Paul's advice to the Corinthians began: "Now concerning spiritual gifts, brethren, I would not have you ignorant.... The manifestation of the Spirit is given to every man to profit withal."

Some ministers, aware of the vast potential of psychic study, but fearful that their congregations might disapprove, have secretly traveled hundreds of miles to seminars conducted by Spiritual Frontiers Fellowship, only to find as classmates some members of their flock who had been afraid to confide to their pastors their own interest.

Throughout the Bible we encounter a world of spirit beings. Therefore, how does a minister explain the transfiguration of Moses and Elijah before Christ and the three disciples, if he does not accept psychic experience? How does the Holy Spirit speak to us, except through psychic awakening? The early Christians knew psychic experience, and took it for granted. Somewhere along the way, the church lost touch with this God-given faculty, but an awakening seems to be at hand.

Arthur Ford cautions that before we try to contact "another world," we should first become integrated in this one, and settle our own personal problems. The best psychics are emotionally stable, sound individuals; neurotics and psychotics have no place in this field. Ford, like Hugh Lynn Cayce, believes that there is safety in numbers. Before trying to develop our psychic gifts, he therefore advises us to join or to organize a small group of interested people in the church, "because if you get a group together for meditation, something will begin to happen." He says the meetings should be held weekly; and, to prepare for them, each member should set aside the same time each day for private meditation. Ford stresses that only like-minded, serious students should be invited to the group meetings. "As you arrive, don't chatter and gossip," he advises. "Go immediately into silent meditation together. After thirty minutes of such God-centered concentration, quietly share your experiences with each other. In this way you will grow in awareness."

For those who seek contact with discarnate spirits, Ford has these specific instructions:

*Seek a quiet spot in some room of your house where you can be undisturbed. Shut out all objective light, or tie a handkerchief across your eyes. Make sure that your spine is straight, whether you sit in a chair or lie on your back on the floor. Then forget your body.

*If there is a particular loved one who has gone on to the next stage of life, focus your attention on his remembered face. Otherwise, visualize an heirloom or other object that has special meaning for you.

*Breathe gently and deeply, inhaling through the nose for a count of eight, and exhaling for a similar count through the mouth, while mentally holding the picture before your mind's eye.

*The rhythmic breathing should begin to wield a self-hypnotic effect as the mental image pulsates backward and forward before your closed eyes. If your mind strays away from the visualized image, and it will, gently bring it back into focus.

After sustained daily practice, you may develop various types of psychic abilities: clairvoyance, in which you see events occurring at a distance; clairaudience, a high level of awareness in which you inwardly hear messages; or a trance state during which a discarnate may speak through you to others. The beginner should practice this type of solitary meditation no more than fifteen minutes a day. The weekly group sessions then provide an essential safety valve.

Prayer healing, which played such a dominant role in the early Christian church, is an integral part of psychic study. Christ healed, and taught his disciples to do likewise. St. Paul lost his sight while experiencing a vision of Christ, and regained it exactly as prophesied. The remarkable success of Alcoholics Anonymous is credited to spiritual healing. Reformed drunkards who have "made love their aim" are able, through prayer and fellowship, to effect a cure for many fallen comrades. As a matter of fact, one of the three founders of Alcoholics Anonymous says that in a psychic dream, while he was hospitalized for his thirty-ninth "cure" for alcoholism, he received instructions on how to form an organization to save others as well as himself.

A resurgence of spiritual healing is springing up in churches across America. The Episcopal Church through its Order of St. Luke's has taken the lead, with regularly scheduled prayer services for the "laying on of hands." Both Spiritual Frontiers Fellowship and the Association for Research and Enlightenment have organized healing groups in every section of the country. Ford gives these hints for conducting your own spiritual healing sessions:

Assemble no more than ten congenial people in quiet convocation. If you have an ailing friend or relative for whom you seek help, take a picture of him to the meeting. Let each member study the portrait, so that he can visualize the person in his inner eye. As you begin the meditation, each member should picture the ailing person as completely well. Never think of the symptoms, but see him only as he should be in perfect health. Become so absorbed in your meditation that you are aware of nothing else.

Ford, in explaining why the results are often miraculous, says: "When you lose self for someone else, or for a worthy purpose, there is a law at work. I don't believe there are any accidents in this universe. Meditation is the key to understanding these laws, and the cosmic force which all of us may tap." Ford says solutions to everyday problems can be found through meditation: "If I face a troubling situation, I meditate on it just before falling asleep. I fix clearly in my mind how I would like to have it resolved for the best interests of all concerned. Almost invariably, on awakening, the solution is presented to my conscious mind. Every problem has a cause. Let the larger, unconscious mind with its stored-up knowledge and access to the cosmic consciousness take over while you sleep."

Mrs. Marguerite Briggs, who conducted a prayer laboratory at the seminar which I attended in Virginia Beach, demonstrated two methods of spiritual healing. In one, the group concentrated its united mental efforts on beaming a healing light toward one person in the room who had a health problem. In the other system, those present meditated on beaming a healing force toward one member, who in turn mentally projected it toward another person who was absent.

Unknowingly, I was the absent person to whom one such beam was projected. The group knew that I was suffering acute muscular spasms in my back, but not until the next day did I learn that at approximately the same time that I was abruptly freed from pain, the prayer group had been meditating on me. Since I did not know of the project, no self-suggestion on my part could have entered into the experiment.

CHAPTER 11

The Man in the Next Room

The Christian Church did not begin with doctrine, but with psychic experience which so stirred the Apostles and their converts that the church was born. Later, the twin impacts of scientific materialism and philosophical rationalism caused the church to disavow its own psychic origins and brand them "superstition," but the wheel is beginning to come full turn. Nearly half of all Protestant ministers who answered a questionnaire distributed recently by the National Council of Churches said they had had some experience with spiritual healing.

The very act of praying is an acceptance of psychical experience, but it is apparently *how* we pray that counts. Three years before attending the seminar at Virginia Beach, I personally witnessed a miracle of prayer. Like many another political correspondent, religion was scarcely in the forefront of my mind during the hectic political campaign of 1960. I was turning out an unending stream of newspaper columns, while crisscrossing America with the jet-age Presidential candidates. The pace was incredibly rugged. We typed on our laps in planes and jolting buses, and when we wearily carried our typewriters and suitcases into hotel lobbies at two or three in the morning, we knew we had to be out again before seven.

In the middle of the campaign, I was felled by excruciating back spasms. The timing could scarcely have been less convenient, nor doctors less cooperative. Had

I been suffering from influenza, a doctor would presumably have come to the house; but even my family physician could not prevail upon the orthopedic specialists to pay a home call. If I needed attention, they insisted, I could call an ambulance and go to the hospital where they made daily rounds.

I endured the agony for a week, but finally gave in and went to the hospital by ambulance. The orthopedic specialist who arranged my admittance did not come to the hospital after all, but an intern strapped me into traction after plastering my legs with many yards of adhesive tape. My legs were then hoisted high above my head, and because of the torturous position and the unceasing coughing of a man in the next room, I did not sleep that night. The next morning a resident physician strode in, took one look at my suspended legs, and snapped at a nurse: "Cut her down out of that immediately. That's the kind of traction for broken legs, not bad backs."

The strips of adhesive were painfully ripped off, and the doctor departed without further instructions. The specialist did not come that day, either, but after eight unattended hours I was finally strapped into a different type of traction by another intern. When my husband arrived that evening, he remarked: "I hope you don't think that you're in traction now."

"Of course I'm in traction," I said peevishly. "Can't you see it fastened to my legs?"

"I see the pulleys," he grinned, "but the weights are lying on the floor." He summoned a nurse and pointed out the obvious. She shrugged that she knew it, but that the ropes were too long. It was Bob who finally shortened the cords so that the weights could function properly. The specialist was still "too busy" to come, but the next morning he sent an assistant, who added another pully to my chin. Thereafter I lay for ten days in double traction, unable to turn in bed.

My mood was dark. I was sleeping very little because of the constant pain and unnatural position. When I did manage to doze off, I was invariably awakened by the rasping coughs of the unknown patient next door. Once a nurse was in the room while he was having a particularly violent coughing spell. I asked about him, and she replied: "He has pneumonia. He won't last much longer."

Submerged in my own self-pity, I rather irritably asked why people with contagious diseases were put in the orthopedic wing. She shrugged that there were a "lot worse communicable diseases than pneumonia" in that wing. I felt extremely sorry for myself. My muscular spasms were as frequent and painful as when I had entered the hospital ten days before, and the political campaigns that I had always found so exciting were progressing without me. I prayed frequently for release from the pain, but the Lord seemed no more interested in me than the absent back specialist was.

Lying in double traction that night, unable to sleep, I prayed long and hard for a cure. I could scarcely concentrate on my prayers, however, because the wracking coughs from next door permeated the thin wall as if it were made of gauze. I knew the sound of a stranger's agony better than my own voice, for scarcely an hour had elapsed since my admittance to the hospital that I had not heard his dreadful hacking. The nurse came in with a pill and offhandedly mentioned that the man with pneumonia was not expected to live through the night.

Suddenly I was filled with shame, and suffused with compassion for him. Almost without realizing it, I began to pray fervently for his recovery. Over and over, I asked God to restore him to good health. I found myself begging that the life of this stranger be spared. At last, about midnight, I fell into an exhausted sleep. Sunlight was pouring through the windows when the nurse awakened me with the breakfast tray. I could scarcely believe that I had slept so soundly for so long. I was almost finished with breakfast, which is a difficult accomplishment when one is lying flat on one's back, when I realized that something was missing. I had not heard the coughing since I had fallen asleep at midnight.

The nurse came for the tray, and with dread I managed to ask if the man next door had passed away. "Goodness, no," she said cheerily. "It's like a miracle.

He hasn't even coughed in seven or eight hours." Silence reigned from the next door throughout the long day and the night that followed. At last I prepared to go home. My back was no better, and the doctors finally agreed that I might as well be in my own bed at home. The nurse helped me into a wheelchair and asked what I would like done with the flowers that filled the tables. On an impulse, I asked her to give them all to the stranger in the adjoining room. She took them in to him, and as she wheeled me past his door, she called out: "This is the lady who gave you her flowers."

A young colored man lying on the bed thanked me shyly and said: "The doctor says I can go home tomorrow." I could not resist asking when he had begun to feel better, and he replied: "Night before last. I thought I was going to die, but about midnight I suddenly felt well all over." It was the exact time of my prayers for him. The Lord had dramatically demonstrated that unselfish prayers are heard.

The Rev. Dr. Edward L. R. Elson, pastor of the National Presbyterian Church where President and Mrs. Eisenhower worshiped during their eight years at the White House, can attest to many instances of the efficacy of prayer. While a student at Asbury College in Kentucky during the mid-twenties, he participated in a weekly prayer session with some other members of his class. One day he received word that his mother was dying, and before rushing to her bedside in Pennsylvania, he asked the prayer group to pray for her recovery at its next session.

Dr. Elson says he later learned that "at the very hour Mother rallied, my classmates were holding the prayer session for her at the college." She recovered, and lived another quarter of a century, until 1952.

After Dr. Elson was ordained in 1931, he served for ten years as pastor of a Presbyterian church in La Jolla, California, where his spiritual ministry attracted so much attention that physicians sometimes appealed to him for help with cases which baffled medical science. On one occasion, he was summoned to the home of a young woman who had been in a trancelike state for ten days following her collapse at the funeral of her fiancé.

"I drove to her house," Dr. Elson recalls, "and before leaving my car, prayed that God would guide me. I then joined the physician at the bedside of the young woman, who was of the Greek Orthodox faith. She was unaware of my presence, but kept endlessly repeating, 'It's so dark! The night is so black, and the rain, and the storm...it's so dark!'

"I went back to my car for a flashlight, and again prayed that I would be shown the way to help her. Then, by reverse suggestion, I began trying to bring her out of trance through a form of hypnosis. At first I whispered softly of gentle breezes and the breaking dawn, gradually increasing the volume of my voice, until I fairly shouted that the sun was now shining brightly. Simultaneously, I beamed the flashlight into her eyes, and as I did so she began talking quite normally. She had occasional relapses during the next few months, but each time the doctor called me, and I repeated the hypnotic suggestion of light, until a permanent cure was effected. She is now happily married, has several lovely children, and is so grateful that she presented me with a beautiful book, into which she had bound four hundred of my prayers."

Dr. Elson's wife is a niece of the late Dr. Glenn Clark, founder of the "Camps Farthest Out" movement that stresses the power of healing prayers. Dr. Elson has no hesitation in expressing his own firm belief that "man is on the threshold of a breakthrough in the field of extrasensory perception and the world of the spirit."

Senate Republican leader Everett Dirksen of Illinois is convinced that "prayer is a direct pipeline to God." During his service on the European battlefront during World War I, he carried a khaki-covered Bible, which he read at night by candlelight. He heavily underscored certain passages that seemed to have particular meaning for him. One of his favorites was an obscure verse from James 5:15, "And the prayer of faith shall save the sick."

Senator Dirksen came to believe that the passage

had healing power in times of crisis, and he put it to the test in 1947, when, as a Congressman, he developed chorioretinitis. Numerous physicians in Chicago and Washington examined his eyes, and because some of them thought he had a malignancy in the right eye, his personal doctor advised that he go to Johns Hopkins Hospital in Baltimore, and have the eye removed.

"I took the train to Baltimore," the Senator says, "and during the forty-minute ride from Washington I stepped out into the vestibule, got down on both knees, and repeated the passage on healing. Then I told God that I felt I had the required faith, and that if He still had work for me to perform here, I would follow His direction if He would manifest His will. Immediately I felt a powerful surge within, and as plainly as if I had heard the spoken word, I was directed to keep both my eyes."

Dirksen continued to the hospital, but after the surgeon examined him and advised immediate removal of the right eye, he said: "No, Doctor, I guess not. I have already had a talk with the Big Doctor Upstairs." The surgeon exclaimed, "Don't tell me you're one of those fellows!" and Dirksen replied, "Yes, He told me not to have the operation, so that's that."

The legislator returned to his office on Capitol Hill, cleared off his desk, and announced that he would not be a candidate for re-election. He and Mrs. Dirksen then returned home to Illinois, where he "slept and prayed a good deal, tended my flowers, and gave myself over to the healing process."

As word spread that he was regaining his eyesight, delegations began beating a path to his door to plead that he run for the Senate. At last persuaded, he challenged the Democratic incumbent, Scott Lucas, who was also the powerful majority leader of the Senate. Dirksen won in that campaign of 1950, has been re-elected regularly at six-year intervals, and since 1959 has served as Republican Leader of the Senate. The "Big Doctor Upstairs" apparently had plenty of work for him to do. Significantly, the right eye which the doctors wanted to remove "is now my good eye," the Senator says.

CHAPTER 12

Love One Another

Dr. Harmon H. Bro, theologian, psychotherapist and parapsychologist who has taught at Harvard and Syracuse universities, says that there is a "growing thirst" inside and outside the Church for psychic experience. The former Dean of the Divinity School at Drake University graphically explains that "thirst" in these terms: "In mid-life, when our families are reared and our earning power is at its peak, something begins to well up inside of us. We begin to hunger for a richer, wiser center for ourselves. We become vaguely dissatisfied with the emptiness within. We say to ourselves, 'Hey, grow!' Finally, something begins to boil up inside. Our stumbling blocks become stepping stones. The first half of life is nature—the establishing of homes and rearing of children. The second half is spirit, and we begin to ask ourselves, 'What else?' This hunger is right on schedule. Don't be alarmed by it. The rich human growth is just ahead."

There is general agreement that meditation can lead the way to spiritual awakening, but like those of many working people in this frenetic world, my good resolutions often failed due to lack of time and will power to carry them through. The Guides for some months had been urging me to write a book on psychic phenomena, so that the lessons which they were painstakingly imparting to me could become available to others who also needed them. Because of my busy schedule I kept delaying that project, and sometimes skipping the daily meditation for weeks at a time. There did not seem to be enough hours in the day. My Guides found this excuse totally unacceptable. Urging me to give time to meditation on first awakening each morning, they wrote:

"Give it your complete attention. Then, refreshed, you will be ready for this period with us at nine A.M. The spiritual values that you receive will more than compensate for the lost time, so do not wonder where you will find the time. It is *here*, and we have told you before that the only real element in the universe is time. That is what develops your progressions, and makes it possible for you to grow in perception. Time, moving forward, never backward, is the staff of the universe on which all else rests. It is the only true reality in your world, and it must therefore be used to the fullest extent in preparing for the next phase, and the next. It is timeless, because it is time itself. The financial progress, the fame, and all else in your world are fleeting. Remember always to utilize time as a precious commodity. Ask yourself many times during each day whether the use you are making of time is the best. If recreation is a part of that usage, well and good, so long as it is the healthful type that fits you for the week ahead. Think always of whether you are benefiting something, or merely stalling."

The Guides often stressed the advantages of using the first waking hour for meditation. Once they wrote: "Use this hour while the mind is fresh, and free from the shackles of the daily schedule. Before rising, let the mind roam to the next plane, and feast itself on the glories to come, for that is the time when you are nearest the Maker—in those first waking moments after a tranquil sleep. The time for meditation is then, rather than after your thoughts are helter-skelter and uncontrollable. This you will remember, and do hereafter."

I am ashamed to admit that I could not seem to hold myself to their prescribed schedule. I was occupied with the writing of a daily political column; the responsibility of a large house, a husband, a maid, and a poodle; and a crowded social schedule. My unseen correspondents were impatient with me, and one day they severely chastised me, writing: "Let us talk seriously to you for a moment about the philosophy that you seek. We are at all times ready to pass along wisdom that we have learned since coming to this side, but unless you are planning to use it for the benefit of others, there is no point in pouring it forth to you, since it seems to make little difference in your own attitudes. That is not what we had hoped. First we must see an improvement in you, before it seems feasible to pass this wisdom along through you to others. The example you set might be bad, unless others could see how the knowledge of this wisdom has also improved *you* who first received it from us. The meditations are a *must* for the same time each day. Let it be on rising, or at a time of your own choosing, so long as it is at the same time each day. That is the way it can develop for real progress."

The Guides kept harping on the book that I was to write. A few days later, they instructed: "We want you to introduce the central theme that the purpose of life in that phase is to prepare for the next and the next and the next. The only way to accelerate one's development is to live in such manner that some of the steps in the long road ahead can be eliminated. This is done through helping others rather than one's self. The spiritual tone of such action so polishes the soul that the progression is rapid. Try always to project this message, because the purpose of the book is to save souls, and leave a mark that will help all who are seeking. This message is overpowering in its significance. It is the force of the universe itself; the interlocking force that powers the planets and supplies all energy. This simple formula will work wonders. By helping others, all are helped. Without helping others, we fragmentize into tiny units. Together we are all-powerful in our quest for perfect union and Oneness with God.

"Were it not that this powerful force exists, this intensity of drive to help others, the world would fall into disunion, and nothing but blackness would exist. The light and life of that planet and all others are dependent on the interlocking force that ties one to another. The will to do for others is more basic than life itself, for it existed before life, and helped to create life. It is the staff of living."

We went away on vacation, and after our return I finally began work on the book, plunging into the task of sorting the mass of automatic writing which I had dated and saved since its earliest beginnings. Some of it was repetitive, but the re-reading of the inspiring passages filled me with shame for having neglected their retelling. The Guides enthusiastically applauded my application to the task, and told me to stress that "other people, by taking a little time and preparing themselves, can actually communicate and learn at first hand the lessons that we are presenting through you."

Dad chimed in with this accolade: "Bravo on getting to work on the book at last. We are ready to help you with it as much as possible on this side, but always remember that you are the one doing it. It is your story, and must be told in the way that best suits you. We want to make sure that this book is entirely your own, told in your own way, but incorporating material which we here are all too eager to impart. Back to work now, ol' girl, and let 'er roll. Dad."

The guides returned to add: "That is right, Ruth. Return to the book, and make some real progress on it while the thought is fresh. *There is no Death.* Let this be the crux of the story. The world is ready for it now, as it struggles to cope with a universe gone mad with power and fear."

From time to time they gave me instructions to be passed along to readers of the book. One of these concerned the best method for establishing contact between our phase of existence and theirs. The Guides stressed that meditation should come first, and that after assuming a comfortable position we should concentrate for twenty or thirty minutes on "one soulful object, whether it be a truth, or a quality, or an image, or an object." They said a shorter time was not sufficient to still the runaway mind, which must be brought into focus while the body is relaxed.

"Next, people should take a pencil in their hand lightly, as you yourself have learned," they continued.

"While holding it on a piece of paper, they should try to empty their minds of all thoughts, while maintaining a spiritual attitude. Let them sit quietly as if in church: receptive, attentive, but unseeking. Let them not push too hard for the words to come; for when they have attained the proper repose of spirit, if their quest is sincere, the flow of words from this side will begin.

"Many here are eager to serve as Guides and help people with their problems, but people are not to begin by self-seeking, or asking questions about their worldy affairs. It is important to reiterate that the purpose of this direct communication with us is not to seek solutions for worldly problems, but to further the development of the soul. What a difference there is between those two strata of human endeavor! The first would perhaps ease the physical body, but the other would free the soul for the things of the spirit. What people think of as life is the mere habitations of a body for a limited period of time. The true life is the unseen one which continues through many phases, and on into eternity. The soul is the only segment of the human being that is salvageable, so why worry about the physical comforts of a body which is inhabited for such a brief period in eternity? The time spent in developing one's psychic qualities is a better investment than diamonds in a safe, for the psychic is the soul, and seeks that which is at the core of the universe—the seed of life itself."

The next day's session produced an impressive discourse on the power of love, which they said "rules the world." They suggested that to test that premise we should try loving someone whom we think that we despise. "This person will so mellow under the influence of your attentive kindnesses that the qualities you loathed will disappear," they declared. "That is what we mean by conquering another by love. To love someone who seems not to be lovable at all is difficult, but the warm glow that emanates from your determination to love him will alter his characteristics, until he becomes the sort of person who could command great admiration by all. The same is true with a wayward child. Pour out to him the love and affection of an unselfish person, and he will mellow before your eyes. This does not mean the consuming maternal love that sees no indignity, but the love of a person who is determined to rescue the little fellow from the clutches of evil.

"Take time to help wayward children. Take time also to love your enemies, or people who seem unworthy of your attention. This is the meaning of true love, not the chemical kind between man and woman, and not the parental love that protects and indulges. Love one another. That is the credo that can alter the world and lift its peoples to new heights. That is something in which everyone can join, for is there one so sheltered that he knows no person who has irritated or disgusted him? Take the test today. The first person about whom you are ready to speak an unkind word should be the subject. Try, instead, to say something loving and kind about him. Your own heart will expand with the unusual effort. The warm glow of it will inspire you to greater efforts. This is the message for today. Learn it well."

Intrigued, I decided to make the test. Carefully selecting the person in our circle of acquaintances whom I most disliked, I began praying for her and sending loving thoughts her way. The subject of my project had such an abrasive personality that, at least once at every party, a group of men and women would heatedly express distaste for her. Now I no longer joined in these discussions. Instead, I meditated on the thought that within her burned the same spark of God as in all of us. Arrogant and overbearing, the woman had seemed never to make an effort to be pleasant, unless the person she was talking to was powerful or wealthy; but the next time I glimpsed her at a large gathering she smiled, waved, and crossed the crowded room to talk to me. She had no way of knowing my changed attitude toward her, and I had told no one of my private project, but something had obviously reached across to her. As my prayers continued, I discovered that my dislike for her was turning to compassion and affection. We are now friends.

Only a handful of people in Washington knew of my growing interest in psychic phenomena. Those who did occasionally urged me to consult the Guides about their problems, but I was reluctant to do so, for two reasons: The Guides discouraged this practice; and I feared that the friends might act on the advice because it came from such a mysterious source and later regret it. I was loathe to assume such responsibility. But friends were sometimes on my mind as I seated myself at the typewriter for the morning session, and this may have influenced what came through. One day the writing began in typical fashion, stressing the need for service to others, and then declared: "The problems which beset earthly people are not ours to solve. We are not given powers to direct or solve specific problems. This would hamper the free choice given those of you at that phase of development. We are here to teach only basic truths, and to try to channel your thoughts into productive paths, so that you may make the most of your time spent there. Do not ask us to tell anyone what to do about earthly specifics. We are concerned with the soul. We can tell you only this: Put the hopes and aspirations of others above your own."

A friend whom I shall call Nan had been particularly in my thoughts, perhaps because she leaned on me so heavily and seemed to be making such a muddle of her life. She would plead for advice and then ignore it. She had a chronic habit of spending more than her income, and at this time was determined to find a house with a swimming pool, where she and the children could enjoy healthy exercise, even though she could not afford it. I did not consciously ask the Guides about Nan, but one day they interrupted the "lesson" to write:

"Now, as to the problems of Nan, she will have to work them out on her own. Let her learn for the first time to face reality. Will she use up all of her principal, and then be penniless, or will she find something that is more suitable to her station in life? Why is it necessary for her to have a pool if you and others are able to forego that luxury? She is an extremely spoiled person who needs to come to grips with reality. She cannot always run to others for the solution to her problems and her bills.

"She will find other houses of more modest stature,
143

where the children will find neighborhood playmates and have a healthy, happy summer. They do not need a swimming pool any more than other children require it. This is a part of Nan's unreality: that she is the only person who absolutely has to have these luxuries or she will die. This is nonsense. If she would do a little housework, she would get as much exercise from that as from swimming. She is too engrossed in herself to need sympathy." Although the crack about housework did not penetrate my conscious mind at the time, I could not resist a chuckle when I later read that part of the automatic writing. Nan always managed to keep servants, even when she was borrowing from friends to pay her living expenses. The Guides said they were "not amiss to giving guidance now and then, but only if it helps a person to understand what the purpose of life is."

"If he will live by the rules we have outlined to you here, this will solve a person's problems more quickly than taking up each of his problems and holding it to a mirror," they wrote. "The service that you perform for others is the candle in the darkness that pierces the gloom. The Higher Guides are awaiting those of you who progress to a stage where they will be able to reach you with their philosophy. Keep trying, and soon you will pass to a higher state in that phase. We are here as beginners in the scale, to tell you how you may advance, even as we hope to do. Remember the Golden Rule."

My father's birthday was July 2, and on that day the Guides announced that he wanted to extend greetings. "Hi, Ruth, this is Dad," the writing resumed. "Thanks for remembering my birthday with that nice prayer for me. On this side over here, we need prayers, just as much as you who are there, so don't forget me in your prayers, any of you. But the message I want to bring you is a little different from that."

He paused, as if wondering how best to express what he wanted to say, and then began: "Bertha [my mother] is wrong in thinking there is danger in trying to establish contact with us here. The only harm comes to fuddy-duddies who would go off the beam in some other way if they did not do so with this. The normal, sane people are not going to be blowing their tops over this, any more than over the headlines in the daily papers, so have no fear of causing harm to anyone by getting him interested in this. A mind so easily lost is already long gone."

Dad obviously had something else on his mind, because the keys played a sharp tap-tap-tap before he began a message for a close relative of ours who is very dear to us both. "He is drifting and worried," Dad wrote, "when all he needs is a little extra faith to shoot him over the top. This is as important as any message I have ever brought you. Tell him that it comes from one who now knows whereof he speaks, for I would have done far better there if I had prayed and had faith in the purpose for which I was born.

"Life is a testing ground for that which comes after death, as you call it there. Prayer is the bridge between, and also the avenue which opens up communication to those who stand ready on this side to contact you with loving care and guidance. It will be amazing what will happen to him and his business if he begins to pray unselfishly each day for guidance and wisdom. He will be surprised to discover that he is actually getting that wisdom and advice from out of the atmosphere, almost. This is what will open the doors for him—prayer. This advice may seem strange, coming from one like me who did not do it himself in that life, but thank goodness I am not quite as ignorant here as I was there.

"Let him open his heart and mind each morning or night at the same hour, preferably at the hour of rising. Tell him at the time of waking to pray deeply and steadily for five or ten minutes, until he feels strength flowing into him. This is the beginning of the wisdom and power that he will need to meet the decisions of the day, and to know what is best to do. Tell him not to take this advice lightly, just because it comes from me; because this old man is no longer a Dumb Dora, but a person who has begun to learn what it is all about. Ruth, I'm counting on you to get this message across to him in such a way that he will take my advice for once in his life. I want that boy to succeed, and he has every talent and opportunity to do so. The only thing which holds him back is that cocky feeling that he knows it all, when the only One who really knows it all is our Creator.

"Those who stand ready on this side to assist him, if he will open up and pray, are legion. Some are darned good businessmen, too, so let him open his heart and mind; and let those ideas pour through him, as they will begin to do if he will but harken to the inner voice that speaks softly, but is always to be heard by those who pause long enough to give it ear. Let him heed the words of a man who loves him deeply, and at least give it a fair shake. Trial will prove the test of the pudding. Now run along, Sis, and have a good day. So long." The breezy yet chiding manner of expression was so exactly like the Dad I remembered that I felt as if I had just had a long telephone conversation with him.

The unhappy subjects of murder and suicide occupied the Guides on one occasion. As these subjects had not previously been mentioned, perhaps the discussion was prompted by a sudden wave of commercial-plane destructions in midair, where heavy insurance policies held by one of the passengers indicated suicide. Now they wrote: "If a soul struggling for release from earthly problems seeks to take the lives of others for that release, he will for the remainder of eternity be blasphemed. The person who kills others in order to take his own life has no hope of salvation. That person, having proved himself totally unfit for life itself, has no place in the scheme of eternal life.

"Now, as to those who take their own lives without destroying others; through God's infinite sympathy they may sometime purge their souls of this horrible blasphemy against God, but the way is dark and long. Having been entrusted with a precious opportunity— the earth-life for testing their mettle—and having been given the priceless opportunity to help others, those persons who would violently lop off that span before God has decreed that they have had their full chance, suffer inexorably for the destruction of that which God has created. Let no man be so dispirited that he thinks his lot will improve by ending the life

146

that God has created. The resultant pangs are so excruciating on this side that the earth-life seems like a blessing by comparison."

One morning the Guides took up the question of how we would recognize former acquaintances when we became a part of the so-called hereafter. "The soul here is so similar to that in your stage," they wrote, "that without the body it is still readily identifiable by those who knew one another there. This is because the same characteristics which make you known to your loved ones there are still wrapped within the soul here. The ways by which we know ourselves and others are too technical to try to explain, because you do not have words for the qualities that are the real substance of the soul. Suffice it to say that the body itself is the least necessary of the factors recognizable between the souls of two people. In the earth phase you are conscious of five senses, but here the senses are so much more acute that those five which you think cover everything are the minutest part of the whole.

"There is no such thing as 'feeling,' for instance, with the soul. That is a purely bodily sense that has no permanence or significance, except as a protection from bodily harm. Like burning or freezing. The important senses are those which encase the soul, warning it of pitfalls which might cause retrogression from the goal of eventual harmony with the whole. The conscience, or voice within, which is the spokesman for the soul, reminds when you are erring, but often is quelled by the louder voices of the senses which protect the physical man. This is only a beginner's lesson on this point."

The question of foreign aid interested the Guides another morning. Emphasizing that the most important rule for society is helpfulness, they declared: "The foreign policy that is directly attuned to helping less fortunate neighbors is an exercise on a broad scale of what each human should be doing in his individual life. The aid money spent to create an atmosphere for advancing the soul of man is good; but when it is used only to clothe the body of the animal man, it is useless. To give man learning, wisdom, spiritual opportunities, is sublime. To give him the mere fruits of another's labor in order to make the physical man more comfortable will breed nothing but discontent, and is of little moment in the long pull toward progression of mankind. The greatest gifts within the power of your nation, or any nation, are lessons in self-help."

A few days later the Guides volunteered to lift the curtain a trifle higher on the mystery that we call death. "When the time comes for a man to cross from that phase of life to this," they wrote, "he will feel no loss of body, but will be at once more free. The problems which beset him there will have vanished with the cast-off shell of body, but the thinking part of him which forms a part of the soul lives on. This thought-producing power is inherent in the particle of man which originally burst forth from the brilliance of the Creator. There is no end to this power, except as certain men so beastfully pervert this magical gift that it must be extinguished for the good of all mankind. These are the brutal killers, the beastlike ghouls who, through their own misuse of power, are rendered so unfit for redemption that the spark is permitted to go out. This extinction is a means of protection for the whole evolution of the soul to its ultimate reunion with the Creator beyond the Golden Door. There is no destruction of any good that these wretched souls may have performed at some time for others, inasmuch as it continues to live with that person who was benefited; but to protect the purity of the eternal reaching for perfection, the rest of that person is extinguished."

Abandoning that unhappy subject, the Guides spoke again of the importance of spending a brief period each day, at the same hour, in meditation and soul-searching. They included an important new tip for establishing direct communication, writing: "Strain always to project the mind to a higher reach. This helps to lift your own dynamic powers to meet the charge which we can send toward you. To receive a television broadcast, you must first connect the electricity and turn on the switch. That is what we ask you to do, in a spiritual way, with us. Turn on the switch by fixing your mind on one channel, while simultaneously raising your electric charge (your reaching power) to the treetops above."

CHAPTER 13

Walk with God

Douglas L. Hatch, a prominent Washington attorney, died unexpectedly of a heart attack in 1962; and when we called at his home before the funeral, his widow expressed the hope that I would be able to bring her messages from him. As one of our early co-experimenters with the ouija board and table-tapping, Ruth Hatch also knew of the automatic writing. Several times subsequently she inquired whether I had received a message for her, and when a negative reply failed to satisfy her, I finally confessed that under the prodding of my family I had discontinued the automatic writing. Bitterly disappointed, she said accusingly: "I feel strongly that he is trying to communicate with me through you. Can't you do that much for me?"

What could I say? I knew how keenly Ruth missed Doug, but I felt strangely reluctant to resume the demanding morning sessions. To complicate my situation, we were packing for a vacation, and I had several newspaper columns to prepare in advance. Touched by her pleas, I finally agreed to try, and the next morning seated myself at the typewriter at nine o'clock. Probably nothing would happen after such a lengthy interval, I thought; but I closed my eyes and tried to lift my mind to a higher plane. Immediately the Guides took over, and without their customary chastisement for my neglect, began:

"This is good, to be back at work together. So much needs to be done, and time is fleeting! We are anxious that you not waste your remaining time there. You have much to give to the world, if you would only utilize your time. Many are clamoring for help, and need you. Why are you turning away? We who are already here wish that you would give us an opportunity to reach those who require help and inspiration. We are intent that you shall utilize your talent for conveying the written word in such manner that all can comprehend. This rare gift was not given to be wasted on empty slogans and tidbits. It is required for nobler purposes, and will die if not used to the limit of your capability. There are those who weep for the ministration and hope that you are capable of giving."

That made me feel rather small. Mustering courage, I asked whether there was a message for Ruth Hatch from Doug. The Guides immediately wrote: "He rests, but, just a moment; he is here now and wants to tell Ruth that he is with her. She is not alone, but sheltered by his loving arms." The message then became so personal in tone that I began to feel like an intruder. Through the Guides, Doug spoke about deals on which he had been working, sounded a warning about a new escort of his youngest daughter's, supplied advice for his son on his career, and added further communications for his wife.

Little of it made sense to me, since I was not close enough to them to know about their family problems and business enterprises; and I was in a quandry. I had promised Ruth that if any communication from Doug came through, I would convey it; yet this message sounded as nosy as the proverbial woman next door. Because we were leaving town in two days, I reluctantly decided to call her, and she breathlessly asked if I had "something from Doug."

I replied that I preferred not to read her the message, but she was so insistent that, with decided misgivings, I reported the long communication word for word. She occasionally uttered exclamations, but made no comment until I had finished. Then came a torrent of words. She said her daughter did have a new escort, ten years older than she was, who had been telephoning and dropping by every day since meeting her at a party two weeks before.

"As a matter of fact, I've been a little worried," she confessed, "because we know absolutely nothing about him except that he recently came here from the West Coast. If Doug were here, I'm sure he would want to know more about him before letting his youngest child get emotionally involved." (The daughter is since happily married to a different man.)

Ruth added that many of the other points raised in the message were subjects about which she had been anxious. I cautioned her, as I had previously, to put no stock in such mysterious advice unless she personally checked it out. She promised, but urged me to consult Doug about some definite problems now facing her, and I finally agreed to do so, provided that she phrased her questions in such a way that I could not know what they were about. I wanted to be sure that my own subconscious played no part in the responses.

She dictated six blind queries, which I put to the Guides the following morning, and then I read their responses to Ruth. She was obviously pleased with the answers. One of the questions, which I had assumed referred to a man, actually concerned land, she said later; and the Guides answered it in the proper context. Another reply warned her not to dispose of the mineral rights to a piece of property, the contract for which she would find if she "pulled the Brazil folder" out of Doug's office files. She did not understand this, but later telephoned me that after finding nothing of interest in a folder marked "Brazil," she was returning it to the file when she found a paper accidentally stuck to the back of it. This was a contract for mineral rights to some property in Latin America. She could not know it then, but six months later, when the J. Paul Getty interests began acquiring all the surrounding area, the value of the Hatch property was greatly enhanced. Ruth says that if the message had not alerted her to the mineral rights, she would have lost them; because in order to validate them she needed the signature of an associate of Doug's, and the man died shortly after signing the paper for her.

Before leaving for vacation, I lent Ruth some books on psychic phenomena; and after our return, she called to ask if I could bring her further messages from Douglas. By then I had decided to resume the regular morning sittings, but I told her that I felt she should solve her own problems, because that is the way the Guides said we humans developed our own potential. Ruth is a capable, intelligent, well-educated woman, and I was sure that as soon as she trusted her own self-reliance, she would make an excellent adjustment to her bereavement.

Ruth is an extremely persuasive person, however, and I finally asked the Guides if they had further communications for her. They replied: "The thing to do about Ruth is to stand ready when she needs a helping hand. But she must not rely on help from this plane until she has learned to stand on her own two feet in that one. To give her too many directions from here would be to weaken her own chance to prove her strength and ability to live her own life. She need have no worries on that score, for she is well advanced in the quality of survival. She needs to study and learn and orient herself to this work if she wishes to profit by it. She must use her own native skills and abilities to solve her problems there. That is the privilege of earth-living, and it is not to be usurped by those who have progressed to the next step. All earth-people must jealously guard their own right to function as free agents in that life. The decisions are theirs to make, but how wisely they make them is the supreme test of their soul's advancement."

I relayed this message to Ruth, but she was so anxious to consult Doug about some loose ends in his business affairs that she came over, and while seated beside my desk dictated some more blind questions. As I typed each one, answers came; but at last the Guides announced that this was all they would acknowledge.

Ruth Hatch was crestfallen. Lamenting that there were other important matters requiring Doug's attention, she phrased another question, but when I dutifully typed it, the Guides wrote: "We said this is all!" The typewriter stopped cold, and nothing more would come from it that day. Thereafter, I declined to consult them about such problems, no matter how vigorous the prodding. Ruth had been seeking guidance on which stocks to buy and sell, and how much to charge clients in settling Doug's accounts. The Guides were willing to help with spiritual, but not financial, advancement. Several years later, happening to think of the Hatches as I was preparing to begin the morning session, I asked the Guides whether there was any news of Doug. Without a moment's hesitation, they typed: "He will not want to tell you anything just now, for Ruth is doing well and should not be disturbed. He is proud of her adjustment."

Back in the summer of 1962, the Guides, having closed the door to further discussion of Ruth's problems, imperturbably resumed the daily lessons. As coolly as if they were conducting a college seminar in philosophy, they wrote: "We want to tell you a little more about the next phase, where we are now. This phase is not unlike that which you already know, but with salient differences. We know when we are wrong. We try immediately to correct any errors, knowing as we do that they will hold us back from the progression that we seek. Here we have more acute awareness of the purpose of life itself. The flowers that provide riotous color in the summer do not drop dead with the frost, but progress to their next phase. This, for them, is a dormant period until the seeds or bulbs burst into new life in the spring. For us there is no dormant period, although some who have met death suddenly, without preparation, will take longer than others to adjust to the change-over. This is why preparation there is important.

"The opportunities there are almost limitless for improvement of the soul. What a marvelous chance to move rapidly ahead! That is why you were born to that phase, to hasten this advancement. It is too bad that consciousness of previous awareness is missing there, for if that faculty were with you, all would strive endlessly for perfection of soul, which would come by a remarkable outpouring of love for one another. No wars would then exist, no fights be fought, no battles waged

The period there would be spent in glorious reaching for opportunities to aid those less fortunate, and the less fortunate would not consider themselves so; for they, like all others, would have the same marvelous opportunity to serve.

"The degrees of bodily comfort would be as nothing, since all would realize that their bodies were but a casting to be discarded when the life span of that phase was done. Who then would care whether he had a fur coat, or merely a cloth to gird himself with, so long as life was sustainable through the bare minimum of food and raiment? This would be all that any could ask. The passions of mankind would be nonexistent, for how silly it would seem to appease the body when the everlasting soul was the organ to be nurtured and preserved."

At the conclusion of that lesson, I dared to mention a subject that had been troubling me for many months. Some people, I knew, believed that automatic writing stemmed merely from one's own subconscious. How, I asked the Guides, could I be sure that the lessons they seemed to dictate were not actually an intrusion of my own thoughts?

"That will be for you to decide," they answered reasonably. Then they added four words that had a rather chilling effect on my ego.

"Were they your ideas?" they asked bluntly, in capitalized type. I had to concede that I could claim no credit for them. I had never thought of them before.

From time to time the Guides stressed that each of us was born for a purpose. "That is why the talents are so varied," they wrote. "God gives to one man understanding, to another knowledge of mathematics or astronomy, to another the saving grace of laughter, to yet another the power to fathom beyond earth's laws and dip into space, or immortality. Each is given this power to use or develop as he sees fit. Those who develop their talents to the utmost, for the benefit of others who will come after them, rise rapidly through the next phases. Those who bury their talents, and fail to utilize this God-given wisdom and power, delay by an appall-

156

ing degree the mission which could carry them more rapidly onward in search of ultimate reunion with God.

"Would that you earth-people had the wisdom and sight of the next step, to guide you there! How rapidly then would war disappear and goodness prevail. This is what the Good Book means about the millennium, when at last the eyes of all are opened to that which we are trying to instill in you; and when evil has no further chance, because all, seeing with fresh eyes the waste and futility of indulging the physical desires, think only of the composite good of mankind.

"When the earth-person learns to put community good above his own, and the happiness of another man before that of himself or his immediate family, then he has stepped across the threshold of spiritual knowledge. The mother who would instill this truth into the minds of her little children blesses them with far more than earthly goods and comforts. The father who would teach his son that what matters in life is helping others, bestows on him a far superior heritage than wealth, or a financial interest in the family business. Learn to love others, particularly those whose avaricious ways repel you. Where is the challenge in loving a saint? There is none. But the one who has goaded you to the point of hysterics, and thwarted every good intention, is the one who must be aided and loved in order for you to reach a higher pinnacle."

The Guides frequently urged that we take time, in our busy lives, to "hear the still, small voice that guides your inner selves." They reiterated that this is best accomplished in a quiet, darkened room at a regular hour each day, but that it can also be experienced on a busy street or in a subway rush, "so long as a person quiets his own tumultuous thoughts and strives to hear the unspoken voice within."

"This built-in prompter has been called many things: the voice of God, the voice of conscience, or the spark of inner man," they continued. "Words are not necessary, for the meaning is clear if you will but listen. Make room for it in your busy lives, for it is the nearest to sublime thought that can be experienced while you are still of the flesh."

The next day they expanded on this lesson, writing: "Before rising, lie quietly for a few minutes to review the errors of the previous day, and resolve to let nothing mar the purity of the as-yet-unsullied day ahead. Resolve to hurt no other person. Walk more closely with God, feeling His presence in the quiet moments before and after conferences, in the smile of a stranger on the street, and in the eyes of a tramp who needs help.

"Walk with God, and you can make no errors of judgment, and commit no sins, for the Presence of God within your daily life insulates you against temptations and deters you from speaking sharply or dishonestly. Walk with God! Feel Him beside you on the busy streets. Touch His hand as you reach into your pocket to give to others. God is there, so why ignore Him? He is more real than your own husband or brother. You are more nearly a part of Him than of your own mother, who nourished and gave birth to you. God is always a part of you, and you of Him, but the complete reunion comes only at the end of the long trail, when you have so atoned for your previous errors that Oneness becomes a reality in truth."

CHAPTER 14

Mystery Stories of the Night

Dreams are the language of the unconscious, and because all of us dream every night, it is important that we learn this language in order to understand ourselves. Psychologists agree that everyone dreams several times during a normal eight-hour sleep, and that we dream in symbols. In Biblical times, an Egyptian pharaoh elevated Joseph to a position of vast power, because the Jewish slave was able to interpret these symbols. Another Joseph was told in his sleep that Mary had conceived by the Holy Spirit, and a later dream advised him to flee with Mary and Jesus to safety in Egypt.

The late Edgar Cayce analyzed many hundreds of dreams during a trance state in which he seemed to tap the cosmic consciousness. In one of those readings, he reported: "Sleep is that period of time when the soul takes stock of what it has acted upon from one rest period to another."

The Cayce interpretations describe four types of dreams: suggestions for improving the physical body, hints for understanding oneself, psychic dreams containing precognitive warnings and clairvoyance, and those containing spiritual guidance and ideas for creativity. Shane Miller, a leader in the Association for Research and Enlightenment, teaches that "when an individual begins his search to know his relationship to the universe and its Creator, he can expect help from the 'other side' in dreams." He says that when this contact is established and recognized by the waking individual, true self-control can begin.

Those who fail to remember their dreams are, at least, missing a more exciting scenario than the "Late Shows" on television. The dreams of a single night are frequently as interrelated as the episodes in a cliff-hanging serialization, and the plot ordinarily thickens around three o'clock in the morning. These dramas can be as engrossing as a James Bond mystery, or as seemingly innocuous as Peter Pan, but they carry a message as fraught with meaning as an Easter Sunday sermon.

In dreams, your subconscious is speaking directly to you. If you dream of a business deal which upset you during the day, or of an argument with your mother-in-law, you are apt to shrug off the nightmare as a mere carry-over of waking tensions. But is it? Many psychologists believe that the friends, relatives, or enemies we dream about are actually symbols for facets of our own personality which need self-examination.

If you dream that you are fishing with a small boy in clear, sparkling waters, but the trout elude your lure, is this simply a suggestion that you need a vacation? Or does it mean that the youngster you used to be is still searching for spiritual enlightenment (the water), and that you subconsciously yearn to recapture the simple Christian faith (the fish) of your childhood?

Dreams are the mystery stories of the night. To solve the whodunit it is necessary to remember and record the dream, and then to understand the symbols by which your subconscious tries to communicate with the waking you. The first phase is easier than the second. To accomplish the first, you need merely say aloud several times before falling asleep, "I will remember my dreams." Call it self-hypnosis if you will, but within a few days you will discover that the undisciplined giant within you, the subconscious, will rouse the slumbering ego whenever the show is over and will supply a vivid recollection of details.

Perhaps you dreamed that you were prancing around in a loincloth while strange dogs yapped at your heels; or that the bleachers collapsed when your father (long since deceased) took you to a ball game. What do you make of it? If you really want to know, keep a pad and pencil on your bedside table and jot down every detail that you can recapture the moment that you awaken. Do not bother at that time to discover some hidden meaning. Roll over and go back to sleep, because if you have only been asleep a couple of hours, you have four more dreams to enjoy before breakfast. The next day you should write out the notes in detail, study the symbols for possible significance, and save them for comparison with other dreams as the weeks pass.

Understanding the meaning of dreams is much more difficult than the simple trick of learning to remember them. To acquire more knowledge in this field, I attended a week's Dream Seminar at the headquarters of the Association for Research and Enlightenment. One of the prominent lecturers who helped to establish the testing laboratory was Dr. Herbert B. Puryear, a psychology professor at Trinity University in San Antonio, Texas, who did the work for his Ph.D. degree in the sleep laboratory at the University of North Carolina. Dr. Puryear has also worked with the sleep patterns and dreams of air force pilots, and has reported on the dreams of our astronauts.

Among the other experts at the seminar were Dr. W. Lindsay Jacob, a staff member of St. Margaret's Hospital, Homestead, Passavant, and Presbyterian Hospital in Pittsburgh, a consulting psychiatrist, and regular lecturer at the University of Pittsburgh; Fred Lathers, who has a science degree from North Carolina State College; and J. Everett Irion, A.R.E.'s resident dream expert. My classmates were business and professional men, housewives, educators, and college students. All were there for one purpose: to discover more about the third of our lives that we spend in sleep.

The director of the unique seminar was Hugh Lynn Cayce, who was eager to test the trance pronouncements of his psychic father that certain colored lights, electrical appliances, diets, breathing exercises, and gems affect one's dreams and psychic process. For the experiment, the enrollees were divided into six groups. Some slept under a harmless violet light to test whether their dream patterns differed from those previously experienced. Some valiantly endured a week of dieting, eating only the food recommended for psychic development by the late Edgar Cayce; this consisted of fresh fruit and "mummy food," a concoction made of equal portions of black figs and Assyrian dates, ground together and cooked with a handful of cornmeal or crushed wheat. One group drank a daily glass of water into which a tiny portion of a drug called Atomidine had been added. Others attached a mechanical device to their opposite ankles and wrists, to set up a positive and negative current within the circulatory system. A fifth group participated in yoga breathing exercises for an hour each day, and the last group wore a blue-green lapis stone taped across the endocrine gland in the lower center of the forehead. The purpose of these experiments was to determine which of the stimuli, if any, most affected the content of dreams.

The next step was to insure that we not only remembered, but recorded, our dreams for further study. Scientists have determined that dreams grow progressively longer and more complicated as the night advances, and that the less frequently remembered dreams occur shortly after 3 A.M. To tap these deep, elusive mysteries, members of the seminar alternated each night as dreamer or moderator. We either permitted ourselves to be roused from sleep, or we sat staring at the eyelids of a slumbering classmate until the active motion of his eyeballs ceased. This was the signal that a dream cycle had ended, and after rousing him we silently handed him a pad and a pencil to which a tiny flashlight had been attached. The producer of the dream then jotted down his scenario, and went back to sleep. In class the next morning we publicly recounted our dreams. Some could recall only one; others, four or five. Sometimes the dreams were brief and to the point, carrying a seemingly obvious impact. Others were complicated in plot and the meaning of certain symbols seemed as cleverly shrouded as the parables with which Jesus of Nazareth often baffled his disciples.

The written word began with picture symbols, as we know through the study of hieroglyphics and Chinese.

It is perhaps not surprising, then, that our subconscious continues to communicate with us through basic forms which may have been as recognizable to primitive man as they are to today's scholar. It is also possible that we dream in symbols so that our subconscious can slip the message past our conscious self, the monitor, who might otherwise censor unflattering thoughts about ourselves.

Under the skilled tutelage of our instructors we gradually began to find our way through the maze; and although we began as strangers to each other, within a few days our dreams were falling into such neat patterns that we began to know the "inner self" of our classmates better than our own families. An older woman from the rural Midwest related unusually long, detailed dreams each morning. Through classroom discussion we decided that her subconscious was warning against her penchant for assuming responsibility for everyone from her college-age sons to her farm hands and fellow church workers. She fought us every inch of the way, protesting that since she thoroughly enjoyed the responsibility, she could not be overdoing it. On the fifth morning her dream symbols were so starkly clear that, after having them pointed out to her once more, she finally had to laugh at herself.

I felt that this heralded a breakthrough in her tussle with herself, and eagerly awaited the next morning's dream report. Sure enough, that night she was no longer scurrying from one project to another in her dreamworld. Instead, she made only a halfhearted search for her lost car, then suddenly was transported to a high mountain, where a monk lived alone. His clothing, household furnishings, and an elaborate silver service had all been provided by others. Feeling no responsibility, she therefore looked around in pure enjoyment, and then entered an adjoining chapel to meditate. Oddly, she did not recognize the import of the dream until we pointed out that she had at last reconciled herself to the fact that she was not indispensable. Freeing herself of the lifelong habit of trying to assume other's burdens and responsibilities, she took time in her dream to meditate and advance her spiritual development. The woman must have accepted the class analysis, because she decided to spend two weeks in Florida before returning to her farm.

Another member of the class reported that for several years she had been dreaming recurrently of a food freezer. She experienced an equally dramatic breakthrough when, during classroom discussion, she realized that she had been subconsciously trying to put a difficult problem "on ice," instead of meeting it head-on to solve it. The freezer has since disappeared from her dreams.

If human beings dreamed only once a decade, imagine the excitement as relatives and friends gathered around to hear every detail and ponder the significance. Because we produce several dreams a night we take them for granted, seldom bothering to recall them; yet it is strange that we are so vitally concerned with what happens in our sixteen waking hours and so indifferent to the other third of our lives. Dreams are elusive, and must be recaptured quickly. If you have trouble remembering them, reach for the pad and pencil; then resume the position in which you awakened. Jot down fragments of the dream as they return, without switching on the light. Note also your mood in the dream. Were you exhilarated or depressed by the action? This is often a helpful key to proper interpretation. The next day, go over your notes and fill in details. Leave a space opposite each person whom you glimpsed in dreamland, and try to analyze your feelings toward him. Which of his characteristics attract, and which offend you? This is important, since many psychiatrists claim that the people we dream about are usually aspects of our own character.

Some symbols have a universal meaning for members of the human race. Clear, sparkling water represents spirituality, and muddy water, intrigue; a bull, stubbornness; flying feathers, commotion or confusion in your daily life; a peacock, self-gratification; a wall, obstacles to the acceptance of a new idea or ideal; a sinking floor, a poor foundation for principles; a snake, either wisdom or temptation, depending on dream context; fish, spiritual food or Christianity; rabbits, sex;

fixing over an old house, changing attitudes and thoughts; crossing a river, an important decision or the start of a new venture.

A burning house suggests that you are angry about something; missing a train means that you should hurry to straighten out your life; a bumpy, rough road means difficult going ahead; shoes, understanding; turning right, doing the correct thing; turning left; making the wrong decision; a beaver, hard worker; baby, new start in life; barbed wire, difficulty.

Dreaming in color suggests emotional intensity, or a higher degree of development. Red usually denotes anger or temper; pink, an infantile attitude toward some problem; yellow, something to be faced at the mental rather than emotional level; blue, a higher plane; gold and white, spiritual development.

A truck or automobile is said to represent the body of the dreamer. A successful merchant who attended the seminar dreamed that he was laying a new tile floor in the garage, because the old one was chipping away and nuts and bolts were pressing upward through the flooring. The tile was deep red in color, flecked with black. A truck entered the garage and passed above the dreamer's body. Then a man offered him a set of new tires exactly like his old ones, "because the old ones had worn so well and were still in good condition."

Irion and Dr. Jacob suggested that he had dreamed at two levels. The physical phase denoted that he should have a medical checkup, since the "tire" could mean "tired"; the truck, his body; and the black-specked red flooring the need for a blood test. In his workaday life the merchandiser had recently been hired away by a rival firm to do the same work as before. Thus, the new-tires-for-old may have represented his material reward for having done a good job in his former work; and the nuts and bolts, unfinished pieces of work that he should complete (put together) before proceeding, as well as a possible lack of iron in his blood.

A woman who dreamed of a hurricane, and then of a little bird lying helpless on the ground, seemed to be undergoing emotional turmoil (the storm) and needed to rid herself of some entanglement so that her spirit (the bird) could soar free. Hugh Lynn Cayce believes that our subconscious sometimes masks us in the role of animals or birds, to symbolize aspects of ourselves. Thus, if we dream of a wolf, a gorilla, an elephant, a bear, a dog, or cat, we should analyze what that animal means to us. To a dog lover, a canine may represent the needed quality of fidelity; to a dog hater, who has been bitten by one, treachery or fear.

The night before leaving for the seminar, I dreamed of engaging in a long philosophical discussion with an Oriental, while eating at a bright yellow counter in his kitchen. Before sitting down to dine I had cut a hole in the screen of his porch so that my little poodle could go in and out without interrupting our conversation. Just as we finished our dreamland dinner, I saw my poodle leave through the opening and begin to walk on top of a huge white dog that continued to sleep quietly on its side. On awakening, I discovered that my poodle was actually walking across my body on the bed, and, since the previous day I had cut a piece of aluminum screening to fit around a pipe, I assumed that the dream was simply a distorted carry-over of waking thoughts.

Dr. Jacob and Everett Irion decided differently. In their interpretation, the big white dog was my slumbering self, which should be concerning itself with philosophical subjects foreign (the Oriental symbol) to my usual workaday world. I was eating (food for thought) at a yellow (this denotes mental activity) counter. My subconscious had used the screen that I cut the day before as a symbol to show that I was letting mundane responsibilities (like the care of my little poodle) occupy too much of my time. In my dream, by cutting a hole in the screen to let the dog look after himself, I was seeking to free myself from trivial demands on my time.

A classmate who dreamed of inspecting a mock-orange bush had similarly paid no attention to it, because the day before she had actually noticed such a bush, loaded with fruit, in her neighbor's yard. Irion said that her subconscious had deliberately used that symbol to tell her that she was "working with false fruit," (mock-orange) and should make a fresh assessment of her goals.

Our instructors emphasized that events of the past twenty-four or thirty-six hours are frequently used as symbols by the subconscious. Consequently, until we learn to analyze the true meaning of the symbolism, we mistakenly assume that a dream has no significance. Irion insists that the subconscious records every minute of our lives, and that if we dream of dirty clothes, for instance, we are being shown that a messy problem in our personal life requires urgent solution. Until we act upon suggestions given to us in dreamland, he says, the subconscious will often deliberately block further dream memories.

We saw a dramatic illustration of this at the seminar. A stunning-looking older classmate met with daily frustration as she vainly sought to recapture her dreams. She could not understand the lapse, because her purpose in attending the seminar was to seek meaning for her exceedingly vivid dreams. Toward the end of the week, she admitted that the first night she had experienced a fleeting fragment of a dream, but had considered it too unimportant to relate because of its brevity. When she told us about it, we analyzed it as an attempt to warn her of the necessity for relaxing her emotional grip on her only grandchild.

Breaking into sobs, she confessed that she was devastated because her frivolous-minded daughter had recently taken back the little girl, who had made her home for several years with the grandmother. She had been yearning to recover guardianship of the child, but after hearing the class evaluation she dried her tears, accepted the verdict of her own subconscious, or higher self, and began dreaming on a more spiritual level.

My own dreams are ordinarily colorful, interesting, and fairly bustling with activity. I live in an exciting dreamland of travel, breaking news developments, and deadlines. I was consequently surprised that during my first night at the seminar, the only dream I could recall was a mere fragment that seemed too drab and unimportant to repeat in class. Urged to tell it anyway, I explained that the announced plan to have a monitor awaken us to record our dreams around three o'clock in the morning was obviously preying on my mind. Therefore, I dreamed that the pretty receptionist at A.R.E. headquarters (who was not to be one of the monitors) kept trying to awaken me to record a dream, but each time that she called me I groggily went back to sleep.

"But Ruth, don't you see the significance of that!" Everett Irion exclaimed in astonishment. "Don't you remember what you said to me yesterday, when you checked in here?"

With some embarrassment I told the class that I had asked not to be awakened, because I needed sleep, and I would probably participate in the nocturnal monitoring no more than once during the week, simply to see what it was like.

"The receptionist was *you,* in your dreams," Irion persisted. "That was your own subconscious telling you to wake up and get-with-it, to participate and be receptive, because you need to learn how to interpret your own dreams." Thus convinced, I promised to enter wholeheartedly into the experiments and to join the yoga breathing classes.

The following night I recalled this dream: I was at a place similar to A.R.E. headquarters, watching some men pull rotted shingles off a high peaked roof, preparatory to replacing them with new ones. As they did so, they kept reaching into the exposed rafters and throwing out dozens of coat hangers, which were covered with thick rust. In my dream I remarked: "I should think the owners would have thrown out those rusty coat hangers when they made similar repairs a year or two ago," and my companion responded, "That would have been too much to expect."

Again Dr. Jacob and Irion apparently solved the mystery of my dream. Coat hangers are used for storing garments when not in use. I had attended the seminar on meditation and dreams two years before at A.R.E. headquarters. Thus, my subconscious seemed to be chiding: "Why didn't you put the challenging ideas that you received here two years ago to better use, instead of placing them in storage and letting them rust? Now you have another chance to replace the rotted shingles (the roof was a symbol for my head or mind) with good shingles; to substitute spiritual goals for material ones. Make the most of the opportunity now."

Who is the older man or woman who sometimes speaks with such authority in our dreams? Experts say that this is our own "higher self," a sort of elder brother or sister who seeks to bring out the best in us. A similar symbol of the "Ancient of Days" is found in the New Testament Book of Revelation. Edgar Cayce taught that the activities of our daily lives are laid before the soul for examination while we sleep, and judgment is passed. This soul, or higher self, is thus both judge and jury; the subconscious is the mind of the soul.

Some classmates at the seminar dreamed of dreams-within-a-dream, or of watching a stage play in progress. Dr. Jacob said that such devices are used by the subconscious to focus particular attention on a message that it wants to get across to the conscious self. He said that emotionally disturbed persons frequently dream of trying to fight their way back along a breakwater from an ocean which threatens to engulf them. "They are afraid," he explained, "of being overwhelmed by their own emotions, and want to get back to firmer ground." He added that dreams of a violent accident or atomic attack are sometimes characteristic of those who are about to suffer a recurrence of severe mental depression, which could lead to suicide.

Several college boys who had driven cross-country to attend the seminar dreamed almost nightly of heavy diesel trucks, road barriers, and construction sites. The dream experts said this related to their inner struggle to overcome "barriers" which were interfering with their "constructive" efforts to understand themselves. To dream of spraying something from a pressurized can, they said, suggests that we are seeking to camouflage ourselves or our intentions. Grains of corn suggest kernels of truth that we are seeking. Fire can represent suppressed anger or a cleansing process of the mind, depending on the emotion felt in the dream.

"Our senses operate at three levels: the physical the psychical, and the spiritual," Dr. Jacob explained, "and all are reflected in various types of dreams. We dream in symbols which have a universal language, because there is a big difference between what we believe and what we know. We know what salt tastes like, but we cannot describe the taste to another. The information in dreams is what we know, although it doesn't always agree with what we believe about ourselves. Thus, the subconscious sends us symbols to get the message through the censor, which is our conscious ego."

Prayer, meditation, and dreams are closely related. As we seek to understand the last by keeping a dream journal, we should pray for guidance and meditate on the meaning of the symbols. Our subconscious is apparently yearning to help us with guidance, prophecies, and subtle warnings. Are we listening?

CHAPTER 15

The Meaning of Christmas

Christmas was approaching, and ten days beforehand Lily let it be known that too many earth-people were confused about its real significance. In the first of several dissertations on the subject, he wrote: "The fact that a tiny Baby was born in a stable in Bethlehem is not the meaning of Christmas. The significant story is that a Man walked among men, teaching them that love is the way to win a seat beside His Father in Paradise. Love is the message of Christ—not the star, or the wise men, or the shepherds. That is sweet and colorful and appealing to children, but the true meaning of Christmas lies in the hearts of men, for without love the Babe was born in vain.

"The purpose of Christ's life was to embed this message in all who would listen: that the ultimate road to salvation is to love one another even as one loves God. Christ died for our sins, yes; and He arose from the dead to teach us of eternal life, but without the message of love that would have been without purpose, for to love is to live forever."

A few days later Lily returned to this theme, writing: "The Christmas season is the most splendid time of the year, not only because it reminds us of the saintly Man in Bethlehem, but also because men's hearts are opened to others. It is the spirit of Christmas to put others' needs above one's own. That is why the spirit of giving must never be removed from the image of Christmas. Mold your thoughts to the true meaning of this holiday season—the blessedness of giving rather than receiving."

The Guides usually declined to answer when I asked specific questions about the plane in which they claimed to be living, or about other mysteries of the universe. They would reply that they preferred to impart the lessons in their own order, waiting until I was ready for the next step. Consequently I was fascinated when, shortly before Christmas, they volunteered the following information: "The souls of those who mingle here and in the stages ahead of our own are not all of the earthly realm. Many are here who have not known life as you know it there. Some are not yet born into the world, and may not need to be, because their remarkable spiritual qualities are so advanced beyond our own, through their dedication to finding reunion with God, that they need not undergo that harassing experience of temptation in the flesh."

At this point, for the first time in their writings, the Guides initiated the subject of possible life on other planets: "Others, who have known life on other planets, are more advanced; but these are unknown to us, because their souls are unrecognizable to us in this lowly stage that we are now in. No doubt the time will come, in more advanced phases, when we will mingle with them and feel a likeness or kinship, but that time is not now. We, here, are still too earth-bound. Perhaps as those in the earth phase progress in intellectual advancement, they will find it possible to communicate with powers higher than ours, and these will perhaps be able to tell them of other life forms which they have encountered from different planets and orbits; but this is beyond our own ken at this stage. We know only those who are here like ourselves, or the ones who have not yet been born on earth, and may not need to be."

I asked whether there is such a thing as reincarnation, and they responded: "We are not trying to withhold information, but we are still seekers ourselves, and wish to tell you only that of which we are positive. This much we can say: Those who feel that they have lived before are not too far off-base. The thing they misunderstand is that no personality is completely reborn. As the soul advances the baser parts are sluffed off as a shell, and the shining parts blossom into new heights. As a consequence, no one is the same person he would have been in an earlier existence, for the baser parts of the personality are discarded, while the higher parts develop. No one person there at this time has lived before in the recognizable form of personality that now exists. The growth of the soul so advances and polishes personality that, were we to be reincarnated, we would not seem to those who knew us to be the same entity as before. Parts of us remain, but not the whole man who sinned and struggled and loved and slaved. We here are not the same entity in its entirety that we were in our earth-life. We have memories and knowledge acquired during that phase, but we are constantly progressing, so that the less important things of the earth are now forgotten by us.

"To us time in the earth-sense is meaningless, except as a measuring stick by which our progress is inexorably marked. We are so uninterested in dates that we find it almost impossible to answer questions about the 'why' of a time element, or the 'when' of our birth and death. These things are so unimportant in the eternity of progress that man while on earth alone needs such guideposts, to mark his years for record there. To us, the basic element of time is how far we have advanced.

"We have millenniums yet to go in our progression toward eternal truth and Oneness with God. This is what time means to us, and our goal is to advance others in such a way that inevitably our own time will be shortened until we are reunited with our Maker, who first gave us birth as sparkling little entities. We were first born in God. God is our ultimate home. It is the cycle of the universe, to seek that of which we once were a glowing part. Our reunion with God will be the ultimate step by which we will obtain the glory of true love and happiness."

Because it was the Christmas season, I had been rereading the New Testament. I therefore asked the Guides whether there had ever been any other true Man of God except Jesus of Nazareth. They replied that "many saintly beings have skipped many intermediary steps," and that all great religions have "their shining examples of goodness and truth embodied in the person of a man who once walked the earth.

"God the Father creates all things," they continued. "He made each and every one of us. The difference between those saintly ones, and those of us who tarry long in our path back to God, is that the former were without sin. The Man of Nazareth was the most holy of all saints. His life was an unblemished page. He loved with such compassion that He gladly died for the sins of those who sinned against His person. This Holy Man was indeed the Son of God. Because of His perfection He ascended directly to His Father, without the intermediary steps that other mortals must take to achieve that perfect union. Jesus lives in God, and because of His earthly habitat for a brief dot of history, He is able to come again and again to that earth without taking on the flesh; but the wonder of your world is that those who wish Him to be there in time of crisis are unable to see His shining Presence.

"He is there as surely as a mother lays a cool hand on a fevered brow. His miracles are never-ceasing, and continue as dramatically as those He performed in the name of the Father while on earth. All who believe in Him are able to experience His wonders of salvation. Open the heart with prayer. Tell the problem unselfishly to Jesus, and the prayer is already on its way to fruition. Take others into your heart, as Jesus took all of you into His own. That is God Incarnate."

Christmas Eve morning dawned bright and clear. When I turned on my electric typewriter at the usual hour, the machine seemed fairly to pulsate with life as Lily wrote: "All of us are gathered here today to wish that you find the true meaning of Christmas and help others to find it, too. Help one another. To have faith in another person is to demonstrate faith in the God of us all, for it was He who created these, your neighbors, in His own image, and proved it by sending His own Son to show that man has the quality of sublimity. To be as Christ was on earth is to be a part of God Himself.

"To live in perfect harmony with all in that plane is to demonstrate that one is ready to join his Maker in perfect harmony. This is so seldom achieved there that one must not be heartsick with the setbacks, for the steps between that phase and eventual Oneness are many, but these can be telescoped as one demonstrates his ability to move forward toward perfection. By this we mean that the soul moves upward each time that an opportunity is seized for helping others. This bounding leap of the soul not only brings great joyousness to the one who performed the good deed, but also lights a candle in the next stage, by which that way is lighted for the soul's progression.

"No one here is so base that he does not rejoice each time that he sees a good deed performed there, in a spirit of pure love and helpfulness, with no thought of personal gain. All of us rejoice when a struggling human is eased along the path toward union with God, for this is the way to observe the laws of God, which are not yet as well understood there as here. You who have been privileged to learn this at first hand have already experienced some of the joy which comes from helping others. Never let an opportunity be lost, for time is fleeting. Always look for the nugget of good in a man, and work tirelessly to develop it into a shining tower of strength. Guide and direct him, not by meddling, but by loving so much that his heart expands with your encouragement. Learn to smile as you spread the message, for it is not a somber but a joyous one. Lift the spirits of those around you, and keep a song in your heart."

We awakened next morning to a white Christmas. During the night the trees and shrubs had been draped in puffy garments, and our statuary in the garden wore tall snow peaks, like chefs' hats. The fairyland scene was enough to instill a song in anyone's heart, and my joy increased when Lily announced, via the typewriter, that my father was "anxious to speak to you on this holy day."

Dad gave me loving messages for Mother, and wrote feelingly of his regret for the times when he had spoken irritably, or in sudden anger. Advising us to avoid similar errors, he cautioned that when we eventually came to his plane we would have to assess the entire pages of our life.

"How much easier the task will be to review your past life," he counseled, "if you live each day as if that was the sole recording of your entire lifetime. Keep that page so neat and tidy, so filled with loving care, that if your life ended that evening at midnight the page would be spotless and blameless. If you take the task of living only one day at a time, keeping some such moral as that in mind, it is easier to progress, for surely even the worst of us can live one day in nearly blameless harmony with all about us.

"The one day lived at a time progresses until many, many days are joined together in like harmony. Therefore, set your goal for perfect living no further than one day ahead. At the end of it, set a like goal for the next day. Thus, you will soon have a string of pearls, each more glistening and pure than the one before; because as we live in this way, so do we grow in beauty and perfection."

Dad paused momentarily in his philosophizing, and with a slight change of pace continued: "Well, Sis, we love you and pray for your continued advancement, just as you are praying for those you love in that realm. Try not to forget me in your prayers, for we need it on this side as we strive to advance, just as much as you need it there. Prayer is the channel by which contact with the higher realm is opened wide, so never hesitate to pray for those who need guidance, and never hesitate to ask wisdom and love and forgiveness and guidance for yourself. There is nothing selfish in that particular prayer, for it merely asks that you be endowed with the qualities which will best fit you for helping others.

"Merry Christmas to you, little Ruthie, and to Marg and Paul and Bertie and all the rest. Our love for those who were near and dear to us grows apace with our own progress, even after we are here. Love is an enduring quality that goes far beyond the tiny barrier, or frontier, that you call the grave. That is the step which permits you to free yourself of the body, but the soul of you—the thinking you—continues here to find its way back frequently to those still struggling in your phase of existence. Be the good girl that your mother and I always wanted you to be. Be good in heart and spirit. Be sweet to those who are less fortunate, and be compassionate in your ways. That is the mark of a true lady. Be compassionate, gentle, and kind. Merry Christmas, Ruth."

Dad expressed regret that my sister, Margaret, was not attempting to communicate with him and with her own Guides. Declaring that she could easily make such contact through the pencil if she would work at it, he added: "Maybe after Christmas she will take the time to discover that there are more important things than having dinner on the table on time. She is missing a lot, my gal Marg, by becoming so absorbed in family that she takes too little time to wonder about her soul's progress. She is a very, very good girl, my Margie is, but she must not let herself be like Martha, instead of Mary, in the Gospels. Let her take time for spiritual things, and she will be surprised how her world will expand. Well, Merry Christmas to all of you, and may your hearts be filled with the joy of living and doing for others. This is Dad, with much love, Ira."

The day after Christmas, the Guides eagerly began to look forward to new projects. "At this close of the old year," they wrote, "we want to show what is possible for all those who will earnestly try to develop their psychic powers in order to better their lives and enrich the souls of others. The first step for them is to try to make contact with what they call The Unknown, so that this power can begin working in their behalf. This power is one of the strongest forces in the universe. With the souls on the unseen side of this imaginary barrier joining with those there who truly seek to advance the cause of others, the powers are almost limitless. Our Father created this force as truly as He created each of His children in His own image."

The Guides were quick to emphasize that such contact between the two planes is good, not evil. "This force could not exist, were it not that God wishes it to be used for the advantage of all of us, His children," they wrote. "Those who mistakenly call it the work of the Devil are shortsighted indeed, for this power would not be suffered to continue through the ages unless God the Father wanted it used. He puts into that world of yours many opportunities for man's creative talents.

177

The space ships could not be built, were it not that God first put there the ingredients for their success. How could man circumnavigate the globe, or orbit the earth, unless God had put into the minds of men the knowledge which could be developed to such a high degree that the discovery at last was made?

"It is the same with the reaches of the human mind in the psychic as in any other field. Were this power of communication not utilized by man, it would be wasted; yet God wishes that it be utilized and developed to the fullest extent, so that at last—as in the Scriptures it was foretold—the veil will drop between the two worlds, and all will be as one. Although some may still be living in the flesh in that day, they will be able to converse at will with those who have passed into the next stage. The time can come as rapidly or as slowly as man views the problem with open or closed mind.

"Were all to follow the steps that you and others have taken to develop this God-given opportunity, the day would be close at hand; but we do not predict that it will come that rapidly, for man is a timid creature when it comes to this field. We know not why. We see only that the exalted ones who have passed beyond the pettiness to a deeper understanding of the laws of the universe are the ones who further the teachings of God and bring ever nearer for all of us that wonderful day when sin can be no more.

"That day can never come until men fully grasp the laws we have been trying to pass along to them through such writings as these. When man fully comprehends that his life is a testing period by which he can rapidly advance himself to the state of utter divinity with God, then sin will have no hold upon him, even though he wears a fleshly body for the brief years that he spends on earth. It is the lack of knowledge, the turning of one's back on the obvious moral of these teachings, which delays the soul's progress. If a man truly understood this principle, how could he indulge in the paltry deceits and indiscretions which would obviously delay his reunion with God?"

CHAPTER 16

A Spirit's Nose for News

Debunkers may find it harder to produce a logical explanation for a series of occurrences in March, 1966, than simply to accept Fletcher for what he claims to be: a discarnate whose awareness is considerably sharpened since he passed to the next stage of life. Arthur Ford came to Washington for a lecture, and I asked him to give a trance sitting for one of my friends. As he was totally unaware of her identity, I felt that this sitting could be a meaningful test of Fletcher's prowess. I myself knew little of Mary's affairs, except that her husband had been a prominent government official prior to his death in an automobile crash several years before.

It was her first experience with a trance medium, and as Fletcher introduced my father, Dad seemed to be speaking more to Mary than to me when he said: "It's difficult to put into words, or to say how free our life is here. It is not something 'out there' or 'up there.' It is all around you. As you walk in the physical body you walk through the dimension that we also are in, and oftentimes we walk through you. That is when we are able to merge our thoughts with yours, and then is when you receive ideas that seem to come from nowhere."

Referring to the book that I was writing, Fletcher said: "Your father wants it to provide hope for people in a world that is rapidly losing hope. Give them hope that there is something real and permanent. Make it clear that the life we live here is not the kind of life we lived on earth, but is the same life with more freedom...because we are not limited in time and space. Give them this message, for if they are without something that they can cling to, they are hopeless. Hope is substance, and there is substance and reality here to justify their hope."

Turning to Mary, Fletcher declared that he had a communication for a friend of hers whose name began with Z. I knew of no such person, but Mary listened raptly as he spoke of "a woman who came over recently." He said she had "a feeling of great relief, because she had suffered very deeply throughout her body and was glad to get out of it." Mary later informed me that this was "unquestionably" the mother of one of her two closest friends, whose name begins with Z. Although wracked with pain, she had been kept alive for fifteen years by expensive medical treatment while cancer spread throughout her body. Her death, Mary added, must have been a merciful release from suffering.

Fletcher next told Mary that she was "interested in food, like a dietitian would be," and I could scarcely have been more surprised when she acknowledged this to be true. "Food for health," Fletcher continued. "This interest is going to grow and expand. I see you in a situation in which the government will also be taking part. I keep getting the thought of experimentation with creating a food supply from the sea. Food for the masses. A chemist is involved in it, although you are not a chemist. I see laboratory experiments, and the project reaching out to Latin America and the Middle East. I see groups in hospitals being used for experiments, and an attempt made to reach a standard for vitamins, in connection with health foods." Mary nodded acquiescence as Fletcher added that she was already carrying on some research begun by her husband, which would concern itself with the world problem of feeding masses of hungry peoples. She subsequently verified this to me in detail, and said that the previous week she had conferred with government officials about conducting experiments with seafood for that very purpose.

"Does the name Sandra mean anything to you?" Fletcher abruptly asked Mary. "She has a mental condition, but it's really more of an emotional problem. She needs analysis and guidance, but does not need to be committed."

A sigh of relief escaped my friend as she murmured: "That's exactly what I wanted to know. What can I do to help her?"

Fletcher quoted by name a "mental-health expert who has recently come over here," and added: "He says Sandra has (blank) tendencies," mentioning a highly technical mental condition.

"That is right," Mary whispered.

While Arthur Ford breathed peacefully in his chair, Fletcher continued to speak through him, saying: "Sandra must learn how to accept herself. This expert says God forgives people, but so many people don't forgive themselves. She feels she has failed someone who has been a victim of her failure. Everyone thinks he does what is right at the moment, so she must not entertain this sense of guilt. If she has a psychiatrist, don't take her to the dogmatic Freudian type. Such a psychiatrist will make her worse. He will blast whatever faith and hope she has left. You can help her, because you have a psychic quality which makes it possible for you to understand people's problems without asking a lot of questions. She is a very brilliant person, who has broken under the confusion of emotional guilt."

I did not know the person of whom they spoke, but Mary later affirmed that Sandra was a close friend who was then undergoing psychiatric treatment at a fashionable clinic. She said the young woman was beset with a guilt complex, suffered from the "tendencies" Fletcher mentioned, and had been a straight-A student in college.

Although Arthur Ford had not known whether Mary was married or single, and no information had been volunteered by either of us, Fletcher next spoke of her husband's death in these significant words: "He wants to tell you that he reached out with both hands to try to save himself, and that's the last thing he remembers. There was an explosion, and he was burned, but he did not feel it. His death was caused by the blast rather than the crash. He is happy here. He wouldn't have wanted to live in the condition that he would have been in had he survived the crash."

Her husband then apparently spoke directly to Mary, via Fletcher, sending love to their two children, encouraging Mary to use her psychic talents, and adding: "The difference between mediocrity and genius is that a genius can dip into a deeper dimension and pick up something out of the pool of knowledge. Every problem you face there, someone has faced before. When that person comes over here after experiencing a problem similar to yours, he has a more enlightened view of it to give to you. That's why some people rise above the level of mediocrity. They can tap this universal pool."

Addressing me, Fletcher announced that "a man named Hilton Brown is very proud of a recent honor which was bestowed on you in his home town." Since the name was unfamiliar I asked for more details, and Fletcher quoted the man as saying that he used to own a controlling interest in an Indianapolis paper for which I once wrote. I remarked that both newspapers in that city belonged to Eugene Pulliam, but because the mysterious Mr. Brown insisted that he also had an interest in them, I agreed to check, and Fletcher continued: "He says you've got one of the best stories in the world. All the other stories are temporary, but it's a wonderful thing when you can get a story that transcends all the problems and has limitless interest. That's what you've got in the psychic book that you're writing."

Two weeks earlier, I had received the Indiana Woman of the Year award from the Indianapolis chapter of Theta Sigma Phi, women's honorary journalism fraternity, so at least Fletcher was partially right. That evening I telephoned my brother in Indianapolis to see if he could shed light on Hilton Brown. He replied that a Hilton U. Brown had been with the Indianapolis *News* for more than a half century; and that at the time of his death in 1958, at the age of ninety-nine, he had been vice-president of Indianapolis Newspapers, Inc. So far as Paul could determine, however, Brown had not owned stock in that corporation, which controls both the *News* and the *Star*.

Strange newspapermen always seem to want to talk to me when Fletcher is around, and the next person to be introduced at the séance was presented in this manner: "A man here says you're going back soon to a place where both of you got your start in the newspaper business. There's going to be a big banquet, or gathering, and people will be praising you. His name is Charles Marsh. He says that long before you came along, he owned the paper on which you worked in Texas."

I protested that the newspaper where I began my career in Waco, Texas, was owned by the Fentress family, but the unknown Mr. Marsh declared: "I used to own the paper, too. Ask Liz. She knows me. The night President Johnson came back from Texas, that terrible night after the tragedy, I was one of the few people who got to speak with him and pledge my friendship again." The name Charles Marsh was new to me, but I promised to check. Then another man, who introduced himself as Dr. John Sutherland, claimed to have been "the only doctor at the Alamo," and said he was a forebearer of Liz Carpenter's."

The next day I telephoned Liz, who is Lady Bird Johnson's White House Press Secretary, and asked: "Liz, have you ever heard of a Texas newspaperman named Charles Marsh?"

"You bet I have," she replied breezily. "He used to be an owner of the Waco and Austin papers before he sold his interest to the Fentress family. He was one of President Johnson's closest friends. As a matter of fact, Charlie Marsh launched the President on his political career; and one of Mr. Johnson's first acts after becoming President was to call on Marsh in Washington and thank him for his friendship. Charlie died not long afterward. Why?"

By now I was thoroughly impressed with Mr. Marsh's knowledge, for, although it had not yet been announced, I had already made plane reservations to fly to Waco two weeks hence, to be the honor guest at Baylor University's annual Woman's Day celebration. I told Elizabeth Carpenter the reason for my telephone call, and repeated the words about Dr. John Sutherland. She called her older brother in Texas and reported back that they did indeed have an ancestor by that name, who, as far as could be determined, was the only doctor at the Alamo during its courageous last stand.

Toward the close of the séance, Fletcher told Mary that her husband was showing him a book. "The author's first name is Adelle," he said, "and you keep referring to it. You have just acquired it within the past month or two."

"Adelle Davis!" Mary gasped. "Yes, I've been using it for frequent reference ever since I bought it six weeks ago. Does he want to tell me something about it?"

"No, he's just giving that to you as a test," Fletcher replied. Apparently by this he meant evidential proof of her husband's continued existence as a complete personality, since Arthur Ford had no normal means of knowing about her interest in a particular book, and I had not heard of it. "He says to you, 'You've been reading it frequently, and when you read a thing that interests me, I read it, too. That's the wonderful thing we share with you even more intimately than we could when we were in the body, because when in the body we can touch you, but the body is a barrier. Now, free of the body, I can merge with you, and two really can become one. Be happy!'"

Fletcher also introduced another man, saying: "His name is Maurice...last name sounds like Pates. He dealt with international problems there. I get the impression that his interest was in children; not in war, but in the victims of war. He had something to do with the United Nations."

Neither Mary nor I recognized the name, but the unearthly visitor proved to be persistent. Two days later, I requested a private sitting with Arthur Ford in order to ask Fletcher some questions relating to the book that I was writing. As I have done before, I made a tape recording of the séance conversation, and one of the first persons to be introduced was a woman whose name sounded like Mary Leeper. "She says she worked with Adlai Stevenson on something having to do with the United Nations," Fletcher declared. "She says she worked with several educational projects for the government, but her last one was working with someone by the name of Maurice Pates—something to do with children and an agency of the United Nations. She hasn't been here very long."

After this second mention of a Maurice Pates, I telephoned United Nations headquarters and asked the personnel director if she knew of such a person. "You must mean Maurice Pate," she replied. "He was executive director of UNICEF, the United Nations children's fund, but he's dead now." She was unable, however, to identify the name Mary Leeper.

Except for Pate, the cast of characters was completely different at this second séance. Fletcher's first performer was a man who introduced himself as Paul Thompson, who claimed to have met me casually at a meeting which had something to do with journalism. When I could not recall him, Fletcher prompted: "He was at the University of Texas and was well acquainted with someone named Leslie." I asked if he referred to Leslie Carpenter, Liz's husband, who is a Texas University alumnus, and he said, "Yes, he knew him very well and wants to give him his best. The person who brought Thompson today said he once worked on the same paper you did; but he later became more interested in photography and did a lot of work in Texas, the Southwest, and Mexico. His name is Mason. Monty Mason. He said that during the last part of his life he was working for the *National Geographic Magazine*. He studied under this Paul Thompson in Texas, and said that at one time he was on the *News,* the same paper you were on."

I asked whether he referred to the Waco *News-Tribune* in Texas, or the New York *Daily News,* and he responded: "The New York one. He says he was there when Cavanaugh was—whoever that is. He says there's another person here named Flowers. I get the impression that Flowers was president of a college. He gave an honorary degree, or something of the sort, when the President was there for a special occasion, and he knew Mason, too. He says that he also knew old Tidwell, whose first name was Joseph—no, not exactly Joseph—but a funny name that sounds sort of like Joseph. Tidwell said his first wife was named Kansas, and they knew you when you were at Baylor. He wants you especially to check out Mason and Thompson, because they will have some significance in your life.

"Mason tells me that his senior editor passed on recently. The *Geographic* editor, that is. He says that he once had something to do with *The Diplomat,* and dealt with a lady there who has been at your house sometime when Ford was here. Name something like Ridings. He says to tell her that Jesse Eubank is here. Monty is interested in what you're doing, because on one of his trips into Mexico he visited the Mayan ruins and talked with some old peons who told him something of their folklore. In the early days before America was discovered, they had practically the same rituals and sacraments that Christians had; when the Catholics came it was easy for Mexicans to accept them, because they were teaching the same things Mexicans had always been taught in their Aztec and Mayan culture.

"You are going to write a book, and he says the important thing to make clear is that these things you are writing about have been a part of every culture. They didn't begin with Christianity, but through that they took on an ethical coloration and morality that they had never had before. People were seeing spirits before they believed in God, and because of that they began to try to picture a God, but they were aware of spirits before they had any conception of a Supreme Being. You must make it clear that the psychic is a constant stream that started when man first began to think, and before he was able to reason; and out of it all the various religions have developed. But Christianity is the only one that made clear that everyone can duplicate the resurrection experience of Jesus; the survival of the complete personality with the same character, and with memory, and with the freedom to make a choice. Men are not the victims of fate. Determinism is not compatible with the teachings of Christ. The

186

concept that men have free will is the major contribution of the Christian religion. Men can choose God, or choose to ignore God. Even after death they have the right to choose. That is why the early Christians were baptized by proxy, because they felt it would help them upward."

The message was interesting, but who was Monty Mason?

At an Iraqi embassy party that evening I saw Franc Shor, associate editor of *National Geographic Magazine,* and asked if he had ever heard of a man named Monty Mason. His eyes lighting with pleasure, Franc exclaimed: "Of course I knew him! His name was Mason Sutherland, but we all called him 'Monty.' He was one of my best friends. He and I were the only ones on the *Geographic* who had previously worked on newspaper desks. Why?" Avoiding the question, I asked where Monty had previously worked, and he replied: "He came originally from Texas, but was on the New York *Daily News* before coming to the *Geographic.* He was interested in art and did a lot of work in the Southwest and Mexico. But he's dead now, you know."

Hope Ridings Miller, editor of *The Diplomat,* could not recall "Monty" without checking her files, but vividly remembered the late Jesse Eubank as a leading citizen of her home town, Sherman, Texas. Through other sources I learned that a man named Flowers had been president of Lyndon B. Johnson's alma mater, Southwest Texas State Teachers College; and Leslie Carpenter readily identified Paul Thompson as a former professor whom he had known at Texas University.

That left "old Tidwell" to be explained. I vaguely recalled that while a student at Baylor University I had taken a Bible course from a professor named Tidwell; and two weeks after the séance, as I strolled Baylor's vastly expanded campus with Mrs. Virginia Crump, assistant dean of students, I noticed a new "Tidwell Bible Building." This reminded me to inquire the name of his first wife, and Mrs. Crump replied that he had had three wives, but she did not know their first names.

I stopped by to see Guy B. Harrison, a professor of history continuously since my own student days there, and he obligingly telephoned several people whom he thought would remember the name of Dr. Tidwell's first wife, but to no avail. We tried several other channels, before finally locating someone who had known the lady. Her maiden name was Kansas Reid! In the thrill of discovery, I neglected to ask about Dr. Tidwell's own first name, but after I returned home and failed to find a listing for him in my volumes of *Who's Who in America,* either new or old, I wrote a query to Mrs. Crump. She replied that his first name was Josiah! As Fletcher had correctly stated it, it was an unusual name that "sounds sort of like Joseph."

During the Ford séance I asked Fletcher about President Kennedy's progress on that plane, and after discussing it at some length, he quoted the martyred President in detail on his views of the Vietnam and Cuban situations, the accomplishments of the Johnson administration and the activities of his two living brothers, Senators Robert and Edward Kennedy. The voice purporting to be JFK's then placed the blame for the Bay of Pigs fiasco squarely on a still-living person, and our involvement in Vietnam on another individual. The voice further predicted that a peace conference on Vietnam would occur "sooner than most people think"; but as there is no intent to embarrass anyone through this book, this intriguing portion of the séance is being withheld.

A few days before these two séances, Arthur Ford had gone to Fort Bragg, North Carolina, at the invitation of a chaplain, to address a group of paratroopers waiting to be shipped out to Vietnam. "These men will mean business when they ask you questions about the possibility of life after death," the chaplain warned Ford, "because they're facing it. They know the statistics. Out of every ten paratroopers who jump behind enemy lines in wartime, only eight return."

For more than four hours the paratroopers eagerly plied him with questions, while Ford did his best to offer proof of personal survival beyond the grave. After the meeting, one of the men asked to speak with him privately. When the others had gone, he told Ford that he had recently returned from Vietnam, where his outfit had been ambushed by the Viet Cong.

"All the others were killed," he said, "and I was left for dead. While lying there, without hope of rescue, I saw the body of one of my buddies rise up, come over to me, and smile. I saw this, even though on the ground I could still see his physical body. Our walkie-talkie and all communications equipment had been destroyed, so I thought that my situation was hopeless; but in less than five minutes a helicopter landed a few yards away. I was rescued, and on the return flight I asked the pilot how he happened to land in such a Godforsaken place at that time. He replied that he was on another mission when a sudden feeling came over him that he 'had' to drop down in that spot. How do you explain it?"

Arthur Ford, with his vast experience in the psychic field, has helped to authenticate many equally dramatic incidents in which the "dead" have seemingly communicated with the living to effect rescues. To those who doubt that life continues after death, he cites the fifteenth chapter of I Corinthians, saying, "If there be no resurrection, then Christ was not raised; and if Christ was not raised, then our gospel is null and void, and so is your faith." Nearly all religions of the world have taught some sort of immortality. The great contribution of Christianity, Ford believes, is the teaching of survival as a total personality. Ford's personal research has convinced him that this "total personality" does not await resurrection "until Gabriel blows his horn." Rather, it continues to function as effortlessly after so-called death as after a good night's sleep on the earth plane.

It will be a great loss to this world when Arthur Ford passes on to the next. His talent is so remarkable that I should think some institution, such as the Ford or Rockefeller foundations, would want to finance research in this field while a man of his caliber is here to help direct the quest. Some of the projects which they sponsor are surely less important to the enlightenment of mankind than an exploration of the possibility of communication between this phase of life and the next.

CHAPTER 17

The Ancient Wisdom

Healing was a vibrant part of early Christian ministry. The Man of Galilee told his disciples that what He did, they could do also, and the New Testament records numerous occasions on which not only Christ, but His followers as well, healed the sick and the lame. What has happened to this miraculous power? Was it intended for use by only one generation of men, or have we simply ceased to listen to the inner voice that would teach us ancient wisdom?

Living today is a man who has effected thousands of seemingly miraculous healings by the laying on of hands. The method that he uses bears no relationship to faith-healing or prayer-healing. He calls it "revitalizing the magnetic field," and he asserts that by placing his fingers over nerve relay centers in the lower abdomen, a human energizing current is transmitted throughout the body. I have seen him work and have interviewed many who can testify to his amazing healing powers; but he does not consider what he does amazing in the least.

"It is actually a lost art," he says simply. "This was the commonly accepted practice of healing in the early church. The laying on of hands was the Disciples' method of distributing human energy; it now sounds miraculous only because the knowledge has been lost through the ages. High priests knew the method in days of old. They thus energized newborn babies, to free them from their mother's tensions and from birth shock, but this knowledge was deliberately kept from the masses."

I asked how he had discovered this so-called ancient wisdom, and he replied: "I didn't. I have always had it." I had to press this modest man to talk about himself, but through repeated proddings he told me this story: As a toddler he used to embarrass his mother by telling her about the ailments of her friends. After one particularly candid recital, when he was five years old, she desperately turned to the family doctor for advice. The old gentleman heard her story and remarked: "Oh, he's one of those, is he? Send him to me. I can use him." Thereafter the boy frequently accompanied the doctor on his horse-and-buggy rounds, helping him to diagnose and treat sick patients. In school he was a lackluster student. Instead of attending classes, he would slip off into the woods to make friends with bears and deer, or sit quietly beside the river, "tuning in."

"Tuning in on what?" I prompted.

"On the ring," he replied. At my look of puzzlement, he declared that a protective ring of energy encircles each planet and stores within it all knowledge since the beginning of time. He said all thoughts and inventions are "taken off the ring," and anyone who will listen properly can pick up whatever information he needs. And how did he receive the wisdom that makes it possible for him to heal patients whom other doctors have pronounced incurable?

"I listen," he said, "and they tell me." Who are "they"? "Why, the Powers," he responded. I wanted to know whether he hears their voices, and he smiled patiently. "I hear nothing vocally. The power is translated into words in my brain." I asked what God means to him, and he responded: "The Power of Powers."

Reliable witnesses, including doctors and nurses, have seen this man stop heart attacks, heal crippled arthritics, dissipate large tumors, arrest glaucoma, and rebuild a disintegrated jawbone, simply by placing his hand on what he terms the "magnetic field"—that is, the lower abdomen or pelvic area.

"This is where you live," he says, as he lays the palm of his hand on that area. "In here is an intricate system, grouping together the main trunk nerves and their branches and relay systems which extend throughout the body. The lungs draw in the energy, but the magnetic field must draw the energy from the lungs in order to radiate it through the body. Everything is centered in the belly." To illustrate, he asked me to rest my fingertips on my closed eyelids. Then he touched a particular spot on my abdomen. As he did so, my eyeballs became as soft and squashy as jelly. "That's how I treat patients who have glaucoma," he said. "The eye tension is released at this spot."

A new patient remarked that he had had two operations for hemorrhoids, and the healer said: "They are caused by anger. We heal those by generating energy through a spot near the belly button. Your left shoulder is here," he added, pressing a different spot on the abdomen. The man winced, grabbed his shoulder, and yelled, "Ouch."

This remarkable man—Mr. A, as I shall call him until he is ready to divulge his identity—walked into my life one February afternoon in 1966. Two friends, wives of an ambassador and a high-ranking government official, were coming for tea. Shortly beforehand they telephoned to ask if they could bring Mr. A whom they thought I should know, since I was writing a book on psychic phenomena. They had met him a year before, and had since made a point of seeing him each time that he came to Washington. They added that his trips here were always arranged by a highly respected member of Congress and a State Department official, both of whom they identified by name.

The women came early to brief me about the out-of-town guest. One said that for the past decade she had suffered such excruciating pain in her left hand that she was frequently kept awake at night, even under sedation; but that after three "magnetic" treatments by this gifted man twelve months before, she had experienced no further recurrence of the trouble.

The other friend told me that after suffering a heavy blow on the head in an accident, she had endured stabbing head pains until the man gave her a ten-minute treatment. The pain promptly vanished, she said, and she had not had a headache since. She also related the experience of a chef at her favorite restaurant, who had slipped on icy steps and plunged to the bottom of an iron stairway. Rushed to the hospital, he was X-rayed and informed that he had a severely wrenched arm which would prevent his working for a month. Badly shaken, he returned from the hospital with his arm swathed in bandages, splints, and a sling. My friend took Mr. A to see him, and after removing the wrappings the healer pressed his fingers on two spots near the elbow. Then he asked the chef to swing his arm, and the pain was gone. Throwing away the splints and sling, the chef immediately went back to work, wielding a heavy cleaver to cut meats. The healer explained that he had simply "taken the shock out," as he had done for my friend after her head injury.

The women told me that this amazing man had been born with a star in his right palm. This is supposedly the sign of a true psychic, and since I had seen the rare marking only once before, in the hands of seeress Jeane Dixon, I was immediately curious. When the doorbell rang, I admitted a massively built, youngish-looking man with blue eyes and clear, unlined skin. Mr. A looked as normal as the man next door, and he had a contagious sense of humor. "Isn't that crazy?" he would remark with a grin, as my friends continued to recite instances of his healing powers.

At my request he showed me his right palm, and I noticed that except for a clearly defined, five-pronged star in the center, it was virtually without other lines. By contrast, Jeane Dixon's palms are so deeply etched and crisscrossed with lines that they could seemingly belong to a centenarian. Noting the youthful appearance of the man's palm and total hand, I remarked: "You are only a boy who has not even begun to live."

His eyes twinkled as he replied: "I am seventy-one years old." My astonishment was not misplaced. When I later asked a friend to estimate the age of the healer, to whom I had just introduced him, he replied: "I'm forty-seven, and he's definitely younger than I am."

That first afternoon at my house, the ambassador's wife said that the man had corrected a "leaking heart valve" which had bothered her since her birth. She related that three doctors were present at her first meeting with the healer, and after listening to her heartbeat, all four men commented on its irregularity. Then Mr. A placed three fingers on a spot behind her upper shoulder for a few minutes.

"When the three doctors listened to my heart action again," she added, "they were nearly overcome with shock. They said it sounded as smooth as a Rolls-Royce motor. Now I can go anywhere without having to guard against a strain on my heart. It has changed my whole life."

I asked Mr. A how he had effected this seeming miracle, and in language which sounded like the shoptalk of a master mechanic, he replied: "I reground the valves. I simply opened the switches, strengthened her magnetic field, tuned her heart, let the energy current through, burned out the rust, and oiled a few joints." Some of that was, of course, done in a subsequent treatment.

Smiling at his colorful manner of expression, I remarked that if he was that good he should be able to fix a hip that had been bothering me constantly for several weeks. "Hand me your thumb," he grinned. Thinking that he was jesting, I held up the thumb nearest him, and he said: "No, the left one. It's your left hip that hurts, isn't it?" He took the thumb in his right hand and gently pressed below the knuckle while simultaneously carrying on an animated conversation. In a few minutes he interrupted himself to ask: "How's the hip?" Suddenly realizing that the ache was missing, I squirmed and wriggled, but could not bring back the stabbing pain that had coursed through it continuously for many days.

Baffled, I offered a more difficult challenge. Chronic bursitis in my right shoulder had defied ten years of medical treatment, including X-ray, deep heat, massage, and cortisone shots. Mr. A strolled around behind my chair and placed several fingers on the nape of my neck. He continued to discourse on other matters for a time and then told me to raise my right hand over my head. I explained that I had not been able to do that for years, but he said soothingly: "All right, just lift it as high as you comfortably can." Gritting my teeth, and dreading the pain, I made the test. The arm effortlessly shot above my head, and even when I began to swing it in a broad arc I could feel no pain. I danced around the room, waving my arm and exercising my hip, with no discomfort whatsoever.

Mr. A watched my antics with amusement and then brought me back to earth by saying: "This is just grandstanding today. I blasted temporary energy through you, but the pain will return. To do it right I would have to work on your magnetic field, tearing down the condition that is causing your trouble, and then build you up again." He was right. For the remainder of that day and evening I was totally free of any twinges, but by the next morning they had returned.

I might have dropped the matter there, except that at a party that evening a youthful friend of mine came hobbling in on a cane. Every step was obviously causing him agony, and when I solicitously inquired about the trouble, Ned said he planned to go into the hospital that week-end to find out. "The top and base of my spine are killing me," he said. "Pains from my shoulder are shooting into my left hand, and two of the fingers are completely numbed. I tried sticking them with pins just before I came, and could feel nothing."

I asked if he would be willing to consult with a man whom I had met the day before, and he said he was in such misery that he would try anything once. I made an appointment for the following day, but when the time approached Ned was unable to get out of bed. With the help of his wife I finally managed to get him to the home of the State Department official, where the healer was staying.

Mr. A placed his ear above Ned's heart and listened to the beat. Then he straightened up and said: "Your difficulty stems from a very difficult birth in which your oxygen supply was affected. As a result, you have never had a normal oxygen intake. As a boy you tried to keep up with your companions, but when you ran you would get a stitch in your side."

The room was silent for a minute. I knew that Ned

had not wanted to come, and I thought that he was disgusted with such a farfetched explanation, but at last he said: "They tell me that I was forty-eight hours being born. My mother had a terrible time, and I was a forceps delivery. The rest of what you say is also true."

Mr. A asked me to listen to Ned's heart, and even I could notice the grinding chug and irregularity of the beat. The man placed his hand on Ned's abdomen for a few moments; then asked him to arch his back above the bed. Ned was frankly afraid to try, but when he reluctantly did so, he felt no pain. Mr. A then moved his fingers to another part of the abdomen, and Ned irritably asked when he was going to begin working on his throbbing shoulder and arm.

"But I *am* working on them," the healer replied affably. "This is your shoulder relay, right here in your magnetic field. Did you ever wonder about the symbolism of the Masonic apron? The ancients who founded that Order knew all about this method of distributing human energy." Ned broke in to complain that he was pressing too hard on his abdomen, but I could see that no pressure was being applied, although through Mr. A's shirtsleeve I observed a powerful pulsing movement in his right forearm. The man explained that from his own magnetic field he was sending energizing current through Ned's relay center to the nerves in his bad arm.

Mr. A's otherwise excellent appearance was marred by a great protruding stomach, which I had assumed to be fat; but when I commented on the pumplike movement of the pulse in his forearm, he stood up and asked me to push my fist into his stomach. I couldn't even make a dent. To my surprise, it was as solid as bone. Mr. A answered my unspoken question by explaining that this was his over-developed magnetic field, from which he transmitted energy to those he healed.

Ned's face was by now suffused with a pinkish glow, and he commented on the feeling of warmth radiating from Mr. A's hand toward his shoulder. "Good," the healer said, "now wave your arm and see if any feeling is returning to that hand." Ned did as instructed. In a moment he reported that he had normal feeling in all but one finger, and the shoulder pain was nearly gone. After his second treatment Ned discarded the cane; and following the fourth visit, two days later, he was walking with the familiar spring to his step. He looked and acted revitalized. The numbness had almost vanished, and his back no longer bothered him. I listened to his heart, and it was as regular as a docile child's.

During Mr. A's week here, I met with him several times. The wife of the State Department official with whom he was staying told me that ten years before, Mr. A had saved her husband's life. At that time he had just returned from an overseas tour of duty, desperately ill with heart trouble and a virulent liver disease which the doctors said would take his life within a matter of weeks. She had heard of Mr. A, and therefore insisted that her husband consent to an examination. The healer gave him a series of treatments, and four days afterward the official not only passed a rigorous medical examination at Walter Reed Army Hospital, but was given immediate clearance for another overseas assignment.

"If he had gone first for that examination, before the treatment by Mr. A," she mused, "the government would have forced him to retire. His career would have ended—to say nothing of his life."

I asked how she had heard of Mr. A, and she replied: "Through my parents. He arrested my mother's glaucoma, and oculists verify that there has been no further deterioration. He healed my stepfather of Parkinson's disease, for which there is supposed to be no cure, although my stepfather had scoffed at the notion that anyone could help him simply by putting a hand on his abdomen. But that was before he was burned." At my startled look, she laughingly added: "The skin on my stepfather's abdomen was actually burned during a treatment. Then it blistered and peeled. This convinced him that some powerful force was at work."

Chuckling at the recollection, Mr. A said: "I had to throw some mighty powerful energy his way to correct his condition. It's crazy, isn't it?"

The official's wife said that during the many hours

she sat in Mr. A's outer office, while her husband underwent treatments, she became acquainted with a number of his other patients. On her first visit she talked with a fourteen-year-old girl who had been paralyzed from the chest down since birth. She was in a wheelchair, but was chubby and healthy looking. The girl and her parents told my friend that when Mr. A had begun his treatments on her six months before, she was "like a skeleton." She had tubes in her bowels and urinary tract, could eat no solid food, and had withered legs that had not kept up with the growth of her body. "But look how she has improved already," the father exclaimed. "The doctors said her case was hopeless, but now she's eating normally, and her legs have grown seven inches in a half-year." When my friend next saw the girl, several months later, she was walking without crutches by holding onto chairs. That was eight years ago. Now she walks without support, is happily married, and has a baby.

I talked with an elderly woman, an osteopath, who had been so crippled from arthritis that she could no longer work at her profession. She said that after two treatments by Mr. A, the curvature in her spine began to straighten, the pain left her hands, and she now treats seven or eight patients a day in her office although she is eighty-five years old. She was so impressed with Mr. A that she brought a group of five other cranial osteopaths to see him. They had been treating each others' ailments for many years, and knew all of each others' aches and pains. What astonished them was that Mr. A correctly diagnosed every condition after merely putting his ear to their chests. He removed pains which had defied them all, and corrected the thumb of one man who had not been able to use it for years—simply by the laying on of his hands.

One of Mr. A's greatest admirers is a middle-aged woman, from whose jaw surgeons had removed a cancerous growth. The remaining bone had nearly disintegrated before she met Mr. A, but during his "magnetic" treatments a usable new jaw formed of gristle, which replaced the bone. Another former patient who becomes lyrical about his strange talent is an eighty-year-old woman who could easily pass for sixty. She says that she had an inoperable tumor "as big as a basketball," and that the doctors told her there was no hope. "That was ten years ago," she boasts. "Mr. A began treating me, and the tumor simply disappeared. My health returned, better than ever. I would gladly give my life for him, because he saved mine."

Nurses who worked with Mr. A noticed that he seemed to sense the disability by the time a new patient walked from the reception room into his office. Thus challenged, he admitted that he psychically grasps much of the problem, and he completes the diagnosis by listening to the heart, without aid of stethoscope. They asked for an explanation, and he said: "There are thirty-six different frequencies. Each individual operates on three waves at different frequencies, making numerous combinations of magnetic field control. The moment that I see a person, I know on which three life rays he operates. With that knowledge, the rest is easy. I then listen to his heart to get the physical picture. The pattern of the heartbeat tells me precisely where the trouble is located, and then I go to work."

"What in the world are life rays?" I asked.

As patiently as a teacher would try to explain the principle of television to a backward child, he said: "The solar rays give us life, but the position of the planets at the time of birth makes us the individuals that we are. Characteristics and personality occur at conception; individuality occurs at birth. Your individuality is governed by your fixed sign. This establishes your magnetic field, which consists of three different frequencies derived from the Power of Powers. You are thereafter influenced by the vibrations of all the planets of this universe. We are no stronger than our magnetic field. Shortness of breath, irritability, and illness are among the signs that insufficient energy is being distributed. When the depletion of the magnetic field continues, the nerves are partially starved for their fuel or energy, creating spasms or nerve tension through the body. This depletion, unless corrected, can develop into serious ailments. Now do you understand?"

What could I say? We accept without argument the influence of the moon on tides, because scientists tell us it is true. We do not dispute the revolving planets and changing seasons in relation to the sun. We have no reason to doubt that a magnetic electrical field governs planetary action; why then is it too strange that a magnetic electrical field might govern human action as well? After all, the atom with its electrons has the same pattern as the sun and planets in a solar system. Remember the old adage, "As above, so below"? Yet we are inclined to view as "superstition" the idea that the position of the planets and the sun can influence our own personality or affairs.

I cannot comprehend how Mr. A, by placing his ear above a heart, can "read" the tensions and know which nerve centers are in spasm. I know that he does it, but how? Mr. A is equally puzzled that others cannot understand something which to him is simplicity itself. He says that for as long as he can remember he has been like a radio station that both sends and receives signals. He tunes in on the source of energy from the Power and then dispatches it to others. Well, how many of us understand the principle by which vibrations carry radio programs through the atmosphere on stated wave lengths? We tune our set to a station and hear a scheduled program. We switch the dial and hear a different one. With television, even a picture is instantly transmitted by means of vibrations, and can be bounced off man-made satellites for viewing on other continents. Our parents would have laughed off such an incredible idea as mere pipe-dreaming, but we believe it because we see the proof in our living rooms. Why is it so difficult, then, for us to accept Mr. A's explanation of an individual's magnetic field, and the mysterious source of his healing knowledge? The proof would seem to be in the cures to which many hundreds can testify.

Some of us are obviously more psychic than others. Mr. A insists, however, that psychic wisdom is available in varying degrees to all who will stand still and listen for the inner knowing. "The ancient wisdom that I pick up from 'the ring,'" he says, "is accessible to anyone on any part of the globe. Thousands would be able to do the work that I am doing. I, of myself, do nothing. The Power does the work, and I am only the tool. Some people have much stronger energy than others. This is determined at conception, and depends in part on how well their parents were mated in terms of energy currents. Individuals with a strong nervous system generate enough fuel or energy to fill their own needs and radiate a surplus. These are the ones best equipped to heal. They could be taught to direct the energy through their hands and release nerve spasms in others. If a baby's pelvic tensions can be released shortly after birth, he can automatically be revitalized by drawing more energy from the atmosphere. Does that make it clear?"

Of one thing I am certain. Mr. A does make it possible for increased energy to restore our tired batteries. As he did with other patients, Mr. A listened to my heart and told me to breathe deeply. I inhaled to the bottom of my chest, and exhaled. He next placed his hand on my abdomen, and I began to feel the vibration and heat that others had described. Then he again told me to take a deep breath. This time I inhaled effortlessly, and it seemed as though a whole new area of my body, which I had assumed played no part in the breathing apparatus, was being aerated as fully as the lungs. I was astonished at the sensation. The new energy which results from this "opening of the switches" must be experienced to be believed. A few such "charges," and a person is seemingly revitalized for months. The busy member of Congress who summons Mr. A to Washington at regular intervals, crowds two or three of these treatments into each day that the healer is here. "I take all of this that I can get when it's available," he told me, "because I find that the supercharge gives me enough extra vitality to last for several months."

At various times while interviewing Mr. A, I asked questions that seemed to puzzle him. A slight frown would pucker his smooth forehead, but then he would say, "Just a minute, I'm getting the answer to that now. Yes, here it is. They explain that..."

There was that "they" again. Mr. A never studied medicine or anatomy. His vocabulary is that of a mechanic rather than a physician. He holds a license to practice, but he does not pretend that his knowledge of ailments is within his own conscious mind. When he examines an ailing person, he says that he tunes up to the higher frequency controlled by "the Powers," and receives guidance directly from them. Instantaneous contact is made, he says, both with "the Powers" and the wave length of his patient, just as with electricity. As the "ancient wisdom" flows into him, his fingers go unerringly to the control centers, and the tensed nerves begin to relax.

Those who know that this man did not complete grammar school are astounded at the depth and breadth of his knowledge. His second wife used to urge him to read books, but he would turn his blue eyes on her in innocent wonderment and ask: "What do you want to know?" He could read the first page or so of a book, then seemingly "tune in" on the author and grasp the rest of the volume's contents. His wife, after their marriage, was worried for fear he would learn a couple of secrets about her past which only her sister, she said, knew. One day Mr. A told her exactly what she did not want him to know. He described the other people involved, even to the color of their hair and eyes.

"Now, stop bugging me with this," he told the startled woman, who had not so much as hinted that she had a secret. "Every time I look at you I see this picture coming between us. Put it away now, and let's forget it." She said she had never known such relief, but she has not dared to try deceptions with him since.

Is it really so strange that this man is seemingly able to pull wisdom from a pool of world knowledge that he calls "the ring"? From time to time, in widely separated parts of the world, individuals are simultaneously working on the same invention. When a patent is applied for, the United States Patent Office is frequently deluged with similar applications before the original product is on the market. Several books with strikingly similar plots may be published within weeks of each other, although the authors have had no communication. Has each tuned in, subconsciously perhaps, on the same cosmic wisdom? Some psychics believe that spirit Guides have sent the idea, which is picked up by human "receiving stations" who live in widely scattered areas; but Mr. A says that the idea has been in "the ring" since the beginning of time. Like Mt. Everest, "the ring" is there, waiting to be tapped.

The next time that Mr. A came to Washington, I arranged for some friends to participate in a demonstration of his technique. Among the guests were a four-star general, a Senator's wife, an intelligence officer and his wife, two pastors, an administration official, several writers, and television commentators. Their names are being withheld only in order to protect the privacy of Mr. A until he is ready to have his identity known.

The general had been suffering excruciating pain for several months, due to a tumor that was pressing on a nerve in his hip. He walked with a decided limp and could not stoop to tie his shoelaces. Mr. A did not know who he was, but as soon as he placed his ear on the general's chest, he said: "You've been under deep emotional strain for the past four months." How true this was! Four months previously, doctors had told him that there was no hope for his wife, who had contracted a rare disease during her foreign travels. She had since died, leaving two small children, and for that reason the general had postponed having an operation on his hip. Mr. A placed his fingers for a few minutes on the general's neck and belly, then asked him to locate the hip pain. All trace of it had vanished, and after several turns around the room the general stooped effortlessly to tie his shoelaces. At this writing, several weeks later, the general reports that his hip is infinitely better, and that he plans to take several more treatments when Mr. A returns.

The intelligence officer who was present told us that he had undergone a shoulder operation two years earlier, but that a spur had developed, which doctors said was causing pain in his arm and numbness in his fingers. After Mr. A had treated the intelligence officer's magnetic center for a few minutes, the latter suffered no further discomfort. The healer then listened to the heartbeat of the officer's wife, and volunteered: "Twenty years ago you suffered a great emotional blow from which you have never fully recovered."

Looking somewhat embarrassed, she verified this statement; and after a treatment, she was so enthusiastic about her improved breathing that she made another appointment; but her husband did not. He had been the cause of his wife's emotional shock exactly twenty years before, and he afterward told me that, as an intelligence officer, he did not dare risk seeing "a man like that who can obviously read minds."

Two cases of deafness showed marked improvement after a single treatment, but a third did not. Several arthritic knees and necks responded favorably to a first treatment, but Mr. A warned that in order to "burn out the rust and accumulation of calcium," several months of treatments would be required, and that "the pain would get worse before the joints got better." This proved true in my own case. The hip pain which I had experienced for several weeks before meeting Mr. A disappeared permanently after three treatments. But the chronic bursitis in my shoulder, which had been of much longer duration, became so acute after I insisted on a "crash" series of treatments, that I abandoned Mr. A's methods and returned to my doctor for hydro-cortisone shots.

My own doctor was incensed that I should have permitted myself to be a guinea pig in such an unorthodox procedure. This medico vigorously pooh-poohed the idea of magnetic healing and declined to meet Mr. A; but I interviewed a brilliant young surgeon, at a famous hospital in another large city, who has frequently consulted Mr. A on difficult cases. This is what he told me: "I was still in medical school some years ago, when my father underwent an emergency operation for what the surgeon thought was appendicitis. It turned out to be carcinoma and a blocked bowel. Mr. A flew down with me, and as we walked into the hospital, it was apparent to me that Dad was dying. He was ashen gray, heaving for breath, and receiving cortisone and Chloromycetin intravenously. He didn't recognize me, but Mr. A went to work on him. Within fifteen minutes Dad's face was rosy, and he was taking long, relaxed breaths. Four days later he walked out of the hospital and has had no further recurrence of the trouble.

"Since I've been practicing, I've had heart cases that rattled like a box of dice, but after this man lays his hand on them, they purr. In patients who have had clotted arteries or ruptured abdomens, which are usually fatal, he has rebuilt the whole wall so that surgery was unnecessary. A man was in shock from internal bleeding, and we were prepared to write him off, but Mr. A pumped juice into him by laying on his hand, and saved his life. No wonder the patients have such faith in him!

"For instance, a woman was suffering an acute attack of appendicitis, and I wanted to operate immediately, but she insisted on waiting until Mr. A could get there. I lost my patient. He gave her one treatment, and she no longer needed the operation. Her appendix was normal! Sometimes I wonder why I spent all those years studying to be a surgeon, when I see what this man can do. He can take the shock out of surgery and the pain out of incisions. It sounds preposterous, and I wouldn't believe it if I hadn't witnessed it several times, but he can even send this strange energy over the telephone to critically ill patients and rejuvenate them. It can't be hallucination, because sometimes the patients don't even know he's doing it. I have simply laid the receiver beside them while he fired this force over the telephone line."

Mr. A does not pretend that the method he employs is infallible, nor does he rule out the value of surgery and orthodox medical treatment in many cases. If an eardrum is gone, he does not try to restore hearing. He reports little success with cataracts, but if an operation is decided upon, he feels that his role is to be available for removing postoperative shock. He considers doctors invaluable in treating diseases. He does not have book knowledge of symptoms and clinical diagnosis, but he has apparently mended scores of conditions for which he does not know the medical terms.

My investigation convinces me that Mr. A is an extremely dedicated man whose sole interest is to aid humanity through the remarkable gift that he believes is given to him by "the Power of Powers." Because he seeks nothing for himself, he has asked me to withhold his identity. He had made a comfortable living in a field totally unrelated to healing and psychic phenomena, and on reaching his seventieth birthday had planned to "treat myself to a year of just plain loafing."

"But they thought otherwise," he says, with a rueful smile. "The Powers ordered me to get to work on a new project that is to make it possible for me to teach others this age-old method of healing." For another year, perhaps, this engaging man can continue to enjoy anonymity. Thereafter, it is a safe bet that this luxury will be denied him. He apparently has a job to do before he rests.

CHAPTER 18

Voices and Visitations

Mrs. William Faulkner, widow of the Nobel prize winning novelist, is convinced that for many years they shared their ante bellum estate, Rowan Oak, in Oxford, Mississippi, with a ghostly feminine spirit. "Mr. Faulkner and I only heard her," she says, "but our two daughters actually saw her; and when I once painted a portrait of an imaginary young woman, they cried, 'Mother, you've painted Judith!'"

Since the death of the towering literary figure, Mrs. Faulkner makes her home with their daughter, Jill (who is married to Paul Summers, Jr.), at an estate on the outskirts of Charlottesville, Virginia. It was there that she told me the story of Judith Shegog, daughter of the first owner of Rowan Oak, who broke her neck in a fall from a rope ladder while attempting to elope with a Yankee officer during the Civil War.

"My husband and I were frequently made aware of Judith's presence," she said, "and on several occasions when we were upstairs we heard an unfamiliar refrain being played on the piano in the drawing room. Sometimes Mr. Faulkner would go downstairs to investigate, and other times I went, but the music invariably stopped when we were halfway down the stairway. No one was on that floor at the time, and we had no cats, but the same tune would resume when we returned to the bedroom."

While in her teens, Mrs. Faulkner seemingly had another experience with a ghost. One evening at dusk, when she was in the kitchen of her parents' house, the Negro cook suddenly exclaimed: "Lawsa mercy, I see Rob comin' up the garden walk!"

As the houseboy named Rob had died two weeks before, the young girl sprang to the window, but she could not see him. "The cook insisted that he was still there," Mrs. Faulkner recalls, "so I rushed out and strolled to the end of the walk, seeing nothing; but as I turned back toward the house, a phosphorescent ball the size of a baseball followed each step that I took. Three times I turned back, then walked forward again, and each time it made the same turns that I did, until I lost my courage and bolted for the house. I firmly believe in ghosts and other psychic phenomena."

Russell A. Alger IV, namesake great-grandson of President William McKinley's Secretary of War, agrees with his wife, Nancy, that the imported Elizabethan drawing room in their country house near Vienna, Virginia, is "occupied by a contented old lady" whose presence they distinctly feel, although they have not seen her. Alger also concedes that Nancy is somewhat psychic. One morning on awakening, she told him she had dreamed that a friend flagged down her car and warned that she could not "get through that way because a broken water main has flooded Glebe Road." Later, at breakfast, Alger switched on the radio just as an announcer alerted commuting motorists to avoid Glebe Road because a broken water main had flooded it.

Shortly afterward the Algers left their boxer, Thor, at a kennel while they went to New York. One evening at dinner there, Mrs. Alger heard a rapping noise and asked, "What's that?"

"It's just Thor. Can't you hear his bell and thump?" her six-year-old daughter, Stacy, replied.

The bell on Thor's collar always sounded when he scratched, thumping the floor with his paw, but they were never to hear it again. On their return to Washington, they learned that on the evening they had seemed to hear him in New York, Thor died.

Nancy Alger had an even eerier experience when

she was about her daughter's age. She and her mother, Mrs. Constance Fox, occupied a first-floor Manhattan apartment on Fifty-second Street near Park Avenue, and one evening after Nancy had gone to sleep, Mrs. Fox asked the doorman to "keep an eye on things" while she went to a nearby movie house. Sometime later Nancy awakened, and when her mother failed to answer her calls, she ran sobbing around the apartment, searching for her. She vividly recalls that as she became almost desperate with fright, she saw a woman lean out of a brightly lighted window across the way, and heard her call: "Go back to sleep, little girl. Your mother has just gone to a movie."

Thus reassured, Nancy went back to bed, but not to sleep. Shortly thereafter Mrs. Fox returned, and when the child told her about the kind lady, she was deeply puzzled. From their apartment windows the only view was a courtyard, surrounded by high brick walls.

Hank Fort, a popular-song writer and entertainer who has composed hit tunes about hostess Perle Mesta, the late Speaker Sam Rayburn, and numerous other friends, says that some of the songs have come to her automatically, in the half-state between waking and sleeping. Both the words and music for "The Spirit of Galilee," a beautiful hymn, were given to her in that manner, and after turning on her tape recorder she immediately sang it, to piano accompaniment. The next day she forgot it until she replayed the recorder.

In the spring of 1966, Hank had to break a business engagement in New York with her long-time friend, Vinton Freedley, Broadway producer of such memorable musical comedies and plays as *Lady Be Good, Showtime USA, Anything Goes, Funny Face,* and *Red Hot and Blue.* When she telephoned Freedley's home two weeks later, to ask if she could see him the following day, she learned that he was in the hospital in deep coma and was not expected to live.

Deeply distressed about him, Hank impulsively called New York astrologer Oric Bovar, told him of the crisis, and gave him the producer's birthdate. In a short time Bovar returned her call, saying: "You don't need to worry about your friend. I've checked his horoscope, and he's not under the death cycle now. He will soon recover." Within a week, Freedley had so miraculously improved that he was dismissed from the hospital.

Hank Fort firmly believes that she has a guardian angel who watches over her welfare. One example that she cites is this: In 1932, living in Nashville, Tennessee, she and two friends were listening to her new radio set when she suddenly thought so strongly of her mother that she switched off the music, saying: "Listen, it's ten minutes to nine. If we hurry, we can catch the rerun of 'Madame X' with Ruth Chatterton. Let's go!" On the way to the theater, Hank explained that Ruth Chatterton always reminded her of her mother, who was then en route to Florida by automobile.

Precisely at nine o'clock, the local radio station to which they had been listening all evening broadcast a call for Hank Fort to get in touch with the station immediately. The summons was repeated at ten-minute intervals for more than an hour, but Hank was blithely unaware of it. One of her closest friends, unable to locate her, called the radio station and learned that Hank's mother's car had collided head-on with a Greyhound bus somewhere in Georgia. She then began telephoning every long-distance operator along the route toward Florida, until she located one who knew of the Greyhound accident and who connected her with the hospital where Mrs. Cornelius (Maude) Hankins had been rushed by ambulance. She then spoke with the doctor, who reported that Mrs. Hankins had miraculously escaped serious injury.

By the time Hank returned home from the movie, the friend was awaiting her and laughingly said: "Lady Maude tried to knock a bus off the road." From this manner of greeting, Hank knew that her mother was all right. She believes that her guardian angel sent her the strange urge to see a movie, in order to spare her agonizing hours of uncertainty until the friend learned that her mother's injuries were minor.

While Douglas MacArthur II was serving as our ambassador to Japan in 1960, his wife awakened at two o'clock one morning with a strong sense of foreboding about their daughter. Slipping into a robe, Wahwee MacArthur rushed down the hall of the Embassy to Mimi's room and found it empty. Although the hour was not unduly late for social activities in Tokyo, and she knew that her daughter had been attending a party at the British Embassy, the feeling of danger proved so persistent that she sat for a half-hour on Mimi's bed, until the young woman appeared at the door. She was covered with blood. After rushing her to the hospital, Mrs. MacArthur learned that Mimi and her escort had been in an automobile collision at the moment she awakened, and that her daughter had refused to go to the hospital without her mother.

Several years later, the namesake nephew of General Douglas MacArthur was serving as our Ambassador to Belgium, when Wahwee had another psychic experience. Wahwee, the youngest daughter of the late "Veep," Alben W. Barkley, had received disquieting news about a close female relative; and she could not shake it from her thoughts even while spending a glorious day at the country estate of friends, outside Brussels. Leaving the others to chat on the veranda, Wahwee wandered alone across the wide expanse of lawn, seated herself on a stump, and closed her eyes.

"Please, God, give me a sign that she will be all right," she prayed. Then, wondering how she would recognize such a sign, she amended: "Dear God, if she's going to be all right, please let me see a deer, as a sign from you."

Recalling the incident later, Mrs. MacArthur said: "I had never before seen a deer outside of captivity, but as I opened my eyes I stared straight at a graceful fawn which stood in a clearing in the nearby forest and seemed to be intently returning my gaze." Wahwee's relative happily recovered.

Gretchen Weber, fashion editor of the Denver *Post,* lost her sister, Frances Siegel, in February, 1965, and her mother, Alice M. Lytle Weber, the following December. The latter was the daughter of George Lytle, discoverer in 1859 of the Caribou mine which launched

213

the silver boom in Colorado. A concert soloist, she was known as Colorado's Schumann-Heink and was a good friend of the famous contralto.

The evening that Gretchen returned to Denver from Boulder, where her mother was buried, she felt a strong compulsion to call her friend Frances Walker, who is woman's editor of the Pittsburgh *Post-Gazette*. During their long-distance conversation, Frances' sister, Clara Walker, picked up an extension phone in their home to add her commiseration, and Gretchen said: "I know Mother is happy, and singing right now with Francie in Heaven."

At that moment, a musical bell that had not been wound or played since Christmas of 1964, and which hung from a bracket on the opposite side of the room from Gretchen's telephone, suddenly began to play, "All is calm, all is bright."

"Oh, Fran, a miracle!" Gretchen sobbed. "The bell is playing!" Both Frances and Clara Walker also heard the refrain from "Silent Night" via the telephone in Pittsburgh.

Gretchen, in speaking later of the incident, remarked: "Although some may say that there was a mechanical reason for the playing of the bell, which I had last heard when I held it to my invalid mother's ear the Christmas before, it still seems a miracle that it played at the very moment I expressed my faith. I can never again doubt the continuity of life."

For some inexplicable reason, certain persons have a premonition of impending danger while others walk unknowingly into peril. Paul W. Murphy, Protocol Officer for the Pan American Union, was relatively new at his job when he made his first good-will visit to Mexico in 1938. He was preparing material for a series of lectures and after a month in Mexico City was assigned to visit Oaxaca, a primitive village in the interior where the natives spoke a little-known Indian dialect, but no Spanish or English.

A day or two before his departure, he had a strong premonition that he would be killed on the flight. He mentioned this to our then Ambassador to Mexico, Josephus Daniels, who strongly advised him against making the perilous trip. But Murphy, who was anxious to make good on his first major assignment for P.A.U., simply said that his papers were "in good order" at the hotel where he had been staying and asked Daniels to notify his mother if anything untoward happened.

A wealthy Mexican philanthropist whom Murphy had met at a party also learned of his premonition, and insisted that he carry with him her priceless piece of shawl that had belonged to Our Lady of Guadalupe. Murphy was reluctant to borrow the relic, since it was mounted in a gold case surrounded by diamonds and pearls, but at her insistence he put it in his right pants pocket. With four other passengers, he then took off in a single-motor plane for Oxaca. At each of the four stops en route, Murphy noticed that when their craft touched down to deliver cargo, the frightened natives hid in the jungles, but as it took off they pelted it with stones.

After completing their last stop before Oxaca, Murphy sat beside the pilot, and while flying above the dense jungle he asked what made the streams so muddy. The pilot was just explaining that it was the breeding season for crocodiles and alligators, when the plane hit an air pocket, spun crazily around, and went into a nose dive.

That was the last thing Murphy remembered until he regained consciousness on the ground, ten feet from the smoldering ruins of the plane. Blood spurted from a four-inch gash on the left side of his head, and for a time he heard the moans of his fellow passengers. Then all was quiet; but suddenly the nearly paralyzed man beheld thousands of iguanas—which he mistakenly thought were baby alligators—advancing toward him from the jungle swamps.

"For the next three days they crawled all over me, drinking my blood and thrusting their long claws into my open wounds," Murphy recalls with a shudder. "The agony was almost unbearable. By day I roasted in the stifling jungle heat and bled profusely. By night the blood congealed, I nearly froze to death, and mosquitoes as big as a fist feasted on my tortured flesh. Naked natives would not come close enough to bring me water, even if they could have understood my pleas, but once a chieftan tossed a can of home-made iodine over my festering wounds. The sting was so excruciating that I longed to die."

Murphy's mother had meanwhile been notified that her son was dead in a plane crash. She asked that his body be returned to the United States for burial, but the Mexican Government informed her that since the plane contained nothing of value, it was pointless to search the nearly impenetrable jungle for it. Her repeated insistence at last prompted the Mexican Red Cross to institute a search, during which another wrecked plane containing ten bodies, which had been missing for several years, was found.

When the searchers at last reached Murphy's plane, his companions were dead. His bleeding body was slung across an emaciated donkey, which carried him to a jungle clearing where the Red Cross plane waited. Murphy was flown to Oxaca and left in a roofless structure containing six beds. The other five beds were occupied by Indian women who wailingly gave birth to babies while Murphy lay unattended. There were no doctors or nurses in Oxaca, only two local midwives. A village priest finally arranged for him to be taken by open truck to the railway station, where he was put aboard a train and fastened into a rubber casing that nearly smothered him. One of his eyes was swollen shut, and the other merely a slit, but he had been gratified to learn that the Lady of Guadalupe relic was safe in his right pants pocket. This fact seemed like a miracle to him, for although his left side was mangled and the clothing gone, the right side of his body was unscathed.

During the jolting journey by train one of the wheels broke down, and Murphy was abandoned for twelve hours in a barn until repairs could be made. When he finally was lifted aboard a ship at Vera Cruz for the week's voyage to the United States, he overheard the ship's doctor tell the captain, "That man will die before you pull out of the dock, so why bother to take him aboard?" An elderly passenger who had been a nurse volunteered to minister to him, and although the sadistic doctor forbade her to come near Murphy, she slipped in each night and dawn to treat his wounds. To her and the relic, Murphy believes he owes his life.

The daughter of Congressman Frank Mondell, long-time Floor Leader of the House of Representatives, had a clairvoyant experience in 1926 at their home in Washington, D.C. Mrs. Marjorie Mondell Astin recalls that the rain had been falling steadily for hours, and that she felt oddly depressed while trying to read a book which failed to command her attention. She abruptly reached for the telephone, dialed the number of a friend, and, scarcely aware of what she was doing, blurted: "I'm so sorry about the death of your brother! I've always felt that motorcycles were terribly dangerous." There was a long pause before her friend responded: "How did you know about it? It happened only fifteen minutes ago."

Helen Sioussat, a consultant to industry who for many years headed the public affairs department of Columbia Broadcasting System, dined with her old friend Bernard Baruch one evening in the fall of 1944. Wendell Willkie, the 1940 Republican Presidential nominee, was then hospitalized; and when elder statesman Baruch wondered aloud how he was getting along, Helen suddenly found herself wailing, "Oh, he's dying, he's dying."

So powerful was her inner prompting that she refused to cheer up, even when her host checked with the newspapers and reported that Willkie was much improved. "I know he's dying," she stated; and because she was too concerned to concentrate on their Gin Rummy game after dinner, she departed early. She had barely fallen asleep when the telephone rang. It was Mr. Baruch, calling to tell her that Wendell Willkie had just died.

Fourteen years later Miss Sioussat moved to Washington, and in April of 1966 she had another premonition, while attending a dinner-dance at the home of former Panamanian Ambassador Augusto Guillermo Arango.

"I was dancing with a charming man I'd just met, who danced divinely," she says, "and I was having a simply glorious time, when something told me to return home immediately. My dancing partner must have thought I was a second Cinderella, the way I abruptly broke away from the tango, murmured that I had to leave immediately, and fled into the hall. Congressman and Mrs. Paul Rogers were saying their good-byes— Becky had a terrible cold—and I breathlessly asked if they would drop me off on their way.

"As soon as I reached my apartment building I dashed across the lobby, and was starting to unlock my door when the receptionist called out, 'Oh, Miss Sioussat, I had just tried to telephone you at the Arangos', but they said you had gone.' I then learned that my long-time maid, Ethel Young, had been carried out on a stretcher a few minutes before, with an oxygen mask over her face. At the moment I felt the strong impulse to return home, Ethel had been gasping for breath and asking the receptionist to call an ambulance. She had been perfectly well when I left, but suffered an acute attack while watching television." The maid fortunately survived.

Mrs. A. Loring Siegener, a well-known Washington hostess, underwent a moving experience with psychic overtones during the war years. Originally from Boston, she was living in Miami in 1943 to be near her husband, who was serving as an instructor in dive-bombing at nearby Opalaka Naval Air Station. When Peggy gave birth to a baby boy, the proud father promptly entered the name of his son, Bruen, for future enrollment at Dartmouth, his own alma mater; but concern tempered the Siegeners' joy when they learned that Bruen had difficulty breathing. His pediatrician thought that a heart malfunction might be involved, and one day while Peggy waited in the overcrowded doctor's outer office, she pulled from the book shelves a large volume on heart diseases.

Opening at random the eight hundred-page book by

Dr. Paul Dudley White, her eyes lighted on a passage describing a rare heart condition on which the medical profession had had so little opportunity to do research that it almost invariably proved fatal. Reading the symptoms, Peggy was stunned to discover how exactly they fitted those of her six-week-old son. When the doctor entered the reception room, she showed him the passage, and he agreed that she should rush the child to Dr. White in Boston. But how could they rush anywhere in wartime, when every means of conveyance was solidly booked out of Miami for weeks ahead?

Through the doctor's efforts they finally secured two train tickets, and the Siegeners set forth with their ailing baby on the long trip north. The remainder of their parlor car was filled with soldiers who had just returned from action in the North African campaign, and who quickly surrendered a compartment on learning of the illness. It was Good Friday when the train pulled out of New York on the last leg of the journey.

"My husband had stepped out into the vestibule for a cigarette," Peggy relates, "when suddenly our little baby, who was lying in his portable crib on the opposite seat, sat up all by himself and looked straight at me. I was terribly shaken, not only because I had never heard of so young a baby raising and holding himself erect, but because of the unfathomable look in his big blue eyes. It was an other-world gaze, wise and adult, which plainly told me that he was not going to live, and that I was not to grieve.

"An ambulance met the train in Boston and rushed us to the hospital, where Dr. White awaited us. Late that night our baby died, and when Dr. White telephoned to break the news, he asked if we would permit an examination in order that other children might be helped in the future. We could not do otherwise than give our consent. We later learned that the hospital arena was crowded with heart specialists while Dr. White conducted the autopsy.

"On Easter Sunday, the day that Bruen was to have been christened, he was buried at the family plot in Boston. A week after our return to Miami, we received a beautiful letter from Dr. White, advising us to have other children as soon as possible, and telling us that many babies of the future could now be saved because of the knowledge gained through examination of Bruen's heart. Perhaps that was what our baby was trying to tell me on that sad Good Friday in 1943."

A year later the Siegeners had a baby girl named Sharon, and in June of 1955, when she was eleven, Sharon went to Camp Illahee in Brevard, North Carolina. During her absence Mrs. Siegener traveled to Washington to investigate schools for her, and her father flew to California to visit his mother and sister. Sharon and her roommate were interested in archaeology, and on the evening of June 15, before retiring, they looked at pictures of Egyptian relics.

That night Sharon dreamed that she was standing in the desert, with the Sphinx and pyramids in the background, watching the approach of some Arabs who were bearing a man on a wooden platform. They were dressed in flowing galabias, but instead of the usual turbans, they wore doctors' headband-mirrors. As they set down their burden, the slumbering Sharon recognized her father lying on the wooden platform; and when the Arab doctors began cutting open his head, the shock of it awakened the child.

The next day, after a campfire session, the director asked Sharon to remain behind. Then she told her that her father had died suddenly during the night. After joining her mother in Boston, she learned that he had dined with relatives at a Los Angeles restaurant, and as they reached the parking lot outside, he collapsed. Rushed by ambulance to the hospital, he died of a cerebral hemorrhage while doctors operated on his head.

Sharon, who graduated in 1966 from Rollins College, recalls another odd happening during that sad period. By the time Sharon reached Boston, Mrs. Siegener had selected a wreath of roses in the shape of a heart to stand beside the urn which held her husband's ashes. Coincidentally, the only dark dress which the youngster had taken to camp was a navy cotton, decorated with red roses and hearts that matched the floral wreath, and she wore it to the funeral. At the close of the Episcopal service, as members of the immediate family vacated the front pew, each paused in the aisle to genuflect to the crucifix. At the precise moment that little Sharon did so, the heart-shaped wreath that matched her dress toppled to the floor. She felt that it was a sign of recognition from her father.

Maxine Cheshire, a featured columnist for the Washington *Post,* believes that she owes her life to a psychic experience which occurred in the fall of 1953. She was working as a reporter for the *News-Sentinel* in Knoxville, Tennesse, and was debating whether to accept a marriage proposal from an attractive reporter for the United Press when she heard a voice say: "You had better go ahead and marry him. If you don't, you won't be alive next year." Maxine says that an auditory nerve seemed to be involved, since she "actually heard" the words spoken by an unseen presence.

Maxine Hall and Herbert Cheshire were married the following April and went to Nassau on their honeymoon. While there she suffered intense pain in the small of her back, but believing that it was caused by a pinched nerve or muscular spasm, she refused to consult a doctor. Soon, however, she developed a raging fever, and her bridegroom rushed her home. They reached Knoxville late that evening, after the drug stores had closed; but they knew of a pharmacy at the hospital and went there to see if the druggist could give her something for the fever and pain. A doctor, noticing her flushed face, took her into the emergency examining room, and after a few minutes said that she had a badly infected kidney which could prove fatal.

"While I was still protesting that I wanted to go home," Maxine recalls, "attendants wheeled a corpse down the hall, and the doctor said the woman had been admitted a week earlier with the same kidney infection as mine. Herbert then convinced me that I should remain at the hospital, and during my stay I learned that one of my kidneys had been injured in an automobile accident several years before. This explained why I had suffered frequent backaches and had lost weight. The doctors gave Herbert little hope for my survival, and while I was in the hospital our switchboard operator at the *News-Sentinel* was admitted with a kidney infection like mine, from which she died the next day. Thanks to my youth and strong constitution, I eventually recovered; but had I not married a solicitous man who insisted that I have medical attention, and had I not drunk some impure water in Nassau, which brought the infection to a head, I would probably have waited until too late."

Maxine comes naturally by her psychic talent. Her great-great-aunt was a clairvoyant, and although she died when Maxine's mother, Mrs. Sylvia Hall, was a child, she apparently played a dramatic role long afterward in saving Mrs. Hall's life. During Maxine's childhood she lived in Harlan, Kentucky, where her father, M. F. Hall, was a prominent attorney. One day in 1939, while he was out of town on legal business, Mrs. Hall took an afternoon nap, during which she dreamed that her great-aunt appeared at the foot of her bed and said: "If you don't do exactly as I say, Mrs. Bates will throw Lysol in your face and smother you to death. Even though she's bigger than you are, she's afraid of you; so, as you sit up, swing your feet around and look her straight in the eye."

Mrs. Hall awakened with a start, swung her feet to the floor, and stared straight into the eyes of the cook, who held an open bottle of Lysol in her hand. Not a word was spoken, but Mrs. Emaline Bates turned quickly and walked into the bathroom. When Mr. Hall returned, Maxine's mother told him of her unnerving experience, but expressed the belief that the strong odor of Lysol, with which Mrs. Bates probably meant to clean the bathroom, had simply triggered the dream.

"The cook was big and mean," Maxine says, "but she was a good cook, so mother kept her for two more weeks, until she returned home one day and found Mrs. Bates drunk on the stairs, with her feet in a mop pan of dirty water."

The discharged cook found another job in Harlan with Mrs. Victoria Gross. Soon afterward she was arrested on a charge of throwing Lysol in the face of her new employer, and drowning her in the bathtub. She was brought to trial, convicted of first-degree murder, and sentenced to life imprisonment. Except for her precognitive dream, Maxine's mother feels that she would have met a similar fate.

Mrs. Hall's remarkable sensitivity to danger has apparently saved other lives besides her own. One Saturday in the early 1930's, Maxine's older half-brother, Dudley Hall, drove to a football game in Lexington, Kentucky. After the family retired for the night, the entire household was awakened by Mrs. Hall's piercing scream. Maxine rushed into her mother's room just as her mother awakened and explained that she had been having a nightmare.

"I dreamed that Dudley had fallen asleep at the wheel of the car," Mrs. Hall said of her stepson. "The car was going off the road, and I was screaming at him to wake up."

A short time later Dudley came in and told his father: "A funny thing happened to me on the way home tonight. I fell asleep at the wheel, and I dreamed that Sylvia was screaming at me to wake up. I awakened all right, just as the car was starting to go over the side of the mountain. That would have meant good-bye for me."

Harlan County, Kentucky, is noted for its blood feuds between rival political factions. Everyone knows everyone else, but relationships are not always pleasant. While Maxine was away at college in 1949, a man came to her parents' house one evening about eleven o'clock and asked her father to accompany him to the office on a matter that required immediate attention. Attorney Hall, who was in his pajamas and bathrobe, asked him to wait while he dressed; but as he turned to leave the room his wife walked in, pointed a .38 revolver at the visitor, and ordered him to get out.

"Why, honey, what's wrong?" the lawyer asked his ordinarily gentle wife.

Ignoring her husband, she said: "Get out of here, or there's going to be trouble."

The visitor laughingly protested that she had known him for twenty years, but Mrs. Hall declared: "If I ever see you near my husband again, I won't ask any questions. I'll just kill you. Now get out and leave Mr. Hall alone."

A year or two later, when Maxine began her newspaper career as a cub reporter on the Harlan *Enterprise,* she visited the local hospital during her rounds and discovered that the man whom her mother had treated so rudely was receiving emergency care. He had been blasted by a sawed-off shotgun. Recognizing Maxine, he apparently decided that confession was good for the soul at such a time, for he confessed that if it had not been for her mother, he would have killed her father that night. "He was marked for death," he said, "and I was the hired assassin."

In those days the Halls lived next door to the local prosecuting attorney. On a bitterly cold morning, when her mother was starting downtown, the attorney offered to give her a lift in his car. Mrs. Hall seated herself in the front seat, but before her neighbor could close the door she suddenly jumped out and returned to her house. A few moments later, as the attorney stepped on the starter to warm up the motor, dynamite hidden in the motor exploded and blew him to bits. It was another Harlan gang killing, of which Mrs. Hall would have been an unintended victim, except that she felt a sudden prompting to return home.

Melvin L. Sutley, an attorney who for many years served as superintendent of Philadelphia's famed Wills Eye Hospital, had a remarkable experience several years ago with apporting. He attended a séance in the home of Edward C. Wood of Philadelphia, with the late Leonard Stott as the medium; and while Stott was in trance, Wood asked the man's Control, Barbara, if she knew where his lost book was. The Control replied: "You are referring to the blue-covered book? We have it over here and will return it to you."

Sutley was not told the name of the book, and he was too disinterested to inquire. Several weeks later, while sitting with an amateur medium in the same city, a discarnate named Daniel Hagy said he was the father of Dr. Reginald Hagy, who wrote the book Wood had previously inquired about. He said its title was

224

Witness Through the Centuries, and he added: "When my son used the word 'soul' in the book, Mr. Wood crossed out the word and wrote above it 'spirit.' Please tell Mr. Wood that I do not approve of substituting the word 'spirit' for 'soul.'"

Sutley was one of a group of eight who sat weekly with this particular medium, but on the afternoon of their next scheduled session, the psychic telephoned that he could not return from Baltimore in time for a session that evening. Sutley tried to notify the others that the séance was cancelled, but two whom he was unable to contact came at the appointed time. They chatted a while and were preparing to leave when the medium unexpectedly arrived, explaining that he had left his car parked near Sutley's, and had just returned by train.

The evening was unbearably hot. The medium was carrying his suit coat, which was taken from him and hung in the closet. He wore thin summer trousers and a short-sleeved light shirt. A drenching downpour had begun and since it was raining too heavily to leave, Maureen Murdoch proposed that they have a séance after all. Recalling the incident recently, she said: "We proceeded to another room which was bare of furniture except for a table without drawers, three chairs for us, and a rocker for the medium. We could not pull the draperies all the way closed, because a window air-conditioner was operating. Therefore, each time the lightning flashed the room was lighted, and we could see the medium sitting peacefully in the rocking chair."

Both Sutley and Miss Murdoch recall that as soon as the medium went into trance, his Control asked them to sing something, while they "tried an experiment on the other side." In a matter of minutes they heard a thud on the floor, as if something had been dropped from a height, and the control said, "We have succeeded. We have brought you the book." Sutley thought of the sitting with a different medium at Edward C. Wood's house, and asked if this was Wood's missing book.

At the affirmative reply, Sutley excitedly told Miss Murdock and Fred Roff (now deceased) about the earlier conversation, and began crawling on his knees to hunt the book. He found it on the floor beneath the table, and when the séance was over they carefully examined it. It was a blue-covered book entitled *Witness Through the Centuries,* by Dr. Reginald Hagy. Leafing through it, they discovered that wherever the author had written "soul," Wood had crossed through it and written "spirit."

"Then we began an objective study of the incident," Sutley recalls. "We tried putting the book in the medium's light-weight trousers and thin shirt, but all agreed that we would have seen it if he had brought it into the apartment. Lightning flashes convinced us that the medium had not moved during the séance. The table had no drawers, and no book had been in the sparsely furnished room before the sitting began. To top it all, we hadn't even planned to have a séance that night!"

Miss Murdoch, who lives in Philadelphia's Society Hill section, not only verifies the impossibility of the medium having brought the book by normal means, but adds: "Nor do I see why anyone of those present would be interested in cheating, because we were all earnest in our seeking for the truth of psychic phenomena. The medium is strictly an amateur who seeks no publicity or personal gain, and is as dedicated as the rest of us. The apporting of the book is incontrovertible, so far as I am concerned!"

Charlotte Woodward, the wife of Vice Admiral Clark Howell Woodward, was a popular member of Washington society until her death in 1957. Those of us who knew her were frequently surprised by her strong psychic bent, which she had apparently inherited from her Irish-born mother, Kathleen Fitzpatrick O'Reilly. Mrs. Woodward's only daughter, Cathalene, who is married to the famous portraitist, Rudolf Bernatschke of New York City, recalls that when her parents were stationed in Samoa during her childhood, her mother used to entertain friends in the American colony by reading cards, using a system which had been taught to her Irish grandmother by a Spanish gypsy.

One day, while reading for the wife of Lieutenant Commander Charles Slayton, Mrs. Woodward said: "Louise, this is odd. I see Charlie and the children taking a trip back to the States, but you aren't accompanying them." Puzzled, she reread the cards three times, but they always came out the same. Shortly afterward, Charlotte and Cathy made a voyage to San Francisco. A week after their arrival, Charlotte suddenly exclaimed: "Something terrible has happened to Louise Slayton. I've just seen her saying good-bye to me." The next day a cable informed them of Mrs. Slayton's death, after an emergency operation for appendicitis. Mrs. Slayton was buried in Samoa, and her husband subsequently returned to the States with his children, as Charlotte had foreseen.

In 1929, while Admiral Woodward was serving as Marine Superintendent of the Panama Canal in Balboa, some of the military wives decided to pool their culinary skills and prepare a typical American meal for a visiting Latin American envoy. The luncheon was to be at the American consul's house; and after the women had assembled in the kitchen, Mrs. Woodward removed her rings to wash her hands and prepare the salad. The rings lay forgotten on the kitchen table until, en route home, she remembered them and asked the chauffeur to drive back to the house. When she told the Panamanian maid where she had left the jewelry, the young woman nearly fainted. In hastily cleaning up the mess left by the amateur chefs, she had scraped off everything on the kitchen table into newspapers and dumped the refuse into the Pacific Ocean, which lapped against huge rocks far below the garden of the house. Mrs. Woodward remained serene, calm, and collected. To everyone, she confidently insisted that she would "get my rings back."

Cathy, on the other hand, was certain that her mother's engagement and wedding rings were gone forever. Logic was certainly on her side, since the ocean sands shifted constantly, and the rise and fall of the tide at that point was sixteen feet. Mrs. Woodward, however, asked native divers to be on the alert for the rings, and the next day one of them miraculously found her square-cut diamond ring on top of a jutting rock. Three months later, on a Sunday morning, Admiral and Mrs. Woodward were reading the newspapers in bed when the telephone rang.

"That will be my ring," Mrs. Woodward announced to her husband and to Cathy, who was lying on a chaise in the room. Lifting the receiver, Mrs. Woodward did not wait for an identifying voice before observing sweetly, "You've called to tell me that my wedding ring has been found." Incredibly, the slim band had been recovered, half-buried in the sand, by a Panamanian shrimp fisherman.

Cathy inherited at least some of her mother's psychic talent. A number of years ago, while living on Tucker's Island in Bermuda, she was preparing to take the boat to New York, and friends had planned a send-off for her at the dock. Just before sailing time, one of them called to say that since her baby had a slight cold, she had decided to stay at home with her, and in that instant Cathy "knew" that the baby would die. She mentioned it only to her husband, but during the voyage to New York she worried and prayed, knowing how deeply the woman loved this only child that had been born to her late in life. Four days after Cathy sailed, the baby died of pneumonia.

In 1962, Dr. Karlis Osis, a New York parapsychologist, was conducting some extrasensory experiments at the Fifty-seventh Street headquarters of Eileen Garrett, the famous Irish-born psychic, using ESP cards developed by Dr. J. B. Rhine of Duke University. Cathy Bernatschke volunteered to be a guinea pig; while seated alone in a screened booth, she had already achieved an above-average score when she correctly called the last eight cards even before Dr. Osis had turned them face up in an adjoining booth.

Impressed, the psychologist asked his secretary to go to another office down the hall and look at one of a number of paintings on the wall, while Cathy remained in her cloistered booth. When the "ready" signal sounded, Cathy said: "I see a French landscape, painted about 1893." Neither Dr. Osis nor his secretary knew the date until they minutely examined the painting she had correctly identified. They found that the artist had executed the landscape in 1893.

Gilbert G. LaGorce, son of the widely known editor of *National Geographic Magazine,* always seemed to have a psychic attunement with his wife, Louise. They were married in their teens after a whirlwind summer courtship at Yellowstone National Park in 1930; and nearly a quarter-century later, while he was in Florida for several weeks on *Geographic* advertising business, the sound of a thunderous crash awakened his wife at their home in a quiet residential section of Washington. She rushed to the window, expecting to see two cars telescoped together, but neither a person nor a car was in sight. A week later, when LaGorce returned home, Louise asked what he had been doing at midnight the previous Saturday.

"As a matter of fact, it was exactly midnight," he replied, "when I ran the yacht smack into the rocks at Baker's Haul over near Miami. Jim Larimore was out in the *Brownie* with me, while I was trying to navigate the turn into the inlet. It made quite a crash."

Their daughter, Betty, noticed that her parents rarely had to complete a sentence with each other. "Did you—?" Mrs. LaGorce would begin, and her husband would reply, "Yes, I read it," or whatever had been on her mind. On awakening Sunday morning, February 15, 1959, Mrs. LaGorce said to her husband, "Let's go out to Great Falls this morning." Somewhat surprised that his devout wife was willing to miss Sunday Mass, he replied: "Anything you want, baby. Let's go."

Recalling that memorable occasion, Mrs. LaGorce says: "We had the whole place to ourselves on that cold, windy February day. No one else had ventured out to the park. For three hours we reminisced about our whole life together, beginning with our courtship in Yellowstone, and Gilbert told me how much I meant to him. Then he kissed me as we walked across the little bridge, and I told him that if he never kissed me again, that would be the best one of my life."

For the next four days they scarcely had a chance to speak, because LaGorce was holding day and evening meetings at the *Geographic* with adverstising salesmen from all over the country. Thursday night he died in his sleep, peacefully, without warning. Mrs. LaGorce found him thus when she tried to awaken him in the morning. She believes that without quite realizing it, each had felt a premonition the Sunday before that it would be their last day together.

George Abell, special assistant to the Chief of Protocol for the State Department, recalls an eerie experience which befell him in the fall of 1963, while visiting Sir Terence Langrishe at his eleventh-century "Knocktopher Abbey" estate in County Kilkenny, Ireland. On a misty September morning George and his host took a pre-luncheon horseback ride across the verdant countryside, and were walking their horses along a country road when Sir Terence abruptly reined in his horse and asked, "Did you hear that?"

"I heard some hounds," Abell replied. Just then, coming out of a clearing at the turn of the road a few dozen yards ahead, they saw a pack of hounds.

"By this time the barking had become louder," Abell recalls, "and we distinctly saw a regular pack of hounds cross the road, followed by a hunt of eight people all wearing pink coats. Sir Terence, who is the master of the Kilkenny hunt and knows of every meet well in advance, exclaimed, 'My God, I can't imagine what this is. I know every inch of this terrain, and I haven't known of a hunt across this area since the old squire hunted those hounds; but he's been dead nine years.'

"He was so curious as to their identity that we pulled off the road at a thatched cottage, and Sir Terence asked the resident who the hunters were. The man replied that no hunters or hounds had been along there that morning—or, for that matter, in nine years. We both told him what we had just seen, and although surprised, he was less astonished than an American would have been. The Irish are like that. In fact, Sir Terence makes no attempt to force his gardeners to trim within several yards of a certain tree on his property, and they wouldn't do it if he did. They 'know' that leprechauns live in it."

Loy Henderson, our former ambassador to such major diplomatic posts as India, Iran, and Iraq, had a strange psychic experience in 1920, while serving as a member of the American Red Cross Commission in Western Russia and the Baltic States. Loy had an identical twin brother, Roy, with whom he was so closely attuned that, to the annoyance of their family, they often communicated with each other by means of an isolated word, rather than needing to complete a sentence.

When they were children, playing Indians together in Colorado Springs, Loy Henderson fell and broke his right elbow. Because the bones were inexpertly set, the arm was so crippled that he was rejected for military service in World War I, but Roy enlisted and was assigned to Fort Riley. It was the first time the brothers had known extended separation. While Loy was abroad with the Red Cross, Roy was mustered out of service after having an infected kidney removed, and he then returned to classes at Harvard College. Loy, in Estonia, was commanding a Red Cross unit at Narva when an epidemic of spotty typhus broke out among Russian ex-prisoners of war. People were dying at the rate of five or six hundred a day, and all members of Henderson's unit contracted the highly contagious disease. One March evening in 1920, while lying in the hospital, Loy Henderson had a sudden feeling that he was dying. At that instant his twin brother appeared to him, and Loy says of the eerie episode: "I was telling him good-bye. Both of us spoke of our deep distress at being separated from each other by death. Then he vanished."

But Loy did not die. In fact, although two of his four teammates died the next day, doctors decided that Loy did not have typhus because he had failed to develop the telltale red rash. Dismissed from the hospital in three days, he returned to his quarters and was taking a bath when a colonel called through the door that a cablegram had come for him. Loy numbly responded that he was sure it contained word of his brother's death; but the colonel, laughing at his fears, offered to open it for him.

"I told him to go ahead," Ambassador Henderson recalls, "and then there was blank silence beyond the door. The cable stated that Roy had died of an infection after having a tooth extracted. His death occurred at the same time as my vision."

Ambassador Henderson's experience was not unlike one that befell Arthur Godfrey in 1923, and which the famous television commentator recounted in *Guideposts* magazine. He said that he was in charge of radio communications aboard a Navy destroyer, having "knocked around a lot since I had left home," when one day, asleep in his bunk, he dreamed that his father, whom he had not seen for years, suddenly walked into the room.

"He offered his hand, saying, 'So long, kid!'" Godfrey recalled, "I answered, 'So long, Dad.' I said some kind of prayer. It wasn't eloquent, but it came from the heart. I never saw him again. When I woke up, my buddies told me that at the exact time while I was asleep, the wires from shore hummed the news of my Dad's death. Don't tell me about science and its exact explanation of everything. Some things are bigger. God is the difference. He gets around."

Elizabeth Fielding, public relations director for the National Federation of Republican Women, had been hesitant to tell her father about her interest in psychic phenomena until recently. When she did so, he gravely related an experience of his own, which he had previously been reluctant to mention. Elizabeth's mother died of a cerebral hemorrhage in June, 1952. The next day Frederick J. Fielding, an employee of the New Haven Railroad, was standing alone near his wife's coffin at a funeral home in New London, Connecticut, when he suddenly saw her standing three feet from him.

"I didn't just think I saw her," he told Elizabeth, "I actually saw your mother standing there. She was exactly like I'd seen her thousands of times before, around the house."

Knowing that her mother's eyes had been removed

and donated to the eyebank, Elizabeth asked whether she had had her eyes open in the vision, and he assured her that she did. "She looked just as natural as always," he replied, "but as I reached toward her, she vanished."

Elizabeth Fielding says of her father: "Dad never takes a drink, and he has great integrity. Until long after this incident occurred, he knew absolutely nothing about psychic phenomena, and had read nothing on the subject."

A similar visitation came to Elizabeth Corey (Mrs. Redmond) Hart, a cultural official with the Kuwait Embassy in Washington, in November, 1965. At five A.M. she received word that her father, managing director of the Far Eastern Division of Ford Motor Company, had died in Ontario, Canada. Five hours later, while driving her car toward Fairfax, Virginia, she stopped for a traffic light, and her father appeared in the front seat beside her.

"I couldn't know it then," the Mt. Holyoke graduate says, "but he was wearing the suit in which he would be buried; and he looked natural in every way, even to his spectacles. He was so real that I reached over to touch his knee, and he vanished; but it left me greatly comforted."

A quarter of a century earlier, Elizabeth Hart was vacationing at a Swiss mountain resort when she had her first psychic experience. Her mother had gone downstairs for breakfast, and since eight-year-old Elizabeth had already eaten, she was standing beside her bed, trying to decide what to do that day, when an inner, male voice shouted, "Move, move!"

"I jumped, and fairly flew to the door," she recalls. "In another instant a towering old armoire that held our wardrobe crashed across the bed, exactly where I had been standing. Both of its front legs were broken off as it fell."

At the age of fourteen, she had another memorable experience. On vacation from classes at Westridge School for Girls, in California, she was swimming in the ocean at Laguna Beach when an inner voice again bellowed: "Get out of the water!" Terrified because of the previous incident in Switzerland, she instantly fought her way back to land and dropped exhausted beside her mother, who was sitting under an umbrella. Then she looked back at the sea, just as a series of three huge waves came roaring in. So powerful was their force that the man who had been swimming beside the young girl suffered a broken back.

Franc Shor, associate editor of *National Geographic Magazine,* had never given a thought to psychic phenomena until the summer of 1964, when he had a dramatic experience which also proved to be a remarkably evidential one. Living as a child with his grandmother, Mrs. Frank Luther, in Cimarron, Kansas, he was fascinated by her fine collection of antique porcelains. A Meissen figurine of a child dressed in a smock, stroking a dog which stood on its hind legs, particularly intrigued him; but his aunt Ethel would tease him by saying, "There's little Frankie wearing a little dress," while he stormily protested that the Meissen child was a girl.

His grandmother, on her death, willed the valuable collection to Ethel. When the latter died, Franc learned that she had left it to him; and after attending her funeral in Dodge City, Kansas, he went to the house which she had shared with his uncle Dick, to pack it for shipment to Washington. Noting the absence of the figurine with the child and dog, he browsed through the premises which he had never before visited, and finally located it in a corner of the basement. The reason it had been removed from the collection was then obvious. The dog's tail was missing. Feeling a sentimental attachment to the figurine, nonetheless, he removed it to his mother's nearby residence until he could locate someone to make a new tail for it.

Back in Washington, he forgot about the statuette until his mother died in June, 1964. Again he flew to Dodge City, and this time he brought the figurine home with him. A week following his return, he awakened at three A.M., "with no sense of having been dreaming."

"It sounds ridiculous, I know," Shor says with some embarrassment, "but I am absolutely certain that Aunt

Ethel was in the room with me. I saw her plainly, and she was wearing one of those loose-fitting silk dresses that she always wore. She looked straight at me, smiled, and said, 'Why don't you look under the piano?' I told her that I didn't understand, and she repeated the remark. After I again said I didn't know what she meant, she replied, 'The dog—Frankie's little statue.' Then, in a teasing singsong, she chanted, 'Look under the piano, look under the piano.' She gradually disintegrated, and I decided that I needed some strong coffee. In fact, I consumed two potfuls before dressing and going to the office. All that day I continued to hear her teasing refrain in my ear. What did it mean? As well as I could remember, there was no piano in the house which Ethel occupied at the time of her death, and which I had visited briefly after her funeral."

That evening Shor telephoned his sister, Camilla Haviland, who is a probate judge in Dodge City, and asked: "Cam, has Dick got a piano?"

"Yes," she replied, "there's an old player piano in the basement."

Franc hesitantly told her of the strange vision and asked if she would conduct a search. It was two weeks before Judge Haviland found time to do so. Then, beneath the old pump-player, a servant found the missing tail intact. Apparently even Ethel had not known its whereabouts until she passed to the "other side," or she would presumably have retrieved it herself.

CHAPTER 19

"Intimations of Immortality"

After the death of President Kennedy, I wrote a book about the new First Lady, entitled *Mrs. LBJ*. Upon its completion, I immediately began work on *A Gift of Prophecy,* the story of seeress Jeane Dixon, who had accurately foretold that dreadful assassination and many other world-shaking events. The production of two books in a single year, in addition to my daily newspaper columns, left time for little else. I therefore abandoned the automatic writing.

Early in 1966, having decided to complete this book on psychic phenomena, I resumed the nine o'clock sessions, briefly turning over the typewriter each morning to whatever mysterious source propelled its keys. The Guides seemed pleased that I was at last on the verge of finishing the book which so held their interest, and the lessons proceeded as before. During the previous few months, death had claimed several of my closest friends, among them syndicated columinists George Dixon and Marguerite Higgins, and H. F. (Hap) Seitz.

One morning, the Guides interrupted a philosophical discussion to write: "George Dixon is helping us to get through to you, and eager to be of assistance in this project. He is as zestful here as there, and understands the purpose of the work. This is remarkable for one who came over so recently, but he is a great soul who never harmed others and was fond of you. He says, tell Meldy [his nickname for his wife, Ymelda Chavez Dixon] that he loves her and will be watching over her the rest of her days, when they will be united here, though in a much closer relationship. He says tell her the thing to do is to take a part-time occupation, where she'll keep the contacts and have her mind occupied, but will not be wearing herself out with the daily grind that wore him down. That, he says, is not for her! She should keep young and pretty, and spruce herself up, knowing that his love for her is everlasting."

I conveyed this message to Ymelda, who had been deeply grieved by the sudden death of her husband, shortly after that of her father, Senator Dennis Chavez. She seemed cheered by its content, and has since begun writing her own weekly column for the Washington *Star*. George Dixon had written a five-times-a-week column, in humorous vein, for King Features Syndicate.

Several weeks later, Bob and I attended a Women's National Democratic Club dinner, of which Ymelda Dixon was chairman; she looked exquisite as she walked onstage at the close of the program. The next morning the Guides closed the daily lesson by declaring: "George Dixon was there last night, and proud as the old one-two punch of his Meldy. He says tell her she was magnificent, and a real credit to the family. Tell Meldy he says not to move too quickly [from their house] until she is sure of her own mind."

Meanwhile, there had been other messages purporting to come from Hap Seitz, and from Marguerite Higgins, whose young son is my godchild. In February, the Guides wrote: "The man that you call 'Hap' is happy here, but he wishes that he had listened to you and saved a lot of time here. He wishes Tania [his widow] to read and study about it all she can, for he missed an opportunity and will pay for it here in tedious tasks that would not otherwise have awaited him." After some personal messages for Tania, they wrote: "He wants her to progress as rapidly there as he could have done if he had opened his mind to the truths you were trying to tell him. He is here with us now; as is George Dixon, who says: 'I'll be darned if you weren't right, Ruthie. Spread the word, kid, and let others know. Don't give a hang what some fuddy-duddies will say about it. They don't count for nuttin' when you see it from over here. Tell Meldy to get with it too, and stop weeping. Tell her she's my baby from here through eternity.'"

The language seemed so typical of the breezy, good-humored George we remembered, that several of us remarked on that fact. A month later, at the close of a morning sitting, I asked for any further news of Hap or George, and the typewriter wrote: "Both are progressing. Hap is taking over a class. He is teaching a class in beginner philosophy for those who did not previously know anything of Eastern religion or thought. This will help him to grow, too." (Hap had spent most of his adult life in China, before the Communists took over.)

"George is a bundle of energy, helping anyone who needs to have a laugh to adjust to his new status here. He is as valuable here as there in showing the light-hearted side, for the long-faced ones who view things with somber solemnity have no place here. Ours is a busy working plane, full of laughter and joy. When the parsons (preachers) come, it is someone like George who can get them to relax and take a shocked new look at the life here, for most of them expect something so different. They think of fine houses and marble halls, and angels with harps, but what they find is a world of activity, with everyone busily at work on projects which are needed to shave off the sharp edges left by the earthly phase and to develop the character."

In early June, when I again asked for a progress report on my former King Features colleague, the Guides wrote: "George Dixon is proving to be a rapid grower, for he was a kingly person there. He helped others, and spoke no ill. Let him be an example to all of you who write. Try not to wound any man or woman, for they are your brothers and your very self."

Marguerite Higgins had been seriously ill of a rare, debilitating infection which she had picked up during her last reportorial trip to Vietnam, and was depleted of energy before her death. Perhaps this physical and mental depletion affected her adjustment to the next adventure of living, because the Guides at first spoke

239

of her confusion at being there. Then, in late January, they wrote: "The girl Marguerite is here, and wants to tell you that she hears it when you speak to her in your thoughts. While not at peace yet, she is beginning to understand, and wishes she had gone into this with you while there. It would have helped her over the rough spots and the shock, for she is a fighter, and does not accept easily when the way is not her own."

Several weeks later, this writing came through: "The girl Marguerite is here, thanking you for the thoughts and prayers, and saying that she is getting a bit of a grip on herself now." She then sent personal messages for her husband, Lieutenant General William E. Hall, her two children, and myself, adding: "She wishes now that she had listened to you, and at least read a little on the subject, so that the shock of coming over would not have been so great."

In late summer, Marguerite sounded as if she had made rapid strides in finding herself, for after commenting on her early confusion, she wrote: "The thing all of us must try to cope with is the problem of making others see a point of view. It is no different with politics or psychic phenomena. To stretch another person's range of vision and understanding is important, but to help him grasp the salient points is paramount, for we like to stay in a comfortable rut and avoid the great issues of our times." She closed with a humorous message for her husband, Bill; then George Dixon took over, with high praise for Ymelda's columns, and the Guides added: "He is proud proud proud of her!"

I had assisted with the funeral arrangements for so many friends during the previous year, that this may have prompted the Guides to write, on May 25, as follows: "When a man feels the call of the Man with the Scythe, he puts on his best raiment and lies down in a coffin; but on this side he will already have arrived, and is being welcomed here. The 'man' who lies dressed for public view is the shell from which the soul has flown; and he, from this side, is able to enjoy the show as they dress up that shell and rouge the cheeks. Those who are performing this task of dressing up the corpse should see the amusement here, for the corpse has as much relationship to the Soul-man, as the casing to a sausage from which the meat is stripped.

"The ordeal of burial is a lamentable waste of time, for when we gather here we are as there, but with ethereal bodies which are perfect duplicates of the other, with the exception that these are without flaws, and need no wardrobes. We take on whatever we choose to wear. As our spirit progresses and the moods here change, we less and less wear the fancy garb that first attracted us, since we soon learn that it has no meaning except vanity. Here, as there, we gain wisdom. The taste will change, and the lowest there may be the highest here, as we automatically seek our own level of spiritual advancement. Funerals are for the living, but never for the so-called dead. The grave will not hold the spirit of man, at any rate; so let the ceremony be brief and sweet, comforting the bereaved; but those left behind should not scrape and pinch to give a fancy burial for one who has no need of it on this side."

The next day the Guides spoke of another aspect of the body, writing: "Those who are born with physical deformities chose those bodies deliberately. If they will therefore accept this truth, and face the fact that by overcoming the difficulty of a deformity they are advancing their souls more rapidly than otherwise, they should never feel sorry for themselves. For it is a brave person on this side who elects to return there as a cripple. He does so because progress is more rapid on your side of the door than ours. If you overcome temptations there, the leap ahead is a remarkably rapid one; whereas here the advance is tedious once we have learned the laws of God and know that it does not pay to disregard them."

One of the oddest messages that I have received from the mystical source came shortly before this book was completed. It reads: "The group here today would like to discuss the meaning of sex, and its part in the life of a human being. For those who wonder whether marriage, or love, continues in this plane after the earth-phase, we would explain this factor: true love is unknown on earth, for too many obstacles bar the path. The body of one is seldom perfectly attuned to another.

Minds are so remote from each other that no human on that plane will ever be able to understand another person totally, as to his moods, thoughts, and motivations. Here we merge with those we love in perfect Oneness, for there are no barriers to thought and body.

"The love here is perfect, and is a process of Oneness known as soul-mating. These souls whom we love here are known to us for many eons, but not until we return here do we realize the object of our seeking. This in no way interferes with the deep warmth of feeling that we continue to entertain for those we loved on the earthly plane; but the soul-mate is truly the other half of our own souls. The part which reincarnates may be male or female, depending on the part that needs more honing and perfection; but no matter how often we return there for honing and growth, the other half of our soul (or soul-mate) eagerly awaits the reunion.

"For this reason, the person who marries several times there need not worry about what his or her wives or husbands will say when that person arrives on this side of the open door; for the soul-mate awaits, and the others are as near or as far away as that soul wishes them to be, or as they wish to be with the newly crossed-over traveler. Our unions here are those of the soul and spirit. There are no ties which require us to continue here a marriage that there was less than congenial, for two souls must equally want a unionship to continue here, or it is so meaningless that the other will not want it either. These are laws which are too deep for explaining at this time, but nonetheless are part of the force which rules the universe. For love is that force: the love of God within each of us that ties us to our Maker and to those He created in His own Image."

On another day the Guides once again returned to the subject of creation, writing: "The immortality of man is not a stream of life that continues from the time he was born on earth, but began with the start of time itself, when, as a little ray, he danced off from the radiant mind of God to seek his path through darkness. As he darted hither and yon, trying to help light the then-dark world, he met challenges from without. These were met in various ways by the little sparks.

Some danced their way through the darkness, virtually untouched by the dangers; whereas others wavered this way and that, afraid to make their way forward until they had probed the dark corners and made sure they would not get lost. This probing led to error, doubts, and temptations, for the way back to God is the straight highroad of purpose, love, and understanding. Those who dallied and became lost have been born and reborn countless times, but as they evolved into human beings the temptations grew greater, until many were tempted to think themselves greater than God the Father who created them.

"This was not the case with others, who shone so purely and radiated such a loving glow that they did not need to be born as personalities there on earth. They were permitted to rejoin the Father and flutter in His reflected glory here as angels and saints; but they will be permitted to go and come to earth without their bodies, for they have overcome temptations to such a degree that they need not wear the earthly form that suffers such temptations. All of you there now are ones who somewhere lost your way and sinned in previous lives, but are now seeking atonement for those mistakes. Not one is there but chose to return and try again. Many there are who are nearing sainthood at the level of earth-beings, and will be able to complete their perfecting here, without being reborn; but the preponderance of the earth-people will come back again and again, each time in different form, but with parts of the personality reborn, so as to work out their salvation—for that plane is the hardest test."

I had ceased asking the Guides for "evidential" that could be checked, but one day they wrote: "When the person who would help others finds that he is groping for the right thing to do, he should turn to the fourteenth chapter of St. Luke, which tells him that the power to 'give' is the most precious gift of all. Therefore, those who would help others must view giving as a rare opportunity for their own souls to progress; for life would be grim indeed if no one needed or wanted our ministrations. To take the hand of a child and guide his little steps is a privilege so rewarding that few

243

would miss the opportunity; yet the little child is more capable of finding his own way than one who has taken so many wrong turns that he is bewildered and finds himself in a maze. The reward of helping people to extricate themselves from the tangled mesh of their lives is more important to the soul's progress than leading a little child.

"Like the child that you were, before you became a man or woman, so we are to you: simply one more progression in the stairs that you too will have to climb. We have in relation to you as much more knowledge than you have in relation to a child, but it is sufficiently advanced for you to profit from it withal. There are many lights in the heavens, but the ones which glow most brightly are those which lighted the darkness when the others were not there. Let your thoughts reach out and grasp the stars, so that when your time there is over, you will find that at least some little corner of the world is brighter because you once passed that way."

Since I am barely aware of the words as they are being typed, it was not until I later reread the complete message that I became intrigued with the Biblical reference. I had not the faintest notion of the contents of the fourteenth chapter of St. Luke, and I must admit that I welcomed this opportunity to "check up on" the Guides. But when I checked the reference, I read this admonition from Christ:

> When thou makest a dinner or a supper, call not thy friends, nor thy brethren, neither thy kinsmen, nor thy rich neighbors; lest they also bid thee again, and a recompense be made thee.
> But when thou makest a feast, call the poor, the maimed, the lame, the blind:
> And thou shalt be blessed; for they cannot recompense thee: for thou shalt be recompensed at the resurrection of the just.

How aptly a Biblical passage which I did not recall, and whose location was therefore unknown to me, had illustrated the lesson of these strange and unpredictable Guides!

CHAPTER 20

This Wonderful Psychic World

The keystone of Christian religion is a belief in life hereafter. The New Testament informs us that Christ died for our sins, rose again from the dead, and appeared numerous times thereafter to His Disciples and to others who had known Him before Calvary. After the Ascension He subsequently appeared to Paul, who was trying to rout the early Christians, and in Acts we read: "He fell to the earth, and heard a voice saying unto him, Saul, Saul, why persecutest thou me?...And the men which journeyed with him stood speechless, hearing a voice, but seeing no man."

The Old and New Testaments contain innumerable references to the spirit world. Albert E. Turner, a Biblical scholar, declares that at least one hundred and forty-five different kinds of psychic phenomena are encountered in the Bible. These range from clairvoyance and precognition to trumpet voices, levitation, and spirit writing. There are numerous instances of materialization. Moses and Elijah appeared on the mount with Christ. An angel appeared to the two Marys at the sepulcher, to the shepherds at the time of Christ's birth, to Peter in prison, and to Paul in a vision.

In the Old Testament we read of the materialized hand, which appeared at King Belshazzar's feast and wrote on the wall: "Mene, mene, tekel, upharsin"—an example of automatic writing. Joshua saw and conversed with a spirit who held a drawn sword in his hand. David received the plan of the temple from a spirit, "and the pattern of all he had by the spirit, of the courts of the house of the Lord."

In Exodus 14:25, the Lord took off "the chariot wheels" of the Egyptians, and an angel went before the fleeing Israelites in a cloud. In Ezekiel we are told: "And the spirit entered into me when he spake unto me, and set me upon my feet, that I heard him that spake unto me." An angel appeared to Hagar, three came to Abraham, and another wrestled with Jacob, according to the book of Genesis. In Jude an angel spoke to all the people, and came and sat under an oak to talk with Gideon. The spirit of Samuel conversed with Saul in I Samuel. An angel came to feed Elija, in I Kings; and angels protected the three Hebrew children from the fiery furnace, in the third chapter of Daniel. The book of Daniel also records that "then was the secret revealed to Daniel in a vision." Exodus recounts that angels spoke to Moses out of the burning bush, and the Lord spoke to him through the trumpet.

These are only a few of many such Biblical references, which would seem to make the Judeo-Christian religion the logical realm for pursuing psychical study. Paradoxically, it is the clergy who most often discount the possibility of spirit communication, while simultaneously warning against making the attempt to communicate.

Fortunately, many brilliant men through the ages have had greater awareness of such phenomena than have cautious men of the cloth. Milton wrote: "Millions of spiritual creatures walk the earth unseen, both when we wake, and when we sleep." Henry Ward Beecher said: "We go to the grave saying a man is dead; but angels throng about him saying, 'A man is born.'" Nathaniel Hawthorne wrote: "When we shall be endowed with our spiritual bodies, I think they will be so constituted that we may send thoughts and feelings any distance in no time at all and transfer them warm and fresh into the consciousness of those we love."

In the eighteenth century, Thomas Paine wrote: "I trouble not myself about the manner of future existence. I content myself with believing, even to positive conviction, that the Power which gave me existence is able to continue it in any form and manner He pleases, either with or without this body, and it appears more probable to me that I shall continue to exist hereafter, than that I should have existence as I now have before that existence began."

Victor Hugo, in *Toilers of the Sea,* declared: "There are times when the unknown reveals itself to the spirit of man in visions.... Those that depart still remain near us—they are in a world of light; but they as tender witnesses hover about our world of darkness. Though invisible to some they are not absent. Sweet is their presence; holy is their converse with us."

Again he wrote: "The dead are invisible, but are not absent.... Death is the greatest of liberators, the highest step for those who have lived upon its heights; he who has been no more than virtuous on earth becomes beauteous; he who has been beauteous becomes sublime."

Immanuel Kant, the great German philosopher, asserted: "It will be hereafter proved that the human soul, even in this life, is in constant communication with the spiritual world, and that these are susceptive of mutual impressions, but ordinarily these impressions are unperceived."

Harriet Beecher Stowe, the famed Civil War novelist, stated that she did not really write *Uncle Tom's Cabin,* but that it was "passed in vision" before her. A psychic from childhood, she said she had to tell the book as it came, and that she suffered in so doing. "One of the deepest and most imperative cravings of the human heart," she wrote, "as it follows its beloved ones beyond the veil, is for some assurance that they still love and care for us. They have overcome, have risen, are crowned, glorified, but they still remain to us, our assistants, comforters, and in every hour of darkness their voices speak to us."

Sir Arthur Conan Doyle, in his two-volume *History of Spiritualism,* asserted: "Spiritualism is the greatest revelation the world has ever known. I have seen spirits walk around the room and join in the talk of the company. We are continually conscious of protection around us."

Henry Wadsworth Longfellow, the patron saint of American literature, attended séances and wrote: "The spiritual world lies all about us, and its avenues are open to the unseen feet of the phantoms that come and go, and we perceive them not save by their influence, or when at times a most mysterious Providence permits them to manifest themselves to mortal eyes."

Similar quotations from other noted writers, scientists, and philosophers could fill volumes, but perhaps these are sufficient to indicate that anyone who, with open mind, is willing to put psychic phenomena to the test is in impressive company. How does one explain how Mozart began to compose music at the age of four, or how some poets have written sublime verse while in their teens? A number of books have been produced entirely through automatic writing, or by means of the ouija board, some having been "dictated" in Elizabethan English to uneducated Midwestern housewives. Knowing of these substantiated cases, one wonders how many other novels, symphonies, inventions, and discoveries were likewise conceived through psychical channels, but never acknowledged as such, for fear that a disbelieving world would be critical of such gems from unseen sources.

David Belasco, the late great theatrical producer, was the son of a clairvoyant mother. He wrote that she notified him of her death in San Francisco, while he was in New York, by appearing at his bedside and telling him not to grieve. Many of his plays touched on the psychic, and shortly before his death in 1941 he wrote an article entitled, "Yes—They Do Come Back."

In *Banner of Light,* published in May, 1896, John Eggleston declared: "Thomas Edison's parents were Spiritualists. I have many times sat in Circles in their home when this great inventor was a mere child." Another family acquaintance wrote that he had known Thomas Edison since boyhood, and that both Thomas and his brother William were believers in psychic phenomena, although "Thomas only discusses the subject with persons of intimate acquaintance." Edison, perhaps with the help of spirit communication, brought us the electric light bulb, the phonograph, and other remarkable inventions.

As children at Sunday School we were taught to accept without question the thesis that life is everlasting. What happens, then, to the soul? Why is it so difficult for us to believe in communication between two phases of life, when we accept without question such wonders as space ships which orbit the earth and the moon, nuclear submarines that pass beneath polar icecaps, the sonic exploration of unseen ocean bottoms, and the splitting of the atom? Our grandparents would have scoffed at the possibility of such achievements, and would not have believed that by turning a switch on a contraption in our living rooms we could see events occurring at that moment in England, France, or Japan, with the pictures bounced off a satellite in space. Television, to them, would surely have seemed as unlikely as conversation between the living and the so-called dead.

The world is full of wonders! Sherwood Eddy, author, world traveler, lecturer, and founder of the YMCA in the Orient, spent many years investigating psychic phenomena before gradually dissolving his doubts and his religious prejudices against it. He finally wrote the book *You Will Survive After Death,* only when one of two matching blue cloisonné ashtrays, which he knew to be securely locked inside his New York apartment, was apported and dropped into his hands by Father Tobe, the other-world Control of a medium named Dr. E. A. Macbeth, at a séance on Long Island.

Anyone interested in exploring the psychic field should acquaint himself with the various kinds of phenomena which were scientifically investigated, and verified to their own satisfaction, by such outstanding British intellectuals as Sir William Crookes, famous chemist and physicist; Frederic W. H. Myers, brilliant scholar and poet; Sir Oliver Lodge, noted physicist; Sir Arthur Conan Doyle, Lord Tennyson, and John Ruskin of the literary world; British Prime Ministers William E. Gladstone and Arthur Balfour; and Alfred Russell Wallace, famed co-discoverer with Charles Darwin of the principle of evolution.

Emanuel Swedenborg (1688–1772) was one of the most brilliant philosophers, mathematicians, chemists, engineers, psychologists, geologists, and anatomists of the post-Renaissance. Suddenly, at the age of fifty-five, he became aware of his psychic powers, and thereafter performed such extraordinary feats of clairvoyance and precognition that Swedenborgian churches still exist, in America and abroad, to carry on his message.

In our own century, California's Stewart Edward White authored forty successful novels and books about his big-game hunting expeditions. Then he wrote the series of "Betty" books, which have won him a permanent place in psychic literature. His wife, Betty, had discovered by chance that she was a sensitive when friends brought along a ouija board, and White's books record her amazing psychical activities while on this plane and through communication from her after she passed to the next.

Since the publication of my book *A Gift of Prophecy,* many have asked me why Jeane Dixon should have a highly developed gift for foreseeing the future, when others do not. Some have doubted that Arthur Ford and other mediums are able to make contact with those on the "other side," since they themselves have not done so. It is as logical to ask why all of us cannot compose classical music like Beethoven and Mozart, paint masterpieces like Michaelangelo and Da Vinci, or probe the fourth dimension like an Einstein. As St. Paul explained a long time ago, each of us is given diverse talents with which to make our way through the brief span allotted to us on the earth-plane. How we use those talents depends on us; and the ability to play the piano well, or to cook a tasty, healthful meal is doubtless as pleasing in God's sight as the more dramatic talent for designing a spaceship or conversing with spirit entities.

We are all psychic. The late great Edgar Cayce, while in trance, was asked whether man should pursue the study of psychic phenomena, and this was his reply: "It is well to study same. It is well to experience same, but in those manners, in those ways that are in keeping with Him who is thy ideal. Not, then, by the communion *only* with discarnate entities, or souls, but rather with that direction which comes from within....Thy body is indeed the temple of the living God. *There* He has promised to meet thee, to commune with thee. *There* is the psychic development, the psychic phenomena that ye seek! The Book of Books is the greater source of psychic experience of individuals, and as to what they did about such, even from Adam to John, or from Genesis to Revelation. These are the living examples that are thine."

When asked how many kinds of psychic phenomena are known to mankind at the present time, he replied: "Almost as many as there are individuals, each entity being a force, or world within itself."

Nearly every American schoolchild is encouraged to memorize these inspiring lines from Longfellow:

> Life is real! Life is earnest!
> And the grave is not its goal;
> Dust thou art, to dust returnest,
> Was not spoken of the soul.

If not the grave, what is our goal? Each of us deliberately chose to be born into this testing period, according to some psychic messages, in order to evolve our soul more rapidly. The earthly temptations are such that one reportedly needs to be stronger in this phase than in the next, where the rules are automatic. Thus, by overcoming these temptations, by rising above the day-to-day turmoil and helping others, the speed of our soul's progress is increased. And by taking a little time each day to meditate on things of the spirit, we can develop within ourselves the wisdom to help others through the obstacle course that we are all traveling together.

Without this spark of oneness, what would be the purpose of the earth-phase? Were we placed here merely to see how much of the earth's surface we could cover with pavement, skyscrapers, and hot-dog stands, or is there a more exalted purpose that led us along this path? Which gives us more pleasure, to help another or outdo him? Where is the satisfaction in "getting even" with a neighbor or business associate? Is our own food tasty, if a neighbor starves?

Unless we take time for assessing our goal, the day may come when our survivors will merely ask, "What did he leave me in his will?" Is it wealth that we wish to bequeath our heirs, or the enduring love and inspiration that will light a torch for those who follow in our steps? The person who aids another is setting off a chain reaction that never dies. One thoughtful deed here is worth more to our account on the "other side" than diamonds in a vault.

Will your son say, "My Dad left me a million bucks"; or will he say: "There lies the man whose life will be a pattern for mine throughout the rest of my days. That man spoke no evil, and bore his burdens lightly; for it was the others' burdens which occupied his time, and each one that he added to his own seemed to lighten his load."

I asked the Guides for a final message for the book. This was their typewritten reply: "To each man the day must come when he 'shuffles off the mortal coil.' Unless he has prepared there for the crossing, the way will be dense for a time; for man creates his own underbrush, through which he must necessarily wade. The noble ones who lose themselves in thought of others will find themselves on a gentle slope here, where the continued climb is made easy by the well-doing they left behind them. We know! We have traveled this road, and because of our heedless behavior there, and our pursuit of worldly fame, the going was rough for us. We seek now to undo that, through this attempt to set forth the pitfalls which others will do well to avoid. Time, for many of you, is running out: the earthly time that numbers days from cradle to grave. A man is reborn each day that he lives for others rather than self. For this reason, it is never too soon to begin the process of daily rebirth. This truth is as old as time itself, and as new as tomorrow's headlines.

"Let no man fail to heed this message: God is eternal, and man is part of that divinity. Within each of you is a part of that divine power that reaches out to God. Touch another person, and you touch another part of

God. Heed this well! He, no less than you, is beloved of his Father. Will you forget the stars as you rush about your mundane duties? They light your way by night as surely as you are a star by day to some other one who stumbles, and would fall, except for that aid from you." They then concluded with this verse:

Let thy light so shine that all may see
Visions of immortality.

My own search for truth is far from ended. It will go on, and although much of what I have learned is not yet verifiable in a court of law, it has been checked as carefully as I, a trained reporter, know how. I have far to go before I can effect the personal improvement that will earn a "bravo" from my unseen Guides. But this much I know:

Now is the time for all of us to begin our spiritual quest, for, as it was written in a Chinese garden a long time ago, it is already later than we think!

A Glossary of Terms Used
in Psychic Study

MEDIUM: A person through whom communication is made between the living and those beyond the grave.

PSYCHIC: One who is sensitive to nonphysical forces, and perceives through means other than the five senses. Also termed a SENSITIVE.

PSYCHOMETRIST: One who can divine facts concerning an object or its owner, by personal contact with the object.

DISCARNATES: Spirits in a different stage of life than our own.

SPIRIT GUIDE: A discarnate who writes through another's hand, or speaks through a medium to convey messages and teaching from the other side.

SPIRIT CONTROL: A discarnate who serves as a kind of master of ceremonies for a trance-medium, to introduce other entities, or relay their messages.

AUTOMATIC WRITING: The production of written messages on paper or other surface, seemingly without the conscious thought of a living person.

SEANCE: A gathering of people to seek communication with the spirit world through a medium.

CLAIRVOYANCE: The seeing of things or events occurring at a distance.

CLAIRAUDIENCE: The hearing of an inner voice or other sounds, without use of the physical ears.

PRECOGNITION: A knowledge of events before they occur.

TRANCE: A state in which the conscious mind rests, while the psychic mind is given free rein.

ECTOPLASM: A supernormal protoplasmic substance which emanates from the body of a medium to produce vaporous or solid substance. The act of producing figures from ectoplasm, or through other supernormal means, is called MATERIAL-IZATION.

APPORT: The movement of objects by supernormal means, sometimes from great distances and through locked doors.

AURA: A radiation said to surround all human bodies, and capable of being seen by many "sensitives."

LEVITATION: The raising of objects by supernormal means.

TELEPATHY: The communication between the minds of two people, without normal use of the five senses.